REA

FRIEND
OF ACPL

DO NOT REMOVE
CARDS FROM POCKET

Gay Midlife
and Maturity

Gay Midlife and Maturity

John Alan Lee, PhD
Editor

The Haworth Press
New York • London

Gay Midlife and Maturity has also been published as *Journal of Homosexuality*, Volume 20, Numbers 3/4 1990.

The Haworth Press, Inc., 10 Alice Street, Binghamton, NY 13904-1580
EUROSPAN/Haworth, 3 Henrietta Street, London WC2E 8LU England

Library of Congress Cataloging-in-Publication Data

Gay midlife and maturity / John Alan Lee, editor.
    p. cm.
    "Has also been published as Journal of homosexuality, volume 20, numbers 3/4, 1990" – T.p. verso.
    Includes bibliographical references.
    ISBN 1-56024-028-8 (alk. paper)
    1. Homosexuality. 2. Gays. 3. Aging – Social aspects. I. Lee, John Alan.
    [DNLM: 1. Homosexuality. 2. Quality of Life. W1 JO672H v. 20 no. 3/4 / HQ 76 G285]
HQ76.25.G42   1990b
306.76'62 – dc20
DNLM/DLC
for Library of Congress
                             90-5285
                                 CIP

The *Research on Homosexuality* series:

Series Editor: John P. De Cecco, PhD, Director, Center for Research and Education in Sexuality, San Francisco State University, and Editor, *Journal of Homosexuality*.

Historical Perspectives on Homosexuality, edited by Sal Licata, PhD, and Robert P. Petersen, PhD candidate.

Nature and Causes of Homosexuality: A Philosophic and Scientific Inquiry, edited by Noretta Koertge, PhD

Homosexuality & Psychotherapy: A Practitioner's Handbook of Affirmative Models, edited by John C. Gonsiorek, PhD

Alcoholism & Homosexuality, edited by Thomas O. Zeibold, PhD, and John Mongeon

Literary Visions of Homosexuality, edited by Stuart Kellogg

Homosexuality and Social Sex Roles, edited by Michael W. Ross, PhD

Bisexual and Homosexual Identities: Critical Theoretical Issues, edited by John P. De Cecco, PhD, and Michael G. Shively, MA

Bisexual and Homosexual Identities: Critical Clinical Issues, edited by John P. De Cecco, PhD

Homophobia: An Overview, edited by John P. De Cecco, PhD

Bisexualities: Theory and Research, edited by Fritz Klein, MD, and Timothy J. Wolf, PhD

Anthropology and Homosexual Behavior, edited by Evelyn Blackwood, PhD (cand.)

Historical, Literary, and Erotic Aspects of Lesbianism, edited by Monika Kehoe, PhD

Interdisciplinary Research on Homosexuality in the Netherlands, edited by A. X. van Naerssen

Psychotherapy with Homosexual Men and Women: Integrated Identity Approaches for Clinical Practice, edited by Eli Coleman, PhD

Psychopathology and Psychotherapy in Homosexuality, edited by Michael Ross, PhD

The Pursuit of Sodomy: Male Homosexuality in Renaissance and Enlightenment Europe, edited by Kent Gerard and Gert Hekma

Lesbians Over 60 Speak for Themselves, edited by Monika Kehoe

Gay and Lesbian Youth, edited by Gilbert Herdt

Homosexuality and the Family, edited by Frederick W. Bozett

Homosexuality and Religion, edited by Richard Hasbany, PhD

Love Letters Between a Certain Late Nobleman and the Famous Mr. Wilson, edited by Michael S. Kimmel, PhD

Male Intergenerational Intimacy: Historical, Socio-Psychological, and Legal Perspectives, edited by Theo Sandfort, PhD, Edward Brongersma, JD, and Alex van Naerssen, PhD

Gay Midlife and Maturity, edited by John Alan Lee, PhD

This series is published by The Haworth Press, Inc., under the editorial auspices of the Center for Research and Education in Sexuality, San Francisco State University, and the *Journal of Homosexuality*.

Gay Midlife
and Maturity

CONTENTS

ABOUT THE EDITOR

John Alan Lee, PhD, is a professor of sociology at Scarborough College of the University of Toronto. A former trade union representative and journalist, he is the author of six books and many scholarly and magazine articles on a wide range of topics including romantic love, sexuality, education, medicine, television, the arts, law, the police, trade unionism, deviant behavior, and aging. One of the first "public" gays in Canadian professional life, he has participated in numerous liberation activities including a three-day "sit-in" in the Ontario Attorney-General's office and the founding of the University of Toronto Gay Academic Union. His current interests include the environment and the work of Amnesty International.

Foreword

The editor's mandate of special issues of the *Journal of Homosexuality* is not simple. The editorial board ranges from advocates of "soft" humanistic inquiry to supporters of "hard" empirical science. The *Journal* aspires to academic credibility but is also expected to be a source of *positive* interpretations of homosexuality. The board straddles numerous academic disciplines and goes beyond, to private practice. It is impossible to please everyone. I lean to the humanistic side, with emphasis on accessibility of ideas to the general reader, and am deeply suspect of "experts" and "specialists" for what they have done to my people — gays and lesbians — for hundreds of years.

Then there is the problem of being "politically correct." For the old-school positivist there is no politics in science. Science deals with facts. The post-phenomenological scientist knows better. Reading the comments of outside (peer) reviewers of articles was often amusing, because politics creeps in, despite academic pretensions. An author's serious concern was a reviewer's triviality, or vice versa. For example, one fellow member of the editorial board reacted angrily to "the suggestion that a cooperative chinchilla might help alleviate loneliness," as if a desire to cuddle animals somehow depreciates the human worth of senior gays and lesbians. Clearly, some of my fellow editors and scholars will not be pleased by this special issue. But they will have their turn at the wheel.

NAG IN CHIEF: THE REAL ROLE OF TODAY'S EDITOR

In writing, an editor plays a variety of roles: initiator, organizer, advisor, gatekeeper, encourager, reviser and polisher. Among an editor's most onerous roles are pleader, soother of hurt feelings, and the bottom-line role of relentless nag. All of the articles published here are worth the reader's attention, but some required far more effort than others to cajole from the author. A few reviewers required repeated reminders before delivering their comments.

Ours is an age of endemic lies. Promising an article by a given date and failing to deliver for circumstances within one's control (such as manage-

xiii

ment of time) is simply a lie. My beliefs are too secular to make me a good Quaker, but one of the principles I've retained from the religion of my youth is "Make your aye, aye, and your nay, nay."

To those authors and reviewers (you know who you are!) who delivered clean copy on time, my heartfelt thanks.

ABOUT OLD AGE: TELLING IT LIKE IT IS

Social science aims to debunk and demystify yet academia can be one of the most fertile sources of new mythology. Gay authors are no exception. It is natural enough that gay academics swing to the opposite extreme and overcompensate for past errors. The time has come for a new equilibrium.

Overcompensation has generated myths in gay gerontology. Striving to erase stereotypes of the miserable, lonely old dyke and faggot, some gay authors argue that gay and lesbian seniors are not only happy, self-fulfilled people, but even more satisfied with their lives than their heterosexual counterparts.

Aside from being untrue, I consider Panglossian views of gay aging unhelpful. There are very few advantages to old age in our society, for gays or nongays. Most of us want to live a long life, but how many would choose to be old, if Mephistopheles offered the alternative? The majority of older men and women are *satisfied* with their senior years, which is not the same thing as choosing them.

The simple fact remains: There *are* unhappy, lonely gay and lesbian seniors. Trying to persuade them that they have superior capacities for adapting to old age (such as "crisis competence") does a disservice. If it is argued that most gay and lesbian elders get as much sex as they did when young, then those individuals who do not share this happy fate must blame themselves for their misfortunes.

Pollyanna mythology leaves the lonely homosexual senior asking "What's wrong with me, if the research says all those other homosexuals are so cheerful in old age?" It would be more helpful for gay gerontology to admit that even the happiest senior sometimes fights loneliness, sometimes looks in the mirror and longs for lost beauty, is sometimes rejected by the young crowd at a bar, and sometimes wishes that sexual adventure were as easy as it once was.

The new mythology has deterred some authors from publishing realistic gay gerontology for fear of seeming homophobic and heterosexist. When I first started organizing this special issue, I asked a friend to submit an article. Instead, this aging gay social scientist wrote a letter. I asked for permission to publish the letter, anonymously if he wished. He put off a final decision until too late. He is now dead.

My friend feared that publication would brand him a turncoat, a senile curmudgeon. Now that he is gone, I cannot refrain from publishing a few passages of his searing denunciation of the Pollyanna approach to gay/lesbian aging. His words express feelings which older gays and lesbians have a right to feel. His situation is not novel—I refer the reader to the bitter denunciation of gay liberationist hypocrisy about the aged in Ralph Schaffer's 1973 article, "Will you still love me when I'm 64?" in L. Richmond and G. Noguera, editors, *The gay liberation book* (San Francisco: Ramparts Press).

My friend's letter begins with a disclaimer, which I discount. I knew him as an accurate observer and dedicated activist. His publications always told it like it was. Neither he nor I argue that the stereotypes of the miserable old dyke or faggot are generally true, but, like most stereotypes, they are not entirely false and had their origins in a reality which is still with us. I realize how vehemently some readers will want to reject these sentiments and I omit his name, since he can no longer defend himself:

I'm too intimately and painfully involved with older gay people to be objective . . . My many personal contacts in gay communities give me a very negative picture of what gay/lesbian aging often entails . . .

Except for those fortunate enough to have a relationship that has survived into mid-life, I don't think aging gay men have much to look forward to in the sexual area. Most of us rely on our porn collections and video screens. A few of the affluent are sugar daddies.

Too many are coping with recurrent bouts of depression and frustration, struggling to maintain their lifestyle and a few close friendships. They manage to keep the fantasies and memories alive enough to assist masturbation.

Some travel and press the flesh with impoverished youth of the Third World. The baths no longer present a viable option. Street hustlers are often dangerous. Going to today's gay bars is usually—for older men—so frustrating as to be little more than masochism.

The fortunate ones can afford to immerse themselves in cultural activities. They fund the battles for civil rights and AIDS relief. They are supporters and patrons of theatrical, musical and other cultural adventures of younger men. We applaud their beauty and skill, and then go home to our electric blankets and VCR's. The *Joys of Gay Sex* belong to a different and younger era.

I really don't think you want an article that portrays the lives of older gay men in these terms, John, and neither my personal nor professional welfare will permit me to write a paper with the candor expressed in this letter.

TOWARD A HAPPIER GAY/LESBIAN OLD AGE

This special issue unfortunately lacks a report from the oldest and largest organization striving to serve older gay men and lesbians. I refer to Seniors in a Gay Environment (SAGE) of New York City. It is probably symptomatic of the difficulties facing gay gerontological practice that SAGE personnel hoped to submit an article, but challenges to the very survival of SAGE made that article impossible.

It was to have been a hopeful article, reporting SAGE experiences to those in other communities seeking to reach out to gay/lesbian seniors. But as this issue goes to press, SAGE has sent urgent appeals to its friends everywhere: "SAGE is facing a financial crisis." SAGE is experiencing "an unprecedented increase in the number of gay and lesbian elders seeking our services" at the same time as government funding has been frozen and foundation grants cut back. I hope that by the time you read this double issue, SAGE will again be firmly on its feet.

The crisis at SAGE (and the absence of equivalent organizations in most gay communities) punches a large hole in Panglossian gay gerontology. An article in *Mandate* magazine several years ago charged that younger men and women of urban gay communities may not be willing to care enough for the pioneers and founders of their community to give them adequate financial support. The terrible drain on community resources created by AIDS has focused attention mostly on the younger community. SAGE's report of "unprecedented numbers" of gay elders seeking help severely tests the mythology of blissful gay aging.

The experience of gay elders in Toronto is no happier. Gays and Lesbians Aging (GALA) struggles to maintain a viable minimum membership and leadership. Its plans are ambitious but its resources pitiful. It is obvious that gay and lesbian seniors will continue to increase in a generally aging North American society. Yet there are good reasons to conclude that gay liberation, as a bitter Ralph Schaffer charged in 1973, is for the young alone, and does not care to find a place in its liberated communities for its older generation.

SAGE's appeal letter pleads "Can you imagine having to say no to some elderly man or woman, so ill or frail that they are confined to their home, who has called SAGE asking for our help?'' Yes, I can imagine that and worse: the terrible loss of personal dignity by elders of our tribe (as Isherwood once put it) whose early struggles for survival laid the foundations for today's liberation, but who find a cool reception in most gay institutions. Even the most Panglossian gerontologists have not denied the fact that younger gays and lesbians have not responded to the needs of seniors dying of old age, as they have to the needs of a younger generation dying of AIDS.

These are harsh words, but we live in a society too accustomed to pushing seniors out of sight and mind. It is time gay gerontology put aside its desire to erase the past by painting too rosy a view of gay aging, and worked instead to marshal the resources of gay communities to meet the needs of our seniors.

LOTS OF RESEARCH WORK TO DO

Seeking ideas for useful research in gay and lesbian aging? Look no further! When this issue was originally proposed, I distributed a five-page outline of possible topics. Some of those topics are addressed here but the majority are not and offer research opportunities.

1. *The gay or lesbian couple aging together.* Do such couples go through recognizable and characteristic 'stages' or develop in characteristic typologies, comparable to those in heterosexual couples research such as the work of Cuber, or Blumstein and Schwartz? Do these stages vary considerably, depending on age equality/disparity in the couple? What are the typical patterns of adjustment of divergent career lines, or divergent patterns in family, attitudes to covert/overt gayness, and sexual fidelity/openness. Special case: gay or lesbian couple with children.

2. *The "gay widow."* A lesbian or gay surviving the loss of a long-term partner. Again, how does this compare with nongays? What is the role of network and support groups? What are the special problems in continuing relationships with the lost partner's networks, specific problems in legal arrangements, etc. Also, research on the gay/lesbian grieving experience. Special case: loss to AIDS.

3. *"Married" or "bisexual" gays/lesbians aging.* Aging experiences in relationships between a gay or lesbian, and a bisexual or nongay married partner. Special case: The role of gay or lesbian as informal "uncle" or "aunt" where the nongay partner has children.

4. *The single older gay/lesbian.* How do gays or lesbians learn to enjoy and prefer their own company as they age, with what costs, benefits,

tradeoffs? Special problems: To stay in or come out of the closet in old age? Is nonconforming behavior more readily tolerated than in the younger adult?

5. *Aged gays and lesbians in the "gay community."* Research is urgently needed on organizations serving gay/lesbian seniors. I have published an article on Toronto's GALA (*Canadian Journal on Aging*, Vol.8, No. 1, 1989) but similar work on such organizations as New York's SAGE remains undone.

6. *Special therapy and counselling needs of the elder gay and lesbian.* What are the special problems of coming out late in life, especially to kin and children, if married? Problems of declining sexual opportunities? Problems of gay "generation gap" experiences and feelings of not being welcome in the younger liberated community? Special case: gays and lesbians who return to heterosexuality late in life, even marrying.

7. *Gay/lesbian death and dying.* How do the gay or lesbian experiences compare with or vary from those typical of nongays? To what extent are nongay typologies such as those of Kubler-Ross, applicable to gays?

8. *Gay power and gray power.* How will senior gays and lesbians interlock with the emerging gray power movements? Special problem: Gay/lesbian retirement centers and living accommodations.

INTRODUCING THE ARTICLES

It is an editor's responsibility to seek the representation of as wide a range of views as possible, so obviously I do not agree with some of the articles published here. It is also apparent from the Introduction that Franklin Kameny doesn't either. Nor do Kameny and I agree on which articles we like or dislike!

I was delighted to get such a feisty introduction from Kameny, one of the great founders of gay liberation, and I am happy that the volume he introduces is no meek recapitulation of conventional wisdom. I will not imitate the example of many editors by summarizing or commenting upon the articles. Let the authors speak for themselves.

One pleasant task does remain. This volume is not only the work of the named authors and the editor, but also of reviewers who contributed to the improvement of earlier versions of each article by their comments and suggestions. My gratitude is owed to Barry Adam, Eli Coleman, Clive Davis, Susan Ellis, Lillian Faderman, Gregory Herek, Joseph Harry, the late Laud Humphreys, Bob James, Mary Laner, Dennis Magill, Victor Marshall, Brian Miller, Stephen Murray, Johanna Stuckey, John Warden, and Ritch Savin-Williams. I am especially grateful for Sanjuana Garcia's meticulous copy-editing of the final manuscript.

Unless this is someone else's book, I encourage you to make comments in the margin. Cheer here, hiss there, violently disagree, and scribble in your own experience. When you've finished, sum up these margin notes and send them to me. They will help my efforts in gay gerontology to continue to "tell it like it is."

John Alan Lee, PhD
Editor
University of Toronto

Introduction

Franklin Edward Kameny, PhD

As a scientist I cannot evade the reality of accumulating years, but as one whom Dr. Richard Friend calls "affirmative older gay persons," I choose to ignore the passage of time. My self-image is much younger than that dictated by the harsh mathematics of my date of birth. I am grateful for an opportunity to comment on these studies of older lesbians and gays; forgive me if I also avail myself of a rare opportunity to indulge in some first-person musings.

A quarter-century ago, I railed against the then-universal tendency of lesbians and gays to let the "experts" and "authorities" pontificate about us. *We* are the best authorities on ourselves. Today journals such as this one publish articles by lesbians and gays about lesbians and gays. Unfortunately, the general public continues to see us through the eyes of psychiatrists and the clergy. The views about gays of some self-styled experts — especially the psychiatrists — have improved significantly in recent years, but others are still wrong.

Lesbians and gays remember the once-universal stereotype of older homosexuals as lonely, frustrated, miserable people. Though still young, we sensed that the stereotype was untrue. The more astute among us recog-

---

Dr. Franklin Kameny lives in Washington, DC. He earned his MA and PhD in Astronomy at Harvard University. He taught there, and at Yale and Georgetown Universities. In 1957 he initiated the first public challenge by a self-admitted homosexual to reverse the long-standing government policy of excluding gays and lesbians from public service. His 18-year battle was finally successful in 1975. He popularized the key sociological concept of *sexual orientation*. In 1963 he initiated the effort which resulted ten years later — as he puts it — "in the mass cure of gays by the American Psychiatric Association." In 1971 he was the first person ever to run for election to government office as an openly gay candidate. During the 70s and 80s his capacity to contribute to the public good has been belatedly acknowledged by appointments to government commissions. Dr. Kameny's participation in gay liberation has not diminished with age; he is still active in the gay movement locally and nationally, and specializes in paralegal consultation in gay-related security clearance cases.

nized that the stereotype was an attempt to convert us to heterosexuality "before it was too late."

Now that I am among those who are older, I do not merely *sense* that the stereotype is wrong, I *know* it from firsthand experience. My 40s were better than my 30s, and my 50s better than my 40s. When I leave my 60s behind they will have been better than my 50s. Life continues to be more rewarding, exciting and satisfying than I could ever have imagined when I was 20. My life is too full to permit time for misery or loneliness.

One of the highlights of my life was founding a gay organization and coining, in 1968, the now familiar slogan *Gay is Good*, by which I meant that homosexuality is affirmatively *good* and desirable in every possible sense of the word. It is fully as good as heterosexuality and in no way inferior. I have always considered my homosexuality a stroke of extraordinary good fortune and I would never trade it for heterosexuality.

My life is based on the absolute belief in the validity of my intellectual processes. Since my middle teens I have taken the position that when society and I differed, I was right and society was wrong. I was perfectly willing to let society go on being wrong as long as it didn't interfere with me. When it did, I would fight to win.

I never tried to adjust to the demands and standards of society. With gratifying success, society has had to adjust to me. Society's language of disapproval — *stigma, deviance* — may have affected my circumstances but never my thinking. Society exists for the individual, not vice versa. Society is the means to an end: the happiness of the individual members of society.

This philosophy, applied "across the board," has particularly shaped my homosexuality. There is one way in which I probably differ from many "affirmative older lesbians and gay men" described in these articles: Their battles for self-affirmation involved resistance to heterosexism, and negative cultural attitudes were often taken as immutable "givens" to be coped with and defended against. Survival required choosing the best strategies for coping and defense. By contrast, I have actively attacked and changed society's negative attitudes. When heterosexism no longer exists, coping and defending will be unnecessary.

Studies of older people provide a glimpse of the past, an opportunity for comparison with the present, and an occasion for speculation about the future. There is a stark contrast between the covert, fear-ridden lifestyles of most lesbians and gays some decades ago, and the more open, relaxed life of a high percentage of homosexuals today. We have moved from a life with little support outside the individual self to a highly structured gay community. That constant theme runs through these articles.

Yet our work is far from finished. Many lesbians and gays feel that survival in a harsh environment compels them to remain "in the closet." Unfortunately, many stay hidden without good reason. They suffer an attitudinal hangover from the days of negative brainwashing and they are too reluctant to act on the belief that *Gay is Good*.

Our progress in the 60s was hearteningly rapid, and continued into the 70s. But in the later 70s the opposition "got their act together" and slowed our advance. In the 80s we have been hit by AIDS. As a scientist, I remain unswervingly confident that medical research will bring AIDS under control as it did with that comparable scourge, syphilis, and we will again move forward.

Even these difficult times have not entirely halted our progress. The moral majority zealots have lost much of their momentum. While it is impossible to predict the tactics of our opposition in the coming decade, I believe that the progress of the past quarter century will not be undone. That is why a compendium of articles about the lives of people still with us, yet already part of our history, such as this one, is useful.

I have mused enough. Let us turn to the articles. They clearly demonstrate the enormous diversity of gays, young and old. The articles range from formal research reports to personal experiences. They begin appropriately with Margaret Cruikshank's survey of previous aging studies, which suffered from inconsistencies in findings but provided tantalizing leads for future research. It is heartening to note how rapidly the field is growing.

John Alan Lee interviewed Don Bachardy to give us insight into one of the best-known 20th century gay relationships between a younger and older man. Personally, I have never "bought into" the creation of a mystique surrounding youth-mentor relationships of the kind which supposedly characterized the classical Greeks. Despite mythology, I refuse to believe that "horny" Greek youths did not enjoy each other sexually, with regularity. That is what *I* see on those Greek vases.

Isherwood and Bachardy had a highly successful relationship of enormous value to both of them, and this article provides information for those who find such relationships important. Yet I would interpret what we are told as first the story of a long-term relationship, and only second the story of an older-younger relationship. Unlike Lee, I do not mourn the passing of age-stratified gay relationships in favor of peer relationships, which are probably better suited to our culture, and to the preferences of most people. Of course, each couple must decide for themselves, and have the freedom to act out their decisions.

Beth Dorrell's article is more a short story than a study on lesbian aging, but it is a gentle and tenderly written story. It gives us insight into the impact that an older lesbian has on the younger women around her. Of course, one example alone cannot tell us much about the vast and varied lesbian world.

Richard Friend's impressive article presents a systematic, structured approach to the diverse ways in which gays and lesbians respond to aging. His reasonable interpretations also indicate areas where further research would be of value.

John Grube's commentary suggests that the gay lifestyles of Toronto and Washington differ sharply. In my experience, the gay left peaked and departed a few years after Stonewall, and now plays only a small role. However, it continues to exercise a divisive, corrosive and counter-productive effect in New York and, in my opinion, has contributed to making that city's gay movement one of the weakest in the country.

I cannot agree with Grube's argument that the highly-structured gay community of most larger cities reflects a "heterosexual reality." The difference between the old, private gay community (an "underground," as Grube correctly terms it) and today's more public gay communities involves more than a mimicry of heterosexual "structure."

Monika Kehoe's article is not only about gays and lesbians; it has generalizable implications for older people. Likewise, Lee's *Can we talk?* is a general "how to do it" piece useful to anyone striving to maintain a relationship in the face of stresses that develop over the years.

Mark Pope and Richard Schulz offer useful reference information on frequencies of sexual relations, as distinguished from the broader sexual *activity*, but I have to quarrel with their inclusion of 40 to 50 year-olds. In my experience, 40 years is hardly midlife, and "older" means over 60.

Richard Steinman's study is a valuable application of sociological theory to age-disparate long-term gay male relationships. It also stimulates my unapologetic critique of our obsessively couple-oriented culture. Gay and non-gay alike (and most authors of this volume) seem to assume that people must couple on more than a short-term basis. Nowhere in the present collection do we find the heretical notion that it might be immature and even psychologically unhealthy to compulsively seek a partner on whom to lean dependently for as long as possible. I remain a staunch believer in the emotional maturity of the self-reliant, and in the joyful promiscuity of the contented single — albeit *careful* — promiscuity for the nonce.

With Keith Bennett and Norman Thompson's paper I may become an ornery commentator indeed. This collection of articles aims to represent a wide range of viewpoints, but I am totally unfamiliar with any experience of "accelerated gay aging." It's certainly not part of my gay reality. I'm also wary of their study on two other grounds. First, we need more comparison with heterosexual males. Second, I think the English (and that includes Australian) attitudes to sex in general and homosexuality in particular often strike Americans as indeed strange.

Livy Visano's careful and extensive study may hopefully replace the patently false picture of male prostitution in former studies (especially Reiss, which remains the classic despite all its glaring errors). In future work, Livy Visano might explore a phenomenon I find interesting: the absence of the pimp in the male hustler world, a role so widespread in female prostitution. I can't go along with Visano in his apparent assumption that it is sociologically desirable for prostitutes to "disengage from this illicit pursuit" and "withdraw from hustling." Those statements are clearly not the hustlers'.

Finally, I am not equipped to assess the accuracy of Winkler's erudite reconstruction of a classical poem from limited fragments. I don't know if she was an "older woman" when she wrote the poem, but there's no denying the lesbian significance of Sappho.

In all, this collection is often at variance with my own point of view but it is a happy advance over the negative, moralistic, value-laden, and defective portraits of gay midlife and aging which once used to depress us.

Stigma, Gay Lifestyles, and Adjustment to Aging: A Study of Later-Life Gay Men and Lesbians

Marcy Adelman, PhD

San Francisco

Researchers of gay/lesbian development have investigated the relationship between adjustment and styles of being gay (Bell & Weinberg, 1978; Weinberg & Williams, 1974), but few researchers have ever examined this relationship as it affects gay men in later life (Berger, 1982; Lee, 1987), and there are no published studies on this relationship as it pertains to later-life lesbians. This article attempts to fill this gap in our understanding of gay development.

Various researchers have suggested that later-life adjustment is not affected by sexual orientation per se, but is made problematic by society's negative attitude toward homosexuality (Berger, 1982; Kehoe, 1985; Kelly, 1977; Kimmel, 1978; Lee, 1987; Minnigerode & Adelman, 1978; Minnigerode, Adelman, & Fox, 1980). These studies report that gay people must deal with the problems related to stigma, which can affect adjustment.

In the study that I co-researched (Minnigerode et al., 1980), we compared the psychological, social, personal, and sexual adjustment of heterosexual and gay men and women 60 years of age and older. Overall, there were few differences and no differences in psychological adjustment as measured by the Life Satisfaction Index (Bild & Havighurst, 1976;

Marcy Adelman is a clinical psychologist in private practice in San Francisco and is the editor of the book *Long Time Passing: Lives of Older Lesbians*.

Correspondence and reprint requests may be addressed to the author, 4112 24th Street, San Francisco, CA 94114.

This article is dedicated to the loving memory of Dr. Fred Minnigerode.

7

Tobin & Neugarten, 1961), the Self-criticism Scale (Lowenthal, Thurnher, & Chirbooa, 1975) and the Symptoms Index (Gurin, Veroff, & Feld, 1960). This article continues the analysis of our (Minnigerode et al.) 1980 data by doing a within-group comparison of the gay respondents from the initial study to determine the relationship between patterns of adjustment to later life and styles of being gay that cope with stigma.

TURNING POINTS IN GAY DEVELOPMENT

Society's hostile attitude toward nontraditional identities shapes gay adult development and renders it more problematic than the usual maturational process (Plummer, 1975). Developmental characteristics and events unique to gay people can be understood as turning points generating different styles of being gay and of coping with this hostility or stigma (Morin & Schultz, 1978). The characteristics or events unique to the lives of gay people have been described by many (Bell & Weinberg, 1978; Cass, 1984; Dank, 1971; DeMonteflores & Schultz, 1978; Lee, 1977; Riddle & Morin, 1977; Roesler & Deisiter, 1972; Simon & Gagnon, 1967; Weinberg & Williams, 1974).

Those processes and events on which data were available from the comparative study and which are described in the literature are: (a) age of first awareness of gay feelings, (b) age of first same-sex experience, (c) self-designation as a gay person, (d) change in the negative connotation of homosexuality/lesbianism, (e) level of satisfaction with being gay, (f) importance of homosexuality, (g) degree of involvement with other gay people, and (h) degree of disclosure of sexual orientation to others.

Various researchers have described the process of gay identity acquisition (Cass, 1984; Kimmel, 1978; Lee, 1977; Plummer, 1975; Riddle & Morin, 1977). These studies differ in the suggested number of developmental phases needed to acquire a gay/lesbian identity, but all agree that certain choices must be made about integration of homosexuality into one's identity.

How gay and lesbian people choose to manage the turning points and stigma unique to their life will generate different styles of being gay (early vs. later age of first awareness of gay feelings; early vs. later age of first same-sex experience; positive vs. other-than-positive connotation of homosexuality/lesbianism). Various researchers suggest that patterns of adjustment across the life course are related to these different styles of being gay (Riddle & Morin, 1977; Morin & Schultz, 1978).

ALTERNATIVE SEQUENCE OF DEVELOPMENT

A typical sequence of the early gay developmental processes is: (a) awareness, (b) experience, and (c) self-designation (Cass, 1984; Dank, 1971; Morin, 1977). Both homosexuals and heterosexuals are socialized by the mainstream culture in which homosexuality is perceived as psychologically and/or morally deficient. Gay people may delay self-designation until after experimentation to allow a period of adjustment to the negative connotations of homosexuality/lesbianism (Dank, 1971; DeMonteflores & Schultz, 1978). In this study, I examined these three events and their relationship to patterns of adjustment in later life.

Because patterns of adjustment to later life are shaped by early developmental and social factors (Erikson, 1959; Neugarten, 1968; White, 1963), we can expect that the resolution of these first three events will affect later-life adjustment for gay people. My study is the first to examine the relationship between the adjustment of gay people to later life and the age and sequence of the resolution of these typically early developmental processes.

Whether a person internalizes or rejects the negative connotation of homosexuality is thought to lead to two different types of gay identity (Morin & Schultz, 1978; Weinberg, 1973). Morin and Schultz (1978) makes the distinction between a well-adjusted gay identity, which rejects the negative stereotypes, and a less well-adjusted gay identity, which internalizes the stereotypes. The relationship between patterns of adjustment in later life and the fourth, fifth, and sixth characteristics investigated in this study (connotation of the meaning of homosexuality/lesbianism, satisfaction with being gay, and importance of homosexuality) reflect these two types of gay identities. Gay people who are better adjusted in later life will be more accepting of their homosexuality/lesbianism.

ALTERNATIVE SOCIAL CHOICES

The last two characteristics or styles of being gay that were investigated are high or low involvement with other gay people, and more or less disclosure to others of sexual orientation. These social styles of being gay have been investigated across the life cycle. Successful adjustment within several life stages—late adolescence (Roesler & Deisiter, 1972); adulthood (Bell & Weinberg, 1978); middle-age (Weinberg & Williams, 1974)—has consistently been shown to be related to high involvement with other gay people and wider disclosure of sexual orientation to others.

The relationship between adjustment to later life and disclosure in gay men has been investigated by Berger (1982) and Lee (1987) with conflicting results; Berger concluded that low disclosure leads to emotional problems; Lee reported a correlation between greater self-concealment and greater life satisfaction. The differences in these two studies can be attributed to the age differences between the two samples; Lee's study included a sample with a larger percentage of men over 60 years of age. Today's generation of gay men and lesbians over 60 years of age is the last generation of gay people to have lived most of their lives before the socio-political changes of Stonewall (1969). Disclosure at a socio-historical time when there was little emotional or political support for being gay would have led to traumatic experiences of loss (loss of children, job, family support, etc.) and damage to self-esteem.

In Berger's study, high social contact or involvement with other gay people was related to greater psychological adjustment. His findings are consistent with those studies with younger samples cited previously.

METHODOLOGY

Sampling Procedure

Research on homosexuality presents serious methodological difficulties regarding sampling procedure. Representative samples of homosexual men and lesbians are difficult to obtain (Morin, 1977). Investigators have been explicit in discussing the nonrepresentative nature of homosexual samples and emphasizing consequent limitations on generality of findings (Bell & Weinberg, 1978). While a variety of recruitment strategies can be utilized in recruiting samples of gay respondents, certain social and psychological characteristics seem related to recruitment source (Weinberg, 1970). Samples obtained through organizations and friendship networks, for example, seldom include socially isolated individuals.

With these considerations in mind, the sample of respondents in this study was not intended to be strictly representative. Presumed differences related to sexual orientation are examined, but conclusions are necessarily limited to respondents in the study.

Three strategies were used to recruit the total sample of 27 homosexual men and 25 lesbians: friendship networks, advertisement, and organizational contacts. (See Minnigerode et al., 1980, for details.)

Sample Characteristics

The respondents in this investigation are 27 self-identified gay men and 25 self-identified lesbians. All respondents are white and live in the San Francisco Bay Area. The two groups, lesbians and gay men, did not significantly differ in age, self-assessed health status, living arrangement, reported income, educational background, religious affiliation, or marital status.

The gay men averaged 65.63 years of age (sd = 4.32) and the lesbians averaged 64.48 years (sd = 4.22).

Most respondents reported their physical health to be "excellent" or "good" (46); only six respondents considered themselves to be in "fair" or "poor" health.

Most respondents (32) were living alone. Gay men were either living alone (17), with a friend (7), or with a lover (3). Lesbians were either living alone (16), with a lover (7), or with an ex-lover (2).

The majority of men (19) and women (20) reported that their present income was sufficient to maintain a comfortable standard of living. Five men and five women reported incomes of less than $5,000; 18 respondents reported incomes of less than $12,000 but more than $5,000; and 22 respondents reported incomes of more than $12,000.

Lesbians were slightly more educated than were the gay men, with the gay men averaging 14.89 years of education (sd = 2.76) and the lesbians 15.96 years (sd = 1.94).

Most respondents (42) were fully retired from gainful employment. Four gay men and six lesbians continued to work full time, while six men and eight women continued to work part time.

The majority of respondents (men, 15; women, 15) claimed no current religious affiliation, although 32 respondents had been raised as Protestants, nine as Catholics, and one as Jewish.

Most gay men (23) and lesbians (18) had never been married, and none of the respondents was currently married. Four gay men and three lesbians reported having children from previous marriages.

Procedure

The present study examined data collected from interviews that generally required four to six hours and two or more sessions to complete. The interview schedule, constructed after component questions had been pilot tested, contained 176 questions, nearly all of which included additional probes. The original study included questions on physical and psychological well-being, work experiences, retirement, leisure activities, friendships, family relationships, marital and nonmarital relationships, sexual behavior, living arrangement, and perspectives on the life course. Between interview sessions, respondents completed checklists and questionnaires.

The data for this article are drawn from the answers to the following questions and/or probes:

1. At approximately what age did you begin to think of yourself as homosexual/lesbian?
2. How old were you when you had your first homoerotic experience?
3. At what age did you first define yourself as a homosexual/lesbian?
4. How important a role does being homosexual/lesbian play in your life?
5. Has being homosexual become more or less important during the past ten years?
6. What does being homosexual mean to you now?
7. How satisfied are you with being homosexual?
8. Have you disclosed your sexual orientation to colleagues at work? How many?
9. Have you disclosed your sexual orientation to close friends? How many?
10. Have you disclosed your sexual orientation to family members? How many?
11. How many of your close friends are gay?

Measures

Gerontological literature indicates that adjustment to later life can best be assessed by using multiple measures to control for the complexities of adaptation and adjustment (Clark & Anderson, 1967; Lowenthal et al., 1975; Maas & Kuypers, 1975; Williams & Wirth, 1965). This article uses the data from three of the instruments used in the comparative study by Minnigerode et al. (1980). These three instruments are used to measure different, although related, aspects or dimensions of adjustment to later life. The Life Satisfaction Index (Bild & Havighurst, 1976; Tobin & Neugarten, 1961) measures satisfaction with past and present life in five areas: (a) enthusiasm or zest; (b) accepting responsibility for one's own life; (c) feelings of having accomplished what one wanted to do in life; (d) positive feelings of self-worth; and (e) happiness or pleasure with life. High scores are interpreted as greater life satisfaction.

The Self-criticism Scale (Lowenthal et al., 1975) measures disapproval with self. Low scores on this scale are commonly interpreted as high approval of self.

The Symptoms Index (Gurin et al., 1960) is commonly used to measure psychophysiological disturbances. Low scores are indicative of few psychosomatic complaints and hence better psychological health.

FINDINGS

Research and theory suggest that adjustment in gay adults is related to style of being gay. In order to assess this relationship in our sample, the eight previously mentioned styles of being gay have been arranged in three categories to facilitate discussion: early developmental styles of being gay; personal styles of being gay; and social styles of being gay.

The following 15 predictor variables were identified, based on dimensions chosen for their ability to discriminate among respondents, and dichotomized to facilitate analysis.

Early Developmental Styles

1. Age when first aware of homosexual/lesbian feelings

   a. early age — 15 years or younger (N = 23)
   b. late age — 16 years or older (N = 24)
      (data unavailable, N = 5)
      Ages ranged from 5 to 27 years of age.

2. Age when first gay experience occurred

   a. early age — 18 years or younger (N = 25)
   b. late age — 19 years or older (N = 23)
      (data unavailable, N = 4)
      Ages ranged from 6 to 37 years of age.

3. Age of self-definition as a homosexual/lesbian

   a. early age — 16 years or younger (N = 23)
   b. late age — 17 years or older (N = 25)
      (data unavailable, N = 4)
      Ages ranged from 5 to 38 years of age.

4. Sequence of early events

   a. self-definition prior to homosexual/lesbian experimentation
      (N = 25)
   b. homosexual/lesbian experimentation prior to self-definition
      (N = 22)
      (data unavailable, N = 4; same age, N = 1)

Personal Styles

1. Meaning of homosexuality in terms of feelings

    a. respondent mentions positive feelings; e.g., enjoyment, satisfaction, relief, etc. (N = 11)
    b. respondent does not mention positive feelings (N = 37)
       (data unavailable, N = 4)

2. Meaning of homosexuality in terms of identity

    a. respondent mentions positive identity, e.g., It is who I am, being me, self-acceptance, etc. (N = 14)
    b. respondent does not mention positive self-identity (N = 34)
       (data unavailable, N = 4)

3. Meaning of homosexuality in terms of friendship

    a. respondent mentions friendship, e.g., companionship, like of or interest in same sex, etc. (N = 13)
    b. respondent does not mention friendship (N = 35)
       (data unavailable, N = 4)

4. Meaning of homosexuality in terms of lifestyle

    a. respondent mentions lifestyle, e.g., way of life, way I live, etc. (N = 15)
    b. respondent does not mention lifestyle (N = 33)
       (data unavailable, N = 4)

5. Satisfaction with being gay

    a. less than very satisfied (N = 17)
    b. very satisfied (N = 31)
       (data unavailable, N = 4)

6. Importance of being homosexual/lesbian

    a. very important (N = 28)
    b. less than very important (N = 19)
       (data unavailable, N = 5)

7. Perceived changes in level of importance of being homosexual/lesbian during past 10 years

    a. less important (N = 13)
    b. more important or same (N = 34)
       (data unavailable, N = 5)

Social Styles

1. Disclosure of sexual orientation at work

   a. disclosed to one or more colleagues (N = 12)
   b. undisclosed (N = 26)
       (data unavailable, N = 14)

2. Disclosure to friends

   a. disclosed to all close friends (N = 30)
   b. undisclosed to one or more close friends (N = 18)
       (data unavailable, N = 4)

3. Disclosed to relatives

   a. disclosed to all living relatives (N = 15)
   b. undisclosed to one or more living relatives (N = 14)
       (data unavailable, N = 23)

4. Involvement with other gay people

   a. low involvement: two-thirds or fewer close friends are gay (N = 21)
   b. high involvement: more than two-thirds of close friends are gay
       (N = 26)
       (data unavailable, N = 5)

These 15 predictor variables indicate a particular style of being gay. Men and women were compared on each style: Chi squares were made, and no significant sex differences were achieved. Men and women were equally distributed in the ages reported for first awareness of being gay, first homoerotic experience, and self-designation as a gay person. The median age determined their style of being gay (early or later).

Questions on satisfaction with being gay and importance of being gay were originally coded by the interviewers using a 4-point Likert scale from "very" to "not at all." Categories were collapsed to dichotomize groups.

I saw a trend in the data on reported number of close friends who are gay and followed through to dichotomize involvement with other gay people based on more or less than two-thirds close friends.

ANALYSIS

A discriminant analysis was performed to evaluate if any particular patterns of adjustment significantly distinguished between the dichotomized dimensions of styles of being gay.

Thus this analysis: (a) determined if any pattern of adjustment is related to any style of being gay by weighting the effect of each adjustment measure in the presence of the other two measures; (b) determined the strength of the relationship between each adjustment variable in the presence of the other two to each style of being gay; and (c) determined the degree of accuracy for each discriminant function or pattern of adjustment in correctly classifying respondents according to the style of being gay to which they actually belong.

RESULTS

Adjustment to Aging

Table 1 shows that adjustment to aging is significantly related to only two styles of being gay: satisfaction with being gay (p < .0001) and the developmental sequence of early gay developmental events (p < .04). Interestingly, the same patterns of adjustment are involved with both groups of styles. High life satisfaction, low self-criticism, and few psychosomatic problems are significantly related to both high satisfaction with being gay and to gay experimentation prior to self-definition as a homosexual or lesbian; low life satisfaction, high self-criticism, and many psychosomatic problems are related both to low satisfaction with being gay and to self-definition prior to gay experimentation.

From Table 2 we can see that high life satisfaction appears to be most strongly related to five styles of being gay: (a) high salience of homosexuality; (b) low disclosure at work; (c) low involvement with other gay people; (d) early age of awareness; and (e) decrease in the importance of homosexuality in later years. High self-criticism appears to be related to early age of self-definition, disclosure to relatives, and early age of awareness. Many psychosomatic complaints appear to be related to not defining one's homosexuality in terms of positive identity. In each case, the inverse level of adjustment is related to the opposite style of being gay.

TABLE 1. Adjustment to Later Life and Style of Being Gay

1. Early gay developmental events

   Age of awareness   Age of first gay experience

   Styles of Being Gay

   Group 1. Early (N = 23)   Group 1. Early (N = 25)

   Group 2. Later (N = 24)   Group 2. Later (N = 23)

Note: From Adelman, M. (1980).

Note: In order to read this table, please note that the sign of the coefficients if negative (-) indicates Group 1 and if positive indicates Group 2.
Thus, the first discriminant analysis would read as follows: high life satisfaction and high self-criticism are related to early age of awareness, while
many psychosomatic complaints are related to later age of awareness. The
adjustment pattern related to early age of awareness, then, is high life
satisfaction, high self-criticism, and few psychosomatic complaints. Also,
the size of the coefficients determines the strength of the relationship
between each adjustment variable and each style of being gay; those
coefficients furthest from zero (0) have the strongest relationship.

Adjustment Variables	Discriminant Function Coefficients	
LSIA[a]	-1.04	-0.21
SCS[b]	-1.10	-1.24
SI[c]	0.03	0.85

---

[a]Life Satisfaction Index A

[b]Self-criticism Scale

[c]Symptoms Index

TABLE 1 (continued)

	Age of self-definition	Sequence of early gay events
	Group 1. Early (N = 23)	Group 1. Self-definition prior to experimentation (N - 25)
	Group 2. Later (N = 25)	Group 2. Experimentation prior to self-definition N = 22)
LSIA	-0.84	0.14
SCS	-1.19	-0.49*
SI	0.09	-0.60

2. Personal styles of being gay

	Satisfaction with being gay	Importance of sexuality
	Group 1. Low (N = 17)	Group 1. High (N = 28)
	Group 2. High (N = 31)	Group 2. Low (N = 19)
LSIA	0.68	-1.15
SCS	-0.48**	-0.65
SI	-0.17	-0.26

	Change in importance of homosexuality in past ten years	Interpretation of one's homosexuality in terms of:
	Group 1. Less important (N = 13)	Group 1. Positive feelings (N = 11)
	Group 2. More or same importance (N = 34)	Group 2. Made some other definition (N = 37)
LSIA	-1.04	0.41
SCS	0.05	-0.80
SI	-0.29	0.08

---

*p<.04   **p < .0001

	Interpretation of one's homosexuality in terms of:	Interpretation of one's homosexuality in terms of:
	Group 1. Positive identity (N = 14)	Group 1. Friendship (N = 13)
	Group 2. Made some other definition (N = 34)	Group 2. Made some other definition (N = 35)
LSIA	0.24	0.21
SCS	-0.75	-0.77
SI	1.18	-0.18

	Interpretation of one's homosexuality in terms of:
	Group 1. Lifestyle (N = 15)
	Group 2. Made some other definition (N = 33)
LSIA	0.85
SCS	-0.44
SI	0.64

3. Adjustment to later life and social styles of being gay

	Disclosure at work	Disclosure to friends
	Group 1. Undisclosed (N = 26)	Group 1. Disclosed (N = 30)
	Group 2. Disclosed (N = 12)	Group 2. Undisclosed (N = 18)
LSIA	-1.15	0.49
SCS	-0.75	-0.84
SI	0.38	0.61

TABLE 1 (continued)

Disclosure with relatives	Involvement with other gays
Group 1. Disclosed (N = 15)	Group 1. Low involvement (N = 21)
Group 2. Undisclosed (N = 14)	Group 2. High Involvement (N = 26)

	Disclosure with relatives	Involvement with other gays
LSIA	-0.96	-1.07
SCS	-1.12	-0.12
SI	-0.08	-0.09

TABLE 2

Adjustment Variables and Related Styles of Being Gay

Life Satisfaction Index A

High life satisfaction is related to:

High importance of homosexuality	(-1.15)
Undisclosed at work	(-1.15)
Low involvement with other gay people	(-1.07)
Early age of awareness of gay feelings	(-1.04)
Homosexuality less important in past 10 years	(-1.04)

Self-criticism Scale

High self-criticism is related to:

Early age of self-definition	(-1.19)
Disclosed to relatives	(-1.12)
Early age of awareness of gay feelings	(-1.10)

Symptoms index

Many psychosomatic complaints are related to:

Interpretation of one's homosexuality in terms other than positive identity (e.g., self-acceptance, it is who I am, being me, etc.) (1.18)

DISCUSSION

Adjustment to Later Life and Early Developmental Styles

The data show a statistically significant relationship between adjustment to later life and the sequence of early gay developmental events (p < .04). High life satisfaction, low self-criticism, and few psychosomatic complaints is the pattern of adjustment related to gay experimentation prior to self-definition (and low life satisfaction, high self-criticism, and many psychosomatic complaints are related to the reverse sequence of developmental events). This style of being gay is not related to stage or age of occurrence but only to sequence.

Studies have found varying time intervals between experimentation and self-definition, but have reported that the typical sequence of events is experimentation first and self-definition second (Dank, 1971; Morin, 1977). This sequence of events appears to be an adaptive style of being gay. According to White (1952), withdrawal into a period of internal readjustment is an appropriate adaptation to a new and difficult situation. The contingencies of stigma and the conditions of internal readjustment are manifested in the relationship between adjustment and delaying self-definition until after experimentation. The results also support Dank's (1971) and DeMonteflores and Schultz's (1978) suggestion that this sequence of events assists in coping with stigma, and, therefore, facilitates further development and self-acceptance.

Adjustment to Later Life and Personal Styles of Being Gay

The data show a statistically significant relationship between adjustment to later life and satisfaction with being gay (p < .0001). High life satisfaction, low self-criticism, and few psychosomatic complaints constitute the pattern of adjustment related to being "very" satisfied with being gay; the reverse pattern of adjustment is related to being "less than very" satisfied with being gay. A major theme of respondents who reported being less than very satisfied was the attribution to their homosexuality of perceived failing in life with respect to careers, friendships, and/or intimate relationships. One 69-year-old woman reported, "It (her lesbianism) hasn't been too successful. I've always picked the wrong people. I picked people for an attraction, not a real caring."

Stigma was also frequently referred to as a reason for being less than very satisfied. One 60-year-old man reported, "I don't feel very (satisfied) because of the disadvantages. Because of the loneliness and intolerance of other people. You cannot just live your life."

Those respondents who reported being very satisfied with being gay tended to speak about self-acceptance and/or the advantages of being gay as follows: "I don't think that anybody, if they cannot accept with good grace whatever they are, can be happy . . . that is important. It's not just important; it's basic. I have fully accepted my homosexuality and embrace it." Another respondent, a 60-year-old woman, commented, "I can be independent and know more about the world . . . I was able to follow a career. I didn't get bogged down in a family thing where I wouldn't have had as much independence."

Whether a person internalizes or rejects the negative characteristics stereotypically associated with being gay (deviant and deficient) is thought to lead to two different types of gay identity (Weinberg, 1973; Morin and Schultz, 1978). The results and themes in this section are in agreement with these gay identity theories.

Adjustment to Later Life
and Social Styles of Being Gay

In this subsection, our data did not show a statistically significant relationship between adjustment and social styles of being gay. In the protocols a major theme running through both disclosure styles was the frustration and anger at either the necessity of secrecy or at the discrimination that was encountered upon disclosure. Clearly, this generation of gay people had little choice but to negotiate between equally demanding alternatives.

CONSIDERATIONS FOR FURTHER RESEARCH

As mentioned, the discriminant analysis can also be used to assess the ability of each discriminant function (or pattern of adjustment) to correctly distinguish between the dichotomized style of being gay.

Table 3 shows those styles of being gay that have coefficients at a magnitude of 1.0 or greater and that have a discriminant function with a correct prediction of 60% or better for the adjustment variables. The high rate of correct prediction in such a small sample suggests that these predictors would very likely be found significant in a larger study.

Taken together, the data of Tables 1 to 3 may be argued to cautiously imply key relationships of lifestyle to aging worthy of further study. A few of these implications are now discussed.

TABLE 3

Proportion of Correct Classification

I. Early developmental styles

   1. Age of awareness

		Predicted Group	
Actual group	# of Cases	1 Early	2 Later
1. Early	23	17	6
		73.9%	26.1%
2. Later	24	7	17
		29.2%	70.8%
Ungrouped cases	2	1	1
		50.0%	50.0%

Percentage of "Grouped" cases correctly classified: 72.34%

  2. Age of first experience

		Predicted Group	
Actual group	# of Cases	1 Early	2 Later
1. Early	25	17	8
		68.0%	32.0%
2. Later	23	13	10
		56.5%	43.5%
Ungrouped cases	1	0	1
		0.0%	100.0%

Percentage of "Grouped" cases correctly classified: 56.25%

  3. Age of self-definition

		Predicted Group	
Actual group	# of Cases	1 Early	2 Later
1. Early group	23	17	6
		73.9%	26.1

TABLE 3 (continued)

		Predicted Group	
Actual Group	# of Cases	1 Early	2 Later
2. Later	25	9	16
		36.0%	64.0%
Ungrouped cases	1	1	0
		100.0%	0.0%

Percentage of "Grouped" cases correctly classified: 68.75%

4. Sequence of events

		Predicted Group	
Actual Group	# of Cases	1 Early	2 Later
1. Self-definition first	25	19	6
		76.0%	24.0%
2. Experimentation first	22	9	13
		40.9%	59.1%
Ungrouped cases	2	2	0
		100.0%	0.0%

Percentage of "Grouped" cases correctly classified: 68.09%

II. Personal styles

1. Satisfaction with being gay

		Predicted group	
Actual Group	# of Cases	1 Low	2 High
1. Low	17	12	5
		70.6%	29.4%
2. High	31	5	26
		16.1%	83.9%
Ungrouped cases	1	0	1
		0.0%	100.0%

Percentage of "Grouped" cases correctly classified: 79.17%

2. Importance of homosexuality

Actual Group	# of Cases	Predicted group	
		1 High	2 Low
1. High	28	19	9
		67.9%	32.1%
2. Low	19	9	10
		47.4%	52.6%
Ungrouped cases	2	1	1
		50.0%	50.0%

Percentage of "Grouped" cases correctly classified: 61.70%

2a. Change in importance of homosexuality in past 10 years

Actual Group	# of Cases	Predicted group	
		1 Less	2 More
1. Less important	13	8	5
		61.5%	38.5%
2. More or of same importance	34	12	22
		35.3%	64.7%
Ungrouped cases	2	1	1
		50.0%	50.0%

Percentage of "Grouped" cases correctly classified: 63.83%

3. Definitions

Positive feelings

Actual Group	# of Cases	Predicted group	
		1 Yes	2 Omitted
1. Yes	11	10	1
		90.9%	9.1%

GAY MIDLIFE AND MATURITY

TABLE 3 (continued)

Actual Group	# of Cases	Predicted group	
		1 Yes	2 Omitted
2. Omitted	37	15	22
		40.5%	59.5%
Ungrouped cases	1	0	1
		0.0%	100.0%

Percentage of "Grouped" cases correctly classified: 66.67%

Positive identity

Actual Group	# of Cases	Predicted group	
		1 Yes	2 Omitted
1. Yes	14	11	3
		78.6%	21.4%
2. Omitted	34	12	22
		35.3%	64.7%
Ungrouped cases	1	0	1
		0.0%	100.0%

Percentage of "Grouped" cases correctly classified: 68.75%

Friendship

Actual Group	# of Cases	Predicted group	
		1 Yes	2 Omitted
1. Yes	13	10	3
		76.9%	23.1%
2. Omitted	35	18	17
		51.4%	48.6%
Ungrouped cases	1	1	0
		100.0%	0.0%

Percentage of "Grouped" cases correctly classified: 56.25%

Lifestyle

		Predicted group	
Actual Group	# of Cases	1 Yes	2 Omitted
1. Yes	15	10	5
		66.7%	33.3%
2. Omitted	33	16	17
		48.5%	51.5%
Ungrouped cases	1	0	1
		0.0%	100.0%

Percentage of "Grouped" cases correctly classified: 56.25%

III. Social styles

1. Disclosure at work

		Predicted group	
Actual Group	# of Cases	1 Undisclosed	2 Disclosed
1. Undisclosed	26	17	9
		65.4%	34.6%
2. Disclosed	12	5	7
		41.7%	58.3%
Ungrouped cases	11	1	10
		9.1%	90.9%

Percentage of "Grouped" cases correctly classified: 63.16%

Gay literature (Kimmel, 1978; Riddle & Morin, 1977) posits a stage sequential model of gay development. However, an early or late development may alleviate some problems while creating or sustaining others. A trend in the data shows that adjustment to later life with respect to level of life satisfaction and degree of self-criticism are inversely related to age of awareness of gay feelings; high life satisfaction and high self-criticism are related to early age (15 years or younger) of awareness; low satisfaction and low self-criticism are related to later age (16 years or older) of awareness.

Gay development need not necessarily occur at a certain age or specific developmental stage for adjustment to occur. Rather, the crucial factor may be understood as the influence of stigma and the person's psychosocial resources to deal with the environmental demands and pressures created by stigma.

In this regard, it is interesting to note the trend in the data between high self-criticism and early age of self-definition as a gay person (Table 1:1: SCS = −1.19). In this sample of old gay people, postponing self-definition until more fully developed affective and social skills had been acquired may have assisted in coping with stigma and increased the likelihood of successful identity resolution. However, for future generations of gay people who grow up in a more accepting and more supportive environment, postponement of self-definition may no longer be either necessary or adaptive.

I believe the course of gay development is secondary to the usual problems and challenges of the maturation process (self-esteem, competence, social skills, etc.). Longitudinal studies would go far in answering questions about and describing gay development and adjustment during the life course.

It is stigma and stigma management that make gay development so perilous. Successfully coping with stigma is not accomplished by a simple attitudinal change, but, rather, is an active lifelong process which coincides with the individual's changing needs and changing social environment. In this regard, it is interesting to note a nonsignificant trend in the data; those respondents for whom the meaning of homosexuality was defined in terms of positive self-identity and acceptance had the fewest psychosomatic complaints (Table 1:2: SI = 1.18).

Those seniors who interpreted their homosexuality in ways other than a positive identity spoke about having had earlier conflicts over self-acceptance but these conflicts had not continued. Since psychosomatic complaints operate primarily as defense mechanisms, it is reasonable to speculate that ongoing identity conflicts could be manifested in increasing psychosomatic complaints.

Since gay development is influenced by social and developmental factors, I would expect that a gay identity and the importance assigned to it would change over time. In nonsignificant trends, high life satisfaction is related both to assigning a very important role to being gay (−1.15) and to the decreasing importance of being gay in later life (−1.04). Those respondents who reported that being gay played a decreasing role in their lives in the past ten years tended to link their age with either a decrease in sexual activity or with being single. One woman matter-of-factly reported that her lesbianism played a less important role in her life because "I'm 70 and I have no lover relationship." Further research is needed to explore the salience of being gay in one's identity and how it changes over the life course.

With respect to social styles of being gay and nonsignificant trends, adjustment to later life (high life satisfaction) is related to low disclosure at work (-1.15). An examination of the protocols revealed that respondents with a low disclosure style reported that work played a "very important role in their lives," while respondents with a high disclosure style reported that work was less than very important to them.

However, some interesting thematic differences emerged between the two disclosure styles which indicate a complex network of intervening variables. For example, those respondents who were undisclosed reported that they felt the need to work harder and/or achieve more in their lives because they were gay, a common adaptational style among stigmatized groups (Becker, 1963; Goffman, 1963). It may be that achievement, as a means of coping with stigma, increases the value of work, and, therefore, increases fear of discrimination and contributes to a low disclosure style.

Compartmentalization was another major theme which emerged from those respondents who were undisclosed at work. It was a familiar and successful means of adaptation. One woman aged 63 reported, "I tried to keep things separate, not just because I'm gay, but because I think things work out better that way. . . . I never discuss my sexuality with anyone." It may be that the compartmentalization of various aspects of one's life is an intervening or conditioning variable in that it represents the socio-historical norm; that is, regardless of sexual orientation, today's elderly rarely discussed sex or sexuality. As a result, compartmentalization may be viewed as a consequence of early socialization practices that defined socially acceptable limits of public behavior.

Concerning the relation of adjustment to disclosure style with relatives, low self-criticism is related to low disclosure style, while high self-criticism is related to high disclosure style (-1.12). The interviews revealed that high and low disclosure styles with relatives cut across levels of importance of work.

Disclosure to relatives ranged anywhere from 20 to 40 years prior to the interview. When respondents did disclose, they were more often than not rejected. One 68-year-old man bitterly reported, "My father was very hostile when I told him I was homosexual. I was 21. We didn't have a positive relationship after that."

Disclosure with relatives often meant lifelong rejection. I propose that such damning responses from significant others at a time when there was little support for being gay could be detrimental to the development of self-satisfaction and self-esteem and would contribute to poor adjustment in later life.

In considering adjustment and involvement with other gay people, high life satisfaction is related to low involvement with other gays, and low satisfaction to high involvement (-1.07). This trend is not surprising if we consider socio-historical factors. Gay subcultures, as we know them today, were unavailable to this generation of later-life gay people (Katz, 1978; Adelman, 1986) and they therefore had few opportunities to resocialize to a more positive identification with other gay people. One respondent, a 68-year-old woman, reported, "I never wanted to identify with a lesbian group. I just like being with women." I would like to suggest that avoidance of identification and minimum involvement with other gays in the pre-Stonewall era operated as a successful adaptation to the negative status assigned to gay people. In other words, the closets of the pre-Stonewall era provided comfort in a hostile environment by allowing one to have a positive self-image. Further, a successful, lifelong adaptation which allowed for such a positive self-image would be resistant, but not impervious, to change.

As discussed, adjustment in adult and middle-aged gays is related to high disclosure styles and high involvement. These generational differences can be attributed to socio-historical factors. Today, homophobic cultural values are offset by visible and viable gay subcultures. Previously, gay people had few alternatives but to attribute a low status value to either themselves or each other. Today, however, gay people no longer have to view themselves or each other as defiant or deficient, but can consider themselves members of an oppressed minority group. This new status brings gay people together and promotes self-esteem through self-affirmation (self-disclosure and identification with other gay people).

The proposed differences are generational, not developmental. What is adaptive for one generation in a specific socio-historical context has become maladaptive for the next generation. Further, I believe that the gay gray movement of the late 1980s (Copper, 1987; MacDonald, 1983) has begun to alter these differences for today's generation of later-life gay people. Old gay people are now becoming a visible and vocal part of the gay subcultures.

In conclusion, the results of this study have raised many questions about traditional theories of gay development. Many of the observations and interpretations from the nonsignificant trends must necessarily be incomplete and fragmentary. Although this article is unable to give a precise description of gay development in later life, it is the author's hope that it has raised enough questions to spur future investigations.

REFERENCES

Adelman, M. (1980). Adjustment to aging and styles of being gay: A study of elderly gay men and lesbians (Doctoral Dissertation, The Wright Institute, 1980). *Dissertation Abstracts International, 40.*

Adelman, M. (1986). *Long time passing: Lives of older lesbians.* Boston: Alyson Publications.

Becker, H. S. (1963). *Outsiders: Studies in the sociology of deviance.* New York: Free Press of Glencoe.

Bell, A. P., & Weinberg, M. S. (1978). *Homosexualities: A study of diversity among men and women.* New York: Simon and Schuster.

Berger, R. (1982). *Gay and gray.* Chicago: University of Illinois.

Bild, B., & Havighurst, R. (1976). Life Satisfaction. *The Gerontologist, 16*(1), 70-95.

Cass, V. (1984). Homosexual identity formation: Testing a theoretical model. *Journal of Sex Research, 20,* 143-167.

Clark, M., & Anderson, B. C. (1967). *Culture and aging: An anthropological study of older Americans.* Springfield: Charles C Thomas.

Copper, B. (1987). *Ageism in the lesbian community.* Freedom: The Crossing Press.

Dank, B. (1971). Coming out in the gay world. *Psychiatry, 34,* 180-197.

DeMonteflores, C., & Schultz, S. J. (1978). Coming out: Similarities and differences for lesbians and gay men. *The Journal of Social Issues, 34,* 59-72.

Erikson, E. H. (1959). Identity and the life cycle. *Psychological Issues, 1,* 18-166.

Goffman, E. (1963). *Stigma: The management of spoiled identity.* Englewood Cliffs: Prentice Hall.

Gurin, G., Veroff, J., & Feld, S. (1960). *Americans view their mental health.* New York: Basic Books.

Katz, J. (1978). *Gay American history.* New York: Avon Books.

Kehoe, M. (1985). *Lesbians in literature and history.* New York: Haworth Press.

Kelly, J. (1977). The aging male homosexual: Myth and reality. *Gerontologist, 17,* (4), 328-332.

Kimmel, D. C. (1978). Adult development and aging: A gay perspective. *The Journal of Social Issues, 34*(3), 113-130.

Lee, J. A. (1977). Going public: A study in the sociology of homosexual liberation. *Journal of Homosexuality, 3,* 49-78.

Lee, J. A. (1987). What can homosexual aging studies contribute to theories of aging? *Journal of Homosexuality, 13*(4), 43-71.

Lowenthal, F. M., Thurnher, M., & Chirbooa, D. (1975). *Four stages of life.* San Francisco: Jossey-Bass.

Maas, H. S., & Kuypers, J. A. (1975). *From thirty to seventy.* San Francisco: Jossey-Bass.

MacDonald, B., and Rich, C. (1983). *Look me in the eye.* San Francisco: Spinsters Ink.

Minnigerode, F. A. & Adelman, M. R. (1978, October). Elderly homosexual women and men: Report on a pilot study. *The Family Coordinator*, pp. 451-456.

Minnigerode, F. A., Adelman, M. R., and Fox, D. (1980). *Aging and homosexuality: Physical and psychological well-being*. Unpublished manuscript, University of San Francisco.

Morin, S. P. (1977, August). Heterosexual bias in psychological research on lesbianism and male homosexuality. *American Psychologist*, pp. 629-635.

Morin, S. F., & Schultz, S. J. (1978). The gay movement and the rights of children. *Journal of Social Issues*, *34*(2), 137-148.

Neugarten, B. L. (Ed.). (1968). *Middle age and aging: A reader in social psychology*. Chicago: University of Chicago Press.

Plummer, K. (1975). *Sexual stigma: An interactionist account*. London: Routledge & Kegan Paul.

Riddle, D., & Morin, S. (1977). Removing the stigma: Data from individuals. *APA Monitor*, pp. 16-28.

Roesler, T., & Deisiter, R. W. (1972). Youthful male homosexuality: Homosexual experience and the process of developing homosexual identity in males aged 16-22 years. *Journal of the American Medical Association*, *219*(8), 1018-1023.

Simon, W., & Gagnon, J. H. (1967). The lesbians: A preliminary overview. In J. H. Gagnon and W. Simon (Eds.), *Sexual deviance*. New York: Harper & Row.

Tobin, S. S., & Neugarten, B. L. (1961). Life satisfaction and social interaction in the aging. *Journal of Gerontology*, *16*(4), 344-346.

Weinberg, G. (1973). *Society and the healthy homosexual*. Garden City: Anchor Press/Doubleday.

Weinberg, M. S. (1970). Homosexual samples: Differences and similarities. *Journal of Sex Research*, *6*, 312-325.

Weinberg, M. S., & Williams, C. J. (1974). *Male homosexuals: Their problems and adaptations*. New York: Oxford University Press.

White, R. W. (Ed.). (1963). *Study of lives*. New York: Atherton Press.

Williams, R. W., & Wirth, C. (1965). *Lives through the years*. New York: Atherton Press.

Through the Looking Glass:
Life After Isherwood —
A Conversation with Don Bachardy

John Alan Lee, PhD

Scarborough College, University of Toronto

BACKGROUND

Christopher Isherwood was a 48-year-old, renowned English writer when he began living with Don Bachardy, an 18-year-old California college student whose youthful appearance caused a minor scandal among Isherwood's friends. Their life together surely fulfills all the disappointed hopes of Oscar Wilde, which he expressed so eloquently at his second trial in this now famous speech (Hyde, 1962, p. 201):

> The love that dare not speak its name in this century is such a great affection of an elder for a younger man as there was between David and Jonathan, such as Plato made the very basis of his philosophy, and such as you find in the sonnets of Michelangelo and Shakespeare. . . . It dictates and pervades great works of art. . . . There is nothing unnatural about it. It is intellectual, and it repeatedly exists between an elder and a younger man, when the elder has intellect, and the younger man has all the joy, hope and glamour of life before him.

Wilde's hopes have been mine too. By 1976, I had already made many attempts to find a partner. In 1977 — a year after Isherwood's visit to To-

---

John Alan Lee is Professor of Sociology at Scarborough College, University of Toronto, Scarborough, Ontario, Canada.

The author is indeed grateful to Don Bachardy, to Tom Steele of *Christopher Street*, and Dr. Stephen O. Murray for their comments on earlier versions of the manuscript.

ronto—I met Devon, 21 years my junior and as different from my background as one could imagine. Twelve years later, I dare to believe he is my partner for life. Isherwood helped me find the courage to hope. In *Christopher and His Kind* (1976) he takes us only to his arrival in New York with Wystan Auden in 1939, but he cannot resist leaping ahead in his final paragraph to share his gratitude for the fate that awaits him in 1953:

> *Each of you will find the person you came here to look for—the ideal companion to whom you can reveal yourself totally and yet be loved for what you are, not what you pretend to be. You, Wystan, will find him very soon, within three months. You, Christopher, will have to wait much longer for yours. He is already living in the city where you will settle. He will be near you for many years without your meeting. But it would be no good if you did meet him now. At present, he is only four years old.*

When one of Isherwood's last autobiographic revelations, *October*, was published in 1981, I eagerly examined it for clues of his success with Bachardy. By then, their partnership was widely celebrated in gay life and media. There's surprisingly little guidance on elder-younger relationships in modern gay literature. I often feel that gay liberation militates against age-stratified relationships, as if they were relics of a pre-Stonewall era. The emphasis in gay life today is very much on peer partnerships. Sure, there are advertisements for "Daddies" seeking "son-lovers," and occasionally younger men seeking "generous patrons," but most such relationships are labeled, fairly or not, as exploitative. Oscar Wilde might find it as difficult to defend the love that dare not speak its name in the 1980s as in the 1880s!

October is not only wonderful reading, but an exemplar of the collaboration between these two men, separated by 30 years in age but joined by three decades of life together. Each page of Christopher Isherwood's prose is balanced by one of Don's famous portraits. But to my great disappointment, there are only two or three tantalizing anecdotes revealing Don's feelings. Through all his writings, Isherwood meticulously respected Don's privacy.

When Christopher Isherwood died in 1986, I felt a personal loss, and pasted all the newspaper accounts into my journal. My relationship with Devon had now settled into that domestic equilibrium of daily habit which a couple must achieve, if the stability of loving friendship is to succeed the glories and tribulations of romantic excitement. Yet there was still much I didn't understand about Devon's side of our relationship, and I remained convinced that I could gain insight from Don Bachardy's feelings for Christopher Isherwood.

The call to edit a special issue of the *Journal of Homosexuality* on aging gave me an opportunity to interview Don Bachardy. The results were so satisfying that I shared them with a wider audience than a scholarly journal can attract, by publishing a version of this article in *Christopher Street* (Lee, 1987). Some readers, conditioned by the survey techniques of latter-day "abstracted empiricism" (Mills, 1959) may argue that little scientific value can come from detailed examination of a single case such as the Isherwood-Bachardy relationship. But the social science of gay aging, especially of age-stratified relationships, is still in its early stages, and the foundation of numerous important concepts in social science is built on careful description of exemplary instances (e.g., feral childhood: Davis, 1947).

The age-stratified relationship is worthy of much more study than it has received (cf. also Steinman and Grube in this issue). Many researchers have ignored age-stratification of couples entirely; a few have gone out of their way to depreciate such relationships. For example, Peele (1988, p. 167) argues that elders who fall in love with much younger partners are displaying "retarded relationship skills" and "psychological dysfunction."

Yet Elia (1987) emphasizes the antiquity of age-stratified homosexual love, including its teacher-student aspects (p. 11). Fang-fu and Yung-mei (1987) remind us of the equivalent importance of age-stratified homosexual coupling in ancient Chinese society. The Isherwood-Bachardy relationship, with its age gap of 30 years, and 33-year duration (until the death of Isherwood) is certainly a "classic" example of age-stratified gay love and therefore worthy of detailed analysis.

METHODOLOGY

Having crossed a continent to interview a total stranger, I was determined not to spoil this rare opportunity, even if that required, in the cause of sociological inquiry, a gentle manipulation of the interviewee. The greatest problem I anticipated was to keep Don talking *about himself* rather than about Christopher. I had heard that he is a soft-spoken artist accustomed to spending most of his hours at home in his studio. I was not surprised when he told me that he and Christopher enjoyed celebrating their anniversaries by themselves: "We never gave parties for dates that we celebrated." I commented that this was unusual, considering how much time they already spent in the same house. Don explained:

> *Well, we liked each other. We really entertained each other. Always the best holiday was to be by ourselves. After all, much of the time we had visitors, or I had a sitter, and in a certain way we lived public lives. We already moved in several worlds—his literary world, my art world, then there was the gay world—and the film world. To be with each other was our most secret, private pleasure.*

Thus, what one might colloquially term Don's "shyness," was, from the point of view of an interviewer, a problem in overcoming information control. Despite the openness of Isherwood about his own homosexuality and the public recognition of Isherwood and Bachardy as a *gay couple* (cf. McWhirter and Mattison, 1984, p. 8) there were numerous reasons to expect that I would have problems in practicing the sociologist's trade as *licensed voyeur* (Berger, 1963).

We learn very little about Bachardy from Isherwood's writings. In *My Guru and His Disciple*, Isherwood (1980, p. 209) reveals his smitten state at age 48 when he "realized [he] had fallen deeply in love with a boy. . . . eighteen years old." He speaks of his reaction to the 30-year gap between them, and the emotional intensity of the relationship. "I knew that, this time, I had really committed myself. Don might leave me, but I couldn't possibly leave him, unless he ceased to need me." Yet, writing a quarter-century later, he devotes only 120 words in all, to this profound event, and almost none to Don's feelings. All we are told about Don is that his face showed "vitality, a shining eagerness for experience."

By the time *My Guru* was written, Don must have held an importance in Isherwood's life at least equal to that of his swami, who is described for scores of pages. There are subsequent brief references in *My Guru* to Don's contact with the swami, but no revelation of Don's character or feelings. This lifelong respect for Don's privacy suggested to me that the information control involved was at least as much Don's wish as Isherwood's literary scruple, and I could therefore expect a difficult interview.

As noted already, little of Bachardy's feelings is revealed in *October*. He appeared briefly in the TV program, *Down There on a Visit* (Granada TV, 1980) but neither his comments nor those of Isherwood revealed much about Don's role in the relationship. Perhaps the most interesting feature of John Lehman's personal recollections of Isherwood, published (posthumously) a year after my interview with Don, is how little he reveals about Bachardy's feelings. Obviously he also knew Don's desire for privacy. Finally, Don's written communications in arranging the interview with me were cryptic, on postcards. I was coming to the interview as a perfect stranger without even a mutual introduction. Why should he trust me?

I decided that the best method for encouraging self-disclosure would be to take the risks involved in the Jourard technique (Jourard, 1964; 1971). This method requires the interviewer to "gain and manage entry" to the private world of the the interviewee (Johnson, 1975, p. 50) through a "research bargain" which, in the case of older gay people, may be more than usually difficult to negotiate (cf. Ponse, 1976).

In the positivist tradition, an interviewer is expected to interact with the respondent as little as possible, so as not to introduce extraneous variables. The ideal, exemplified in the Milgram experiments (Milgram, 1973), is to tape-record the interview questions so that there is no interpersonal effect at all. But Jourard argues an opposite approach, consistent with qualitative methods in sociology. The interviewer fully participates in the interview by offering to expose as many and as revealing "secrets" about his private life as he is asking the respondent to reveal.

The early stages of a Jourard-type interaction may find the interviewer doing more of the talking than the interviewee. If the technique works, the respondent slowly begins to feel obligated to match the interviewer's revelations with his own, to keep up his side of the implicit research bargain. There are considerable risks. The interviewee may regard the interviewer's self-disclosures as a violation of privacy rules (Ponse, 1976). Rather than become complicit in the violations by matching self-disclosures, the respondent may stick to noncommittal remarks, or even break off the encounter. Or he may sit back and let the interviewer do most of the talking.

Happily, the Jourard method worked to our mutual satisfaction. I revealed a lot about myself and my partner and Don fully reciprocated. More important, he was very happy with the ensuing transcript of the interview (which I had promised to check with him before use, another key element in establishing the trust-bargain of a Jourard interview). I removed most of the revelations about myself and my partner from the first draft of the *Christopher Street* article since they had served their methodological purpose. But Don urged me to restore them because they made the report of our encounter more personal. He and his friends were delighted with the *Christopher Street* publication. Thus, the need to be concerned about the reciprocal impact of sociological investigation on the person studied was fully discharged. Mission accomplished!

THE INTERVIEW

When did you first know you were gay?

I knew very early. I have an older brother who is also gay. He came out with trumpets blaring. That made it much easier for me. I was always perfectly content with being gay; it was never a struggle.

Tell me about meeting Christopher.

We met on the beach . . . probably about 1951. My brother and I used to go down to the beach on weekends. Chris and I said hello to each other for several years; he knew my brother better than me; I met him through Ted. One weekend my brother and I were on our way down to the beach and we decided to stop and have breakfast with Chris; it was along the way. That was so enjoyable Chris decided to come to the beach with us, and we spent the day together, and that was so nice we decided to have dinner together, and at the end of the day we all agreed to do it again the following weekend.

Did you have any personal agenda, at that time, about where these encounters on the beach might eventually lead? I realize it's a long time to reflect back. . . .

No, it seemed perfectly natural to me, the way we got to know each other. We enjoyed each other's company and just naturally wanted to be together.

There was never any revelation, maybe five or ten years later, that either of you had a different agenda than the one that came about?

How do you mean?

Well, I'll give you my own case as an example. I met my lover, Devon, by approaching him three times in three hours on the Toronto gay beach. The first two times he just said two words and went back to sleep because he'd had a particularly good time the night before. Finally I got him talking to me. He was so much my type that I was determined to make an impression. Much to my amazement he eventually asked "What are you doing for dinner?" It wouldn't have mattered if I was having dinner with the Queen; I would still have said "nothing." It wasn't until five years later, at an anniversary party where we exchanged these rings, that I first thought to ask him, "Why DID you invite a pestering stranger to dinner that night?" He told me that he was just breaking up with a previous affair, who was at this dinner party, and he wanted to make it very clear the affair was over, by arriving and leaving with a new companion. Of course, he had no intention of ever seeing me again afterward, because he thought I'd been rather obnoxious in pushing myself on him at the beach. So his agenda at the time was really quite different from what eventually came about. We became lovers!

I remember that it was I who proposed that we live together. It seemed perfectly natural to me.

That was in 1953, after you'd known each other to talk to, for about two years. Do you recall his response to your proposal?

I think he was a little surprised, and apprehensive. You see, people my age weren't at all his thing. I was much the youngest person he'd had any dealings with. He was seeing a person at the time who was in his middle thirties. A boy of 18 was really way out of his line.

He was worried you weren't mature enough?

Oh no, he was sure I was mature; he said I was surprisingly mature for my age, but it was illegal, you know, and he was a cautious man. He didn't want to get in trouble, and of course people were quite scandalized. When we first went to New York together it went around town that Christopher had brought a 12-year-old with him. I did look very young.

You did indeed. Your picture with Christopher at 48 makes you look about 14, not 18. Perhaps the gap in your ages, not merely your youth, must have made him wonder about any future relationship. Had you always been attracted to much older men?

Well, I had very little experience at that age, and I'd never spent very much time with people my own age. In fact at school I was a loner. It was quite natural to me to prefer the company of people older than myself.

Can you recall, when you first met Christopher, if there was a particular image or type in your mind, of the person you'd like to love?

I hadn't really thought about it. I wasn't looking for anyone to live with, it wasn't a goal. I wasn't looking for love, but here was this man who was so much fun to be with. It seemed perfectly natural we should spend as much time together as possible and I knew he felt the same way.

Was there any unevenness about who was taking most of the initiatives? Were there times when one of you seemed to feel more committed to keeping the relationship going than the other? You know what the French say—a bit cynically—"in every marriage, one person loves and the other allows himself to be loved?"

I think in a healthy relationship those roles are interchangeable; it goes back and forth.

Did a time come when you began to think there was too big an age gap between yourself and Christopher?

Oh no, never. Chris regretted the age difference, but I often said to him, 'I don't think it would have worked nearly so well for us, if there hadn't been that difference.' We offered each other the contrast of a younger and an older perspective, and it kept any kind of competitiveness out of our relationship.

You never felt any competitiveness with him?

Not at all.

That's really interesting to me, because Devon and I often have competitions and power struggles. Did you not have power struggles with Christopher?

Very few; I think far less than most people. You see, Christopher was old enough that he didn't have to worry about power. He was glad to relinquish it. He was pleased whenever I showed initiative. When I took the lead he was perfectly willing to let me run the show as I wanted to. He didn't have to keep proving himself.

I think I only began to come to that situation two or three years ago, when I realized I was getting too old to carry the canoe on portages. Devon has been going to the gym and is actually in much better shape than when we met, so I'm rather glad now to relinquish the canoe. It's a real pleasure to watch him carry it over a mile-long portage. But I still find it difficult to surrender direction of the relationship—or even of the route we're going to canoe. I wonder if something the same wasn't true of Christopher? I don't mean to be offensive, but I seem to remember reading somewhere that there was a time when you were afraid of becoming a sort of "Mrs. Isherwood." In other words, no more than a supportive figure in a great man's life?

Oh yes, that's true too. You see, Christopher's surrender of power to me was between us. In the eyes of the world, he would be the leading figure in our relationship, but that never bothered me. He was distinguished when I first knew him, so I was fairly used to that. I took pride in his reputation.

Do you recall if there was some particular time when you finally felt this relationship could last, perhaps for many years?

Oh, I presumed from the beginning that it would last. Christopher was the reticent one in the first years. I think he expected the 30-year difference between us would eventually mean I'd leave and find someone my own age, but I never saw it like that, and indeed I was right. You see, I have always lived more in the present. It was Christopher who worried about what was coming, more than I ever did.

And there never did come a time when you felt like looking at men your own age as partners?

Yes, I did occasionally, and he allowed me my freedom. He'd had all that experience before he knew me. It wasn't fair for him to deny experience to me, and if you do love somebody, you want them to be happy, to have what makes them happy.

That's interesting, because that's exactly the approach I took with Devon. We're talking pre-AIDS, of course. He's very grateful now that I let him have all the fun he wanted with other guys. I think if I'd tried to insist on monogamy, then even if he'd stayed with me, he'd resent me now, for making him miss so many opportunities to fool around in his late twenties. But there is always the fear of the partner meeting somebody else who would be more than just fun. Didn't that fear occur to Christopher, or you?

No. Christopher was a difficult act to follow.

That's a wonderful compliment to him. You mean physically too?

Yes.

(There was a long, meditative pause between us at this point. Don had begun the interview very shyly, often looking away from me, into the distance, as he talked. His hand often seemed to be protecting his mouth, so I quietly worried if the tape recorder was catching his voice. But with this last "Yes" there was a flash in his eye and a firmness in his voice that made me feel he had lowered his guard for the first time. I broke the silence by deciding that now was a good time to ask a question I'd originally planned for much later in the interview.)

This is difficult to ask. Is there going to be another act? I mean, you're younger than me, with a life expectancy of another 20 years . . . .

Who knows? I'm not ruling anything out.

But on the other hand, not looking yet?

Some . . . (another long pause). I'm very busy, life is very full, the day isn't long enough to get everything done . . .

And obviously any new partner would have to be a very special person indeed.

Well, I would think under all circumstances a partner must be very special.

Quite so, but if one has a partner for a year or so, he may not be all that difficult to replace, and I have certainly replaced short-term partners, several times. But after ten years with Devon, I can't think what I'd do if I lost him . . . to say nothing of being together thirty years. I couldn't imagine what another partner would be like.

Well, I've been lately seeing a young man who is almost exactly 30 years younger than I am, and that's been very interesting for me, because seeing this young man reminds me continually of my early years with Christopher, and now I know so much better how he was feeling.

So you've sort of gone through the looking glass, into a world in which you occupy the other role, looking back?

And I remember so much of what happened with us, and I find myself saying "Ah, ah, now I know." I know what he meant when he said certain things.

So that a younger man, who had the wisdom you had at 18, might realize that because of your experience, you would be particularly empathetic as an older lover, having once been the younger lover of an older man?

I hope that may be so.

But these days are so different from the 1950s. One of the problems of many of the older men I've interviewed is that the gay world, "the life" they knew, has been short-circuited. Younger gays can meet each other easily in bars and discos, without the intermediation of the older men who used to control the networks of parties. Nowadays, many older men feel left out in the cold, as if gay liberation was only for the young. Do you have that feeling at all?

No, it never occurred to me.

Then how do you meet a man thirty years younger—at a bar or disco?

No, I never go. I don't attempt to be part of a younger crowd. You see, I have somebody sitting for me every day; it's easy for me to make contact with people.

Devon never went to college—while I have a doctorate. It's often a problem. Was a difference in education ever a problem for you and Christopher?

Oh, he took pleasure in educating me, and I was a very good pupil. I was going to college when we met, but I never finished college, and I learned so very much more from him than I could have learned in school.

Didn't you resent that? I mean, students may learn a lot from a teacher, but resent the teacher at the same time.

He was an unusual man.

And you were an unusual student?

Yes I was, and I realize that more lately. He often told me that I was, but at that age it takes a long time to develop confidence in oneself—belief in oneself. He kept reassuring me, but I would reply that it was because he loved me that I seemed special to him. But lately I've realized I really was special.

Does that mean you went through your 30s, maybe even your 40s, not entirely sure of yourself?

It took me a long time to invent myself as an artist. I really had to start from scratch. That took a lot of doing.

But worse than that, you had to start by getting out from someone else's shadow?

Yes, and at the same time, trying not to blame that person for his shadow, which he couldn't do anything about. I had to be independent but I couldn't blame him for his celebrity because he had it before I knew him and he deserved it. But I also had the need to be somebody in my own right.

When did you finally feel that way?

Oh, when I started working professionally as an artist, by gradual degrees, I came to believe in myself more.

Have you kept track of your own growth over the years?

Christopher always encouraged me to keep a journal. He said 'You'll never regret it," so I kept one largely to please him. He always kept one. When he died I started reading all the journals he'd left behind and that was a wonderful experience for me. I'd never read them before, other than the parts he'd published. So here was a history of our relationship written by this wonderful writer over 30 years. It was an extraordinary experience for me, and a lot of it is written directly to me. He knew I would read it one day.

Did you ever have a situation during those 30 years, where you read each other parts of your journals, to reassure each other? I'm thinking of my own experience. Devon used to think I was writing things in my journals that were critical of him — things I didn't want to say out loud — so I gave him several years of my journals and said "Read this and see."

No, we very early on agreed we wouldn't have access to each other's journals, and even as young as I was, I realized that if he let me read what he was writing, he probably wouldn't write as much about me. I wanted to encourage him to write about me as much as he felt like doing, and indeed I am in his journals a great deal.

But that means he never read yours?

Alas, you know, it never occurred to me. When I finished reading his journals I started re-reading my own. That's the first thing that hit me, that I'd never shared mine with him. Of course he always knew I'd read his. It never occurred to me to give mine to him, and he would have enjoyed them. I remember once or twice I read certain passages to him, and he was always interested, but I never let him just read at his leisure, and it's one thing I very much regret. I wish I'd thought to share them with him because he would have very much enjoyed them.

Yes, the journals would have complemented each other.

Indeed, they do. I've been very pleased to discover that often we have written about the same things. We were both very happy from different points of view.

In reading both sets of journals, have you discovered times when you and Christopher felt radically different about something, but didn't say so at the time?

No, we always shared our feelings at the time; we were always close, we talked a lot to each other. We had the same reactions to people. We loved the same movies. I knew exactly what he'd feel about any movie, for example.

That is amazing, considering your age difference, and your difference in education. Weren't there things you really differed about, for example one liking ballet, the other something else?

No, we were really extremely compatible. He was naturally more literary, and I more visual, but when we collaborated, for instance on certain film projects, it was a very good balance. He saw things in terms of his literary interests, and I saw the scenes visually.

Yes, I love October *for that reason; it's such a wonderful collaboration and I'm very envious of it, because Devon and I have difficulty collaborating.*

Well, it's tough for heterosexuals too, you know. If you can work with somebody, that's an extraordinary bonus. We wrote a lot of screen plays together, and it was very enjoyable for both of us. He got to a certain point in his life where he didn't want to take on screen writing any more. It was just too much of an effort to do by himself, but if I was willing to work with him, then that made it fun for him. We'd get up earlier in the morning than usual, and often we'd have our day's writing stint done by 10:30 or 11:00 in the morning and we'd have the rest of the day to do our own things. I'd have a sitter in the afternoon and he'd work on whatever book he was writing.

And you never felt any conflict in these collaborations? There must have been times when you wanted a word in, and he wanted it out?

Oh, but you see I was never silly in that way. He was always the writer. We would discuss scenes, work out the progression of a story, but when it came down to the actual writing I just sat at the typewriter and took dictation. In that way it seemed I had the best of the deal. I had all the pleasure of the writing without any of the responsibility.

That's a wonderful way to put it.

And I'm a good typist. It was really the most useful thing I learned in my entire schooling, and when I first knew Chris, he was working on a book called *The World in the Evening* and I helped him with the final draft. I typed it, so we started collaborating when I was 18.

And you didn't see that as somehow demeaning?

Oh no, in fact there's a party in the opening section of the book, and he names the last names of the guests, and he put in the name Bachardy.

I guess it's obvious without saying, that you and Christopher were pioneering a kind of relationship which is still not common today.

It's funny, we were pioneers of a kind, but it never occurred to us that we were setting an example for anyone. We were only doing what came naturally.

Were there any other gay partnerships around that could serve as role models for you—people you could watch to see how they were handling things?

No, there really wasn't anyone else around us with the kind of relationship we had.

Auden and Kallman didn't strike you as an example of the older and younger gay man in relationship?

Well, they were a long way off in New York. Christopher didn't really like New York, and we didn't often go, so we didn't see much of them, and often when we did see Auden in New York, Kallman would be away somewhere.

There must have been times when you asked yourself 'How am I going to work this problem through?' Did you look around in literature or movies, or was there someone you could talk to?

I've had very few confidants in my life. Christopher was my key confidant and I told him far more than I told anyone else. I sometimes felt the need to have people who were my friends rather than his but it was just a mental idea of mine. When it came right down to it I didn't really want a confidant other than him. I knew he was very wise. He never gave me bad advice. Occasionally I wouldn't do what he suggested, just to be independent, and I always regretted it!

But that can also be an annoying experience, to find someone else is right after all.

Oh, he was so tactful. He handled me brilliantly.

And your very choice of words there suggests that if you have a relationship now with a younger man, you'll feel competent to handle it?

Yes, I learned a great deal from him, and if I can do as well as he did I'll be doing very well indeed.

I take it you never sought any kind of professional counseling in difficult times? There must have been times when Christopher saw that you had problems he couldn't do much about. Do you think now, looking back, that there were times when you posed a difficult problem for him?

Oh, gigantic problems. His journals are full of them, but he did have that recourse. He was a natural writer and for him, writing was a cure in itself. And he's very kind to me in the journals, much kinder than I deserved. Yes, I rocked the boat a good deal.

It's obvious one of the things you want to emphasize is these journals . . .

I couldn't recommend it more strongly; he was absolutely right about keeping one.

And would you add to his advice, in retrospect, that it would also be a good idea to exchange journals once in a while?

No, because as soon as you give somebody access, you're not writing it for yourself, but from the point of view of the person who's going to be reading it. When I say I regret not showing him mine, I mean very late in life; it would have amused him in those last years. One reason I didn't think of it was that my journal is rather messy, handwritten on bits of paper, because I didn't want to feel I was officially writing something. That way I didn't feel the responsibility. If it was more like a book it would have. . . .

Moved into Christopher's territory?

Yes, exactly. I was very respectful of Christopher's territory. He gave me a real respect for writing. He cured me of all amateur notions about writing. I knew it was a really tough job that cost him the maximum of effort. I knew what effort he devoted—he wrote and rewrote.

What about his journals, were they like his books?

His journals are very interesting. What makes them so fascinating is that everything he put into print was considered down to the last comma, but the journals are spontaneous. He never rewrote the journals. And that spontaneity gives him a voice that isn't in his published work. There is a freedom and energy that is to me quite exciting, and the material—he was a natural diarist and these journals may be his very best work.

But they also pose something of a problem, don't they? Do you have to decide whether you want to see those published, and Christopher's image continued, or whether you need to be yourself and work on your own life?

I'm certainly going to see to it that his journals are published. They're too good for me to keep to myself.

But you're not going to publish yours for the same period?

I wouldn't even think of publishing mine until all of his are published. I'm in no hurry to even make a decision about that. What I am doing is gradually typing mine, so at least they're legible.

And in the process, reliving them?

Yes, and I'm keeping journals of my current experience.

Did you ever have a room of your own?

No, we always slept in the same bed, and always very, very close. That was a basic part of our relationship.

Christopher makes a wonderful comment in October *that the one time when your distance in ages was least obvious was in sleep, as if you were communicating in your sleep.*

Yes, we often felt most intimate in bed, sleeping together. I think it's essential in a relationship. I can't imagine sleeping in another bed, or in another room. To have that basic physical contact seems to me the whole point of a relationship. And, you see, we never had animals, because we both instinctively knew that we each wanted the affection that would go to any animal we might have. We gave it to each other rather than an animal. And we had animal personas with each other. I think when you examine most intimate relationships you'll find that all sorts of people act out animal personas. Having pets would have weakened that.

So you've never had a room of your own?

No, I've never wanted one. Christopher used the big bedroom as his writing room; the other bedroom was our only bedroom. I have a little workroom with a desk, and my studio attached to the house. We were not only in each other's voice range, we were very close, and yet, we could spend an entire day on the premises and not necessarily see each other. I could be out in my studio and he in the back of the house writing, but we always had that sense of each other's presence, and it was always so encouraging. Knowing that he was there doing his work made mine more appetizing to me, and I believe he felt the same way.

Do you think the specialness of your relationship depended on the fact that each of you had an independent profession; neither had to go and work in an office?

Oh, he allowed me that freedom. Imagine being able to invent oneself as an artist right from the very foundations; it was a great satisfaction. He took such pride in my work, and when I started having success he was so pleased. He often said it was one of the great joys of his life to participate in my career as an artist. He was as proud as any father could have been.

Was there that aspect to it?

Yes, that too. We really had a wide range and cultivated every aspect of our relationship.

And that didn't make you uncomfortable?

Well you see, I'd never been close to my own father. Chris was a year older than my real father and I was still young enough to be interested in a real father figure and Christopher was such a wonderful one.

But what about when you were, say, 38?

No, I never got tired of him in that role. I think it kept me young for a long time. For years I was often the youngest person present.

But there must have come a time when both of you, even by silent agreement, understood that in addition to this father-son relationship, there was also a peer relationship?

Well, you know Chris always told me I was very sophisticated for my age. I think he treated me as an equal in those early years. He never condescended to me and I don't think he felt the need to. We had a curious rapport from the earliest times.

So you felt both a peer and a son at the same time?

Yes, these weren't in conflict; they enriched the relationship rather than narrowing it down.

What about toward the end? Weren't you more the burden-bearer?

Yes, I was, but that didn't alter anything. It seemed a perfectly natural development when I started taking on more responsibility. In fact, one of my earlier complaints used to be that I did everything, because I ran the house, and 'did this and that and that.' And then, when he got sick and couldn't do anything, I suddenly realized how much work he used to do. He just hadn't drawn attention to it.

For example he had kept the accounts?

Yes, he almost always kept the accounts.

That's often a big problem, particularly between two men in our culture, each raised to be self-supporting. It's one thing Devon and I haven't worked out yet; we still have separate accounts. We haven't got to the point where it's ours, rather than yours or mine.

Oh, for a long time we just had the one bank account because I wasn't earning any money to speak of. When I started earning money as an artist I had to have my own account from the point of view of taxes, but that was just an outward form. We always thought in terms of pooled resources.

But he bought this house? Was his name always on the deed?

Yes.

And that didn't bother you? There weren't times when you thought 'I'm living in Chris's house, not in our house'?

No, we just didn't split things up like that. I knew that what was his, was mine. It wouldn't have impressed me to have my name on the deed — it might have done —

It wasn't just the deed, was it? He might want a leather couch, and you one covered in cloth?

Oh, he always deferred to me in anything visual.

What about travels? I might want to go to Costa Rica, and Devon somewhere quite different.

Well, I made some trips by myself, to do with my art work, but I would only be away a few weeks at the most.

What of vacations together?

We always seemed to want to go to the same places.

Please excuse me, but this all seems much too successful! I find it hard to believe everything worked so smoothly. There must have been times when you disagreed, aside from that time mentioned by Christopher in October, about whether to have curtains in the bedroom . . .

We fought like crazy. I think any relationship can't be worth having if its all sweetness. If there isn't some friction then maybe there isn't very much interest.

Then what did you fight about?

(A very long pause, broken by several 'ahs.') Well, I think I often invented things to fight about just for the sake of fighting. I pretended to care more about a thing than I really did, just to increase the energy level. We both had highly developed temperaments.

And who would be the peacemaker at the end of those fights?

We both were capable of making peace. That wasn't a role one or other played more often. I was often the first to say I was wrong. . . .

But you also enjoyed the energetic workout of a fight?

Yes.

Were these fights over serious things, touching your very being as a person?

I sometimes felt that way while the argument was going on, but the core of our relationship was always strong.

So there was never, ever a time when you reviewed things in your mind, and considered that this relationship had gone its natural span?

No. (*long pause*) No. Well, I'd never met anyone like him. He was really unique, and I had the sense to know that very early on. And also there was a great bond between us. We were both Vedantists . . .

Ah, so your philosophical and spiritual feelings grew together?

Yes.

But that involved one of you before the other.

Yes, and he never pushed it. He never tried to persuade me to 'join up.' He was never a proselytizer. We did often go together to the temple, but I wasn't initiated for a good 10 years.

That's a long time to make up your mind.

Yes, I'm glad that I didn't rush into anything. Once I did become a Vedantist I know it was a great satisfaction to Chris. He felt it was an extra bond, an extra closeness, and indeed it was, for the rest of our lives together.

Did you ever need the services of an intermediary, someone to go from one of you to the other during a misunderstanding or conflict?

No, we never did. You see, as much as we could, we didn't weaken the bonds between us by sharing with anyone else what we could have by ourselves.

So even though you had a number of celebrities and guests here over the years, they never got much of a glimpse of your private world?

No.

That's interesting, because one of Devon's complaints about me is the violation of too many of our privacies. He says I'm "too public." Do you think your mutual privacy was an important thing in a lasting relationship?

Oh yes indeed, Chris and I were very, very private, and we didn't talk about ourselves to anyone else. That's something we instinctively understood. It was natural to us both to be very closed about what went on between us.

One of the things Devon has told me is that he had to make a choice about whether to 'live in John Lee's world or not.' He had a feeling of crisis about whether to live in my cultural world of books, theatre, politics and so on, or to find his own world. Did you ever feel you had to choose Christopher's world?

Well, his was established already, and it seemed to me a wonderful world, glamorous, with very interesting friends. The people who sought him out were very interesting to me. I was glad to be part of his world.

Did you ever feel threatened that it would swallow you up?

Yes, that's why I had to become an artist. I had to have my own identity and credentials, I couldn't keep riding on his coat tails. By gradual degrees I did develop my own personality and identity and as soon as I did, his world was even more interesting to me, because I felt I had a genuine reason for being there.

Were there times when you told Christopher not to come too far into 'your world'? I'm thinking, for example, of a time when Devon didn't want me in the same gay-lib group he'd chosen to join. Were there such times? Perhaps not wanting him at a gallery opening where he'd steal the limelight?

Oh no, he was very interested to meet my artist friends and entered into my world with great appetite, and in later years we saw every bit as much of my artist friends as his literary friends. You see, he didn't particularly want to share his writing experience with other writers. His instinct was always to be with people who weren't writers. He wanted to get away from that small literary world and experience others. It was a pleasure for him to meet my artist friends and many of them became as good friends of his as mine.

But it didn't threaten you that he might take over in some way—that they might talk to him and ignore you?

Well, by the time I was a known artist we'd already coped with that problem. I was proud of him, and glad to introduce him to my artist friends. He was a jewel, and they realized it too. He was amusing and made them laugh. He was always an asset to me, never a weight or drawback, never. He was so charming. He didn't take himself seriously as so many writers do.

Were there rituals you developed over the years, to celebrate the fact that you were together so long?

We had our anniversaries, and our way was always to be by ourselves. We never gave parties for dates that we celebrated.

Not even the round numbers, like 10 or 20 years together?

No, what we most wanted to do was to be by ourselves. We'd stay home together and cook supper.

Did the changes in the gay world after Stonewall make much difference to your relationship?

No, we were public in the '50s. We quite often went to Hollywood parties where we were the only gay couple. We heard later that some people were quite scandalized. I still looked very young, and in the '50s, it was quite unusual for two men to openly go as a couple. So when the '70s came, what was there to do that we hadn't been doing all along? The only difference it made to Christopher, and that was quite a large difference, was that he could come out in his writing, and that freedom meant a great deal to him.

But what about you? How did it feel to have your relationship out in the open?

Oh, I always went with him on speaking engagements and had my share of notoriety. For instance *The Advocate* put a picture of me on the cover, which horrified my father. He was bitterly ashamed. His attitude was 'you can be queer if you want to, but do you have to advertise it?'

Did you lose important friends over this new public stance?

Well, if friends dropped me for something like that, they couldn't be really important to me, could they? I was sad for them, but they were depriving themselves and behaving idiotically. Most of my friends had known I was gay anyway.

But it's one thing to know it privately, and another for you to announce it in the papers, isn't it?

I would have dared anyone to challenge me on that point. If they couldn't be my friends on that basis, that was their problem.

(We stopped for a second round of tea for me, coffee for Don, and our moments of sharing that ritual allowed me to move to a difficult question.)
Were you able to prepare yourself for Christopher's death?

I knew when he fell sick that I had to get ready for it, but when it really happens, you realize there is no way to prepare for it. It is my personality to cope with things as they happen. Chris was a worrier by nature; he foresaw situations and worried, but I'm quite the reverse. I thought I was used to the idea of his dying but once he was gone, it was very much different than I had expected.

Do you want to say more, or is that too painful?

When someone isn't there, it's just very different. You can accept it psychologically, but the physical absence is very impressive.

Have friends helped?

Friends have been very supportive. When Chris died I was invited out a great deal and people were most kind. I almost had to fight for an evening to myself. But no one could fill Chris's absence. There would be no way for anybody to fill his role or even approach it. My whole instinct is not to try to repeat that relationship. It would be impossible. To me it is important to have completely different kinds of relationships, as I was telling you earlier, about this young man I've been seeing. That, to me, is interesting because it is completely different from my experience with Christopher. And in fact it's casting me in Christopher's role.

But AIDS has changed life so much since the gay world you knew when growing up with Chris. Do you think your experience will be relevant?

Things are very different and it's very difficult to be a young gay person these days. I was fortunate to have had all that freedom. But you know, safe sex is an awful lot of fun!

It seems obvious that you don't feel oppressed by having been gay all your life?

Oh no, it's always seemed to me an enormous advantage.

An advantage?

Yes, being gay is one of the very best things that could have happened to me, and if my parents were responsible, then they have my undying gratitude. My life without my gayness would have been intolerable.

That's amazing—I'm sure you know that's not what a lot of gay people believe?

Well they should, and I'm sorry if they don't.

Many gay people worry that their relationships are basically physical ones that won't last long. I've read that Christopher was fond of young men with goodlooking legs, like yours. How did that work out? As you got older, what happened to that attraction? Did the physical attraction just quietly suffuse into friendship?

I don't think we either of us lost it. He was always to me a very beautiful man, and he got more beautiful as he got older, and I told him so repeatedly. He would scoff sometimes, but I believed it.

And he said the same thing to you?

Oh yes.

Didn't you find that remarkable?

Well, we were remarkable people. Something enhanced our physical attraction. I believe physical contact at night, sleeping closely in the same bed, keeps that attraction alive.

So it becomes not so much a sexual thing as a physical closeness?

We were always physically close to each other, and if you are, the sexual thing is just so natural.

Was Vedanta helpful in that? Was there a sort of spiritualizing of the flesh?

No, neither of us spiritualized the flesh. We enjoyed the flesh for its own sake.

Even when Christopher was in his 70s?

Oh yes.

Well, you certainly make me feel very hopeful.

ANALYSIS

The Jourard method of interviewing produced such a revealing disclosure of Don Bachardy's perspective on his 33 years with Isherwood and his hopes for the future that it would be insulting not to let the reader draw insights and conclusions without my help. Here, I propose only to link some of the key insights with general social science concerns related to gay aging, with the hope of stimulating further research into age-stratified gay male relationships.

1. The Multiple-Role Matrix of Age-Stratified Love

The key characteristic of the age-stratified relationship is not the absolute ages of the partners but the gap between those ages relative to the absolute ages (cf. Steinman in this volume). Thus, a gap of 10 years is much greater in its effects when the partners are, say, 22 and 32, than when they are 52 and 62. What counts is not the age gap, but the perception of that gap. Don Bachardy's recollection of his and Christopher's experience of the gap between them at the outset is especially revealing of the way they managed that gap throughout their relationship.

Even though he was falling in love with a man as old as his father, Don (at least in retrospect) did not perceive that as out of *his* line. Instead, he has perceived the gap as out of line *for Christopher*, whom he calls a "cautious man." Don recalls the gap between Christopher and himself from the point of view of his own youthfulness (looking like "a 12-year-old") and with "little experience at that age" with gay relationships. He recalls that the age gap was not a problem for him; it was "quite natural."

Don reconstructs in reminisence a partner for whom the age gap was a problem: "People my age weren't at all his thing. I was much the youngest person he'd had any dealings with. He was seeing a person at the time who was in his middle 30s. A boy of 18 was really out of his line." Now we know from Isherwood's autobiography that, factually speaking, this is not the case. Christopher had been far from cautious in relationships with young men such as Heinz, a German boy whom he loved and attempted to bring to England (Isherwood, 1976). John Lehman, a biographer of Isherwood, reports that when Christopher first visited America he asked his literary agent, George Davis, to "find him exactly the kind of American boy he dreamed of. . . . a beautiful blond boy, about 18, intelligent, with very sexy legs," and Davis obliged. Lehman (1987) continues:

> Christopher . . . became infatuated with him. "Vernon". . . . became the representative "American boy" . . . He occupied the place in Christopher's emotional life that had been left vacant when Heinz had been wrested from him. When he returned to England "Vernon" continued to haunt him. (pp. 44-45)

It would be a mistake to regard Lehman's memoir as "true" and Don's recollection as a mistake or fabrication (Goffman, 1959). Don is certainly as familiar with the facts of Isherwood's biography as Lehman, but in life review with me, he is not reporting facts, but perceptions shaped by a long and intimate relationship (Butler, 1977). These perceptions ought to be instructive to older gay men in love with younger partners. In my research (Lee, 1986; also cf. Steinman in this volume), the *elder* often worries about the gap of an age-stratified relationship. What Don tells us, in many ways through this interview, is that the age gap may be unimportant for the younger man. Thus, the older man may be well advised to look at other aspects of the relationship when problems occur rather than jumping to the conclusion that the age gap itself is the problem.

The members of any intimate dyad interact on a number of levels with varying awareness of alternative role scripts (McCall & Simmons, 1966). But an age-stratified relationship adds special challenges and problems to this interaction, and when it is additionally a mentor-protégé relationship, there are still further opportunities and risks. As Lehman notes in his *Memoir* (1987, p. 84) the 30-year gap between Don and Christopher "would have been great even in Ancient Greece."

At least in retrospect (the accuracy of which in Isherwood's case is strengthened by his life-long habit of keeping a journal) Christopher realized that his relationship with Don would have a "responsibility which was almost fatherly" (Isherwood, 1980, p. 209). He says nothing, then or later, about Don's attitude to a *son* role. Now, in retrospect, Don tells us he felt himself a peer and a son at the same time, and in addition a "student." Presumably there were interfacing roles in Christopher's mind for all three of Don's roles. There were also "animal personas," and roles as co-believers in Vedanta.

Don is clearly aware of the way his 30-years-older partner manipulated him tactfully but effectively, and Don manipulated in return. They "fought like crazy" when Don "invented things to fight about." There are already some interesting analytical models of these multi-leveled "role transactions" in psychology and sociology (e.g., Simmel, 1953; Blau, 1964; Berne, 1964; Bach & Wyden, 1971). But to my knowledge, even those which analyze gay male dyads (e.g., McWhirter & Mattison, 1984) and the strains caused by "stage discrepancy" (Mattison and McWhirter, 1987) pay little if any attention to the dynamics introduced by age stratification.

An elder partner has some advantages of experience and access to resources when manipulating interaction with a junior partner (cf. Foner, 1984; Brecher, 1984) but there are disadvantages too in a youth-dominated culture (Berger, 1971). Further research could usefully examine the resources each partner can call upon and distinguish dyadic interaction into at least three types (approximate parity, advantages of the elder, and of the younger). Then overall routine patterns of interaction could be analyzed according to type, and frequency distribution in proportion to total interaction.

For example, Christopher apparently took care of the accounts as long as he was able, while Don saw to furnishings. In the early years, advantages of income would obviously have placed more power in Christopher's hands, while choices of furnishings, paid for by Christopher in any case, would have given Don little leverage on direction of the relationship. But over time, the furnishings would have created an environment dictated by Don, while the financial imbalance diminished. These processes slowly led to a balanced dyad (peers, rather than patron/protégé) and link nicely with processes outlined by Steinman's "Social Exchanges Between Older and Younger Gay Male Partners" (in this volume).

In some areas Don leaves us with puzzles rather than explanations: By what decision-making processes did two such disparate partners arrive at "both always wanting to travel to the same places" at the same point in time? Don appears to be overly modest in his recollection of his early contributions to the relationship, leaving us with the impression that he got more than he gave from the older, famous Isherwood. But we could guess that Christopher, at 48, found in 18-year-old Don a vital recapitulation of his tragically fated pre-war relationship with Heinz. Can it be coincidence alone, that just prior to "falling deeply in love with a boy" (Isherwood, 1980, p. 209), Christopher had a happy reunion with Heinz, who had survived the war, and married? (Lehman, 1987, p. 83)

Being in love with a teenager again was probably a way for Christopher to rediscover his own youthful energy. There are hints of this as John Lehman (1987, p. 84) recalls his fascination and distress when, in 1952, Isherwood allowed him to read his journal of the early post-war years.

> What astonished and perplexed me . . . was the sort of schizophrenia. . . . between the new Vedanta beliefs . . . and the unchanged . . . life of the old Christopher . . . I was also struck by how terribly little he had recorded about his pre-occupations as a writer. . . ."

Lehman believed that Don's youthful energy was an important stimulant to Isherwood to begin working hard again (Lehman, 1987, p. 86). Having a loving partner to dictate his writing to (Lehman, 1987, p. 87) would have made Christopher's hours as author infinitely more appealing than a lonely struggle to get the words out. His previous lover, Bill Caskey, was a sailor, and often away from home. By contrast, Don eventually became a collaborator in the planning of certain film scripts. Confirmation of my argument must await Don's publication of Isherwood's journals, and then his own, but I would expect those journals to confirm that in their early years, Don contributed his full share to the vitality and endurance of their relationship, despite his youth and son/student roles.

2. Power in the Marriage

Power in intimacy has fascinated some students of relationship (Blau, 1964; Komarovsky, 1962, p. 229) but again, remarkably little is available on power in nongay age-stratified relationships, let alone gay couples. For example, Jessie Bernard's splendidly foresighted *Future of Marriage* (1962) discusses both power in marriage (pp. 147-55) and the impact of age stratification on marriage (p. 188), where she particularly notes the ancient regard for the advantages of a teacher/student pairing. Yet Bernard never links the factors of age and power in her analysis.

The landmark study of American couples by Blumstein and Schwartz (1983) is very much concerned with power, including the effect on the balance of power exerted by sexual behavior, money, occupations, and other factors. But again, there is no report of the correlation of these factors with age gaps in relationships. One of their five exemplar gay, male couples is mildly age-stratified (ages 37/47) and is reported as having to "work at keeping a balance of power" (p. 543). Since the authors have much data still to analyze, more detailed reports on power in age-stratified couples is to be hoped for.

Power dynamics in marriage are often exquisitely complex. I have argued elsewhere that sexual play may help clarify them (Lee, 1980). Dominance and submission are classic dynamics of marriage models, but are made even more complex by age gaps. Christopher was not only much older than Don, but also, at least in the early years, more famous in his work. Komarovsky (1962, p. 229) found that both educational difference and social rank affected the "margin of power" in marriage.

The bargaining position of each spouse depends in part on the degree of emotional involvement in the marriage (p. 229; cf. also Blau, 1964). Komarovsky assessed power according to outcomes of marital disagreements, deference, and decision-making (p. 221). In the case of Don and Christopher, there appears to have been a remarkable, though probably implicit, pact, that "Christopher's surrender of power was between us. In the eyes of the world he would be the leading figure. . . . I was fairly used to that." The last words obviously hide years of implicit and/or explicit role accommodation and negotiation.

This problem of power in intimacy is especially relevant to the "Pygmalion myth" in age-stratified relationships. As Galatea discovered her own identity, she became independent and eventually left Pygmalion. (Shaw portrays the problem admirably in his play, *Pygmalion*, later produced as the film *My Fair Lady*.) I strove to gently uncover the Pygmalion-Galatean dynamics in the Isherwood-Bachardy relationship, not least because of interest in the problem in my own relationship with Devon.

One of the mechanisms by which a partner of inferior social power in the relationship may assert independence is in "teasing" and "fighting,"—or best of all, a form of fighting which is also teasing—that is, not about real differences, but for the sake of ritual conflict (cf. Bach and

Wyden, 1971). Such ritual fights emotionally distance the partners from each other for a period of time, but without lasting damage. Thus, they help to establish, during the period of "distancing," the personal *independence* of the partner holding inferior power. The implicit inferiority of the protégé/student/son role is at least temporarily negated, and even permanently attenuated.

Ritual fights about nothing serious, memorable or of lasting impact, appear to have helped Don slowly win his struggle to "invent himself" and move out of the shadow of his famous lover. This process was essential for both lovers, and the relationship. No one can accept the love of another who does not fully respect himself (Laing, 1970, p. 18). Isherwood could not abandon his role of father/teacher/patron, for that was clearly part of his attraction to Don, but had he remained only those, and not helped/allowed Don to become a *peer*, the relationship as lovers could never have endured.

Through tact, collaboration, and mutual respect, negotiated again and again in daily adjustments which must remain hidden from us until the publication of their journals (and perhaps even then) these two men, divided by nationality, age, occupation, education, and social rank, eventually negotiated roles as peers/partners/lovers into Don's middle age and Christopher's old age. This is a remarkable process, and its social mechanisms merit much more study.

"He expected that . . . I'd leave and find someone my own age. . . . " says Don of Christopher. A relationship must eventually cement, or come unstuck, and Christopher knew long before meeting Don that most human intimacy forever retains a quality of social bargaining (Blau, 1964). Christopher, reflecting back 30 years, observed that until a relationship became fully cemented between peers, it was always a calculated matter of bargaining (Isherwood, 1980, p. 41):

> The parties might keep up [the bargain] for a short or a long time, or even until death, but they could never regard it as absolutely firm. Neither party could be trusted not to violate it at any moment without warning.

Yet Don assures us that he felt "from the beginning" that it would last. Such a sentiment may be forgiven as romantic optimism when expressed early in a love affair, but the retention of this conviction 33 years later is not to be ignored. The dream that a "marriage," gay or nongay, can eventually achieve a kind of solidarity in which bargaining is no longer inherent, is clearly an ancient hope that two may become "one flesh." One does not bargain with one's own arm or leg.

There were certainly early bargains between Don and Christopher, especially about the long and costly stages necessary for Don to "invent himself." But what kinds of early bargains are most likely to assure that later, bargaining itself become superfluous? How do early bargains affect the chances of long-term solidarity, versus the repeated struggles of negotiations? These are yet more topics for research on age-stratified gay relationships.

CONCLUSION

The intimate mentor-protégé relationship is one of the great historical patterns of the traditional gay community (Lee, 1987; cf. Grube, this volume). At one time both partners could look for guidance to similar relationships institutionalized in the gay world, but today such dyads are rare and widely devalued among gay men. The emphasis today is on age-peer gay lovers (but cf., Denby, 1985, p. 176). There are still younger men who like older men, and elders who seek juniors, as any casual examination of gay advertising will confirm, but there is far too often a note of defensiveness in those who seek such pairings.

Don Bachardy today has the advantage, as he fully recognizes, of turning to good use the obverse side of his own experience with Christopher. Many older men have no such advantage, and few younger men have access to the information and role models which older gay men, once happy protégés, could provide. The gay community must recognize that its contemporary depreciation of age-stratified love is no more valid or justifiable than society's rejection of homosexual love itself. To provide guidance and hope for those who still seek Wilde's *Love that dare not speak its name*, we need more stories like this of Don and Christopher.

REFERENCES

Bach, G. R. & Wyden, P. (1971). *The intimate enemy*. New York: Avon Books.
Berger, B. (1971). *Looking for America*. New York: Prentice-Hall.
Berger, P. L. (1963). *Invitation to sociology*. New York: Anchor Books.
Bernard, J. (1962). *Future of marriage*. New York: Bantam World.
Berne, E. (1964). *Games people play*. New York: Grove Press.
Blau, P. M. (1964). *Exchange and power in social life*. New York: Wiley and Sons.
Blumstein, P. & Schwartz, P. (1983). *American couples*. New York: William Morrow.
Brecher, E. M. (1984). *Love, sex and aging*. Boston: Little Brown.

Butler, R. N. (1977). Successful aging and the role of life review. In S.H. Zarit, (Ed.). *Readings in aging and death*. New York: Harper and Row.

Davis, K. (1947, March). Field note on a case of extreme isolation. *American Journal of Sociology*, pp. 432-37.

Denby, R. *American lives*. Stamford, CT: Knights Press.

Elia, J.P. (1987). History, etymology and fallacy. *Journal of Homosexuality 14*(3/4), 2-19.

Fang-fu, R. & Yung-mei, J. (1987). Male homosexuality in traditional Chinese literature. *Journal of homosexuality, 14*(3/4), 21-33.

Foner, N. (1984). *Ages in conflict*. New York: Columbia University Press.

Goffman, E. (1959). *The presentation of self in everyday life*. New York: Anchor Books.

Grube, J. Natives and settlers: An anthropologic note on early interaction of older homosexual men with younger gay liberationists. *Journal of Homosexuality 20*(3/4), 119-135.

Hyde, H.M. (1962). *The trials of Oscar Wilde*. New York: Dover Press.

Isherwood, C. (1952). *The world in the evening*. New York: Farrar Straus Giroux.

Isherwood, C. (1976). *Christopher and his kind*. New York: Farrar Straus Giroux.

Isherwood, C. (1980). *My guru and his disciple*. Markham: McGraw-Hill Ryerson.

Isherwood, C. & Bachardy, D. (1981) *October*. Los Angeles: Twelvetrees Press.

Johnson, J. M. (1975). *Field work*. New York: Free Press.

Jourard, S. (1964). *The transparent self*. New York: Van Nostrand.

Jourard, S. (1971). *Self disclosure*. New York: Wiley.

Komarovsky, M. (1962). *Blue collar marriage*. New York: Random House.

Laing, R. D. (1970). *Knots*. New York: Random House.

Lee, J.A. (1980). The social organization of sexual risk. *Alternative Lifestyles* 2:1, 69-100.

Lee, J.A. (1986). Report to the Social Science and Humanities Research Council of Canada, file number 492 80 0009.

Lee, J.A. (1987). What can homosexual aging studies contribute to theories of aging? *Journal of Homosexuality, 4*, 43-71.

Lee, J.A. (1987). Life after Isherwood, an interview with Don Bachardy. *Christopher Street, 10*(4), 50-58.

Lehmann, J. (1987). *Christopher Isherwood, a personal memoir*. London: Weidenfeld and Nicolson.

Mattison, A.M. & McWhirter, D. P. (1987). Stage discrepancy in male couples. *Journal of Homosexuality, 14*(1/2), 89-100.

McCall, G. J. & Simmons, J. L. (1966). *Identities and interactions*. Glencoe: Free Press.

McWhirter, D. P., & Mattison, A. M. (1984). *The Male Couple*. Toronto: Prentice-Hall.

Milgram, S. (1973). *Obedience to authority, an experimental view*. New York: Harper and Row.

Mills, C.W. (1959). *The sociological imagination*. Oxford University Press.
Peele, S. T. (1988). The romantic ideal. In R. Sternberg & M. Barnes, (Eds.). *The psychology of love*. Yale University Press.
Ponse, B. (1976). Secrecy in the lesbian world. *Urban Life, 5*(3), 313-38.
Simmel, G. (1953). The social role of the stranger. In E.A. Shuler (Ed.). *Outside Readings in Sociology*. New York: Crowell.
Steinman, R. Social exchanges between older and younger gay male partners. *Journal of Homosexuality, 20*(3/4), 179-206.

Accelerated Aging
and Male Homosexuality:
Australian Evidence
in a Continuing Debate

Keith C. Bennett, BA

University of Western Sydney, Nepean

Norman L. Thompson, PhD

Macquarie University

SUMMARY. The evidence of research looking at accelerated aging among gay men is contradictory. In this study the issue of accelerated aging is addressed by accounting for the duality of the gay man's lifestyle as he interacts in both the homosexual community and the larger society where heterosexuality is the presumed norm. The onset of middle and old age as self-perceived by gay men and as perceived by other gay men in the homosexual subculture is contrasted. The results indicate that existing contradictions and debates about gay men and accelerated aging are largely a function of their referent perceptual worlds.

Aging can be stressful and problematic for all individuals in Western societies. Certainly there are difficulties which many elderly people en-

---

Keith C. Bennett is Senior Lecturer in Behavioural and Social Sciences in the School of Health Studies, University of Western Sydney, Nepean, PO Box 10, Kingswood, NSW, Australia 2750.

Norman L. Thompson is Senior Lecturer in the School of Behavioural Sciences, Macquarie University, Sydney.

The research was supported by grants to Norman Thompson from the Macquarie University Research Committee and the Australian Research Grants Committee.

Reprint requests should be directed to Keith Bennett.

counter, such as reduced income and problems of housing and transporta-
tion. In addition, persistent negative stereotypes, often unsupported by
research findings, shape attitudes and behaviour toward older people, and,
in turn, influence the elderly's behaviour in a detrimental manner (Bengston, Kasschau & Ragan, 1977; Atchley, 1977).

Homosexual men share many of the stresses of aging with their heterosexual counterparts, as well as additional problems associated with their
sexual orientation. These additional problems are related to stigmatization
by members of the wider society and their involvement in the homosexual
subculture, where youthfulness is a major criterion for socio-sexual success (Hoffman, 1968; Weinberg & Williams, 1974). Nevertheless, the
traditional stereotype held by many younger gay and nongay people is that
the older gay man is lonely and depressed, a view rejected by a growing
body of international research in the United States, Canada, Australia,
The Netherlands, and Denmark (Bennett & Thompson, 1980; Berger,
1982; Francher & Henkin, 1973; Friend, 1980; Kelly, 1977; Kimmel,
1978; Lee, 1987; Minnigerode & Adelman, 1978; Weinberg & Williams,
1974). Research workers have found that older gay men cope well with
the aging process and are comparable to younger homosexuals in social
and psychological adjustment.

CONTRADICTORY EVIDENCE ON ACCELERATED AGING

Because of the gay community's emphasis on youth, homosexual men
are considered middle-aged and elderly by other homosexual men at an
earlier age than heterosexual men in the general community. Since these
age-status norms occur earlier in the gay subculture, the homosexual man
thinks of himself as middle-aged and old before his heterosexual counterpart does.

The evidence from studies looking at the notion of accelerated aging
among gay men is contradictory. Two investigators who used very different data sources came to opposite conclusions from their findings. Friend
(1980) advertised for older gay men to participate in a research study in
Philadelphia. Since over 90 percent of the men who responded were under
the age of 64, with the youngest being only 32, he concluded that this was
support for the belief in accelerated aging among gay men. On the other
hand, Laner (1978) concluded that there was no support for this notion
when she looked at newspaper advertisements through which homosexual
and heterosexual men sought companions or dates. Contrary to predictions from the accelerated aging position, she found that older advertisers
were underrepresented in both the homosexual and heterosexual groups,

and a majority of the gay men stated their age as between 18 and 34 years. However, the fact that a third of the gay men and only a tenth of the straight men did not state their age casts doubt on her conclusion.

Turning to studies which deal directly with age-status norms among homosexual males, we also see results that are contradictory. Minnigerode (1976) asked gay men between the ages of 25 and 68 when they believed middle age and old age began, and to place themselves into an age category (young, middle-aged, or old). He found that all men in their 20s, 80% in their 30s, and 28% in their 40s considered themselves young. The remainder thought of themselves as middle-aged, including all the men in their 50s and 60s. The mean ages for their perceptions of the onset of middle age was 41.29 years and 64.78 years for old age. Since these latter figures are similar to those found among heterosexuals by Neugarten, Moore and Lowe (1965), Minnigerode concludes that his data contradict suggestions of accelerated aging among gay men.

Kelly (1977, 1980) asked homosexual males between the ages of 16 and 79 when youth, middle age, and old age began and ended. The "majority and plurality" saw youth as beginning before 18 years and ending around 30. Middle age spanned the years between 30 and 50, while old age was 50 and over. Kelly's findings support the contention that social aging is accelerated among homosexual males since these age-status norms for middle and old age are considerably earlier than those stated by heterosexuals in the study by Neugarten et al. (1965).

DUAL EXISTENCE OF THE HOMOSEXUAL

In the present study we explore the issue of accelerated aging among gay men. We believe the earlier research has not accounted for the duality of the gay man's lifestyle as he interacts in the two worlds of the homosexual community and the larger society in which heterosexuality is the norm. Accelerated aging among homosexual men can be considered only by examining the total range of an individual's social experiences in both the homosexual and heterosexual worlds along with his perceptions of these events.

The very notion of subculture combines ideas about social structure and differential social interaction as identified by interactionist theorists (Fine & Kleinman, 1979). The symbolic interactionist approach suggests that some homosexual men may accept and internalize widely-held beliefs about the expected course of their aging process. This means that "a person's feelings about himself are derived from imagining how others regard him—regardless of whether these imputions are accurate or not" (Weinberg & Williams, 1974, p. 153). The attitudes and opinions of people in both the heterosexual and homosexual community have an impact on the gay man as he deals with his own aging (Bennett, 1979). Harry and De Vall (1978) conclude that the degree of emphasis on youthfulness will depend largely on which segment of the heterogeneous gay world one observes.

The reality of any alleged emphasis on youthfulness within the gay subculture is irrelevant; what is important are the perceptions of homosexual men about their own aging and whether they report the loss of youthfulness as a factor to be dealt with.

Previous research on accelerated aging seems to have assumed that the perceptions of age-status norms are either primarily influenced by the gay subculture, or they reflect an averaging out of those in the homosexual and heterosexual worlds. We propose to take into account the pervasiveness of the *duality* of the gay experience. Specifically, we will determine and contrast the age of onset of middle and old age as *self*-perceived by gay men and as perceived by *other* gay men in the homosexual subculture.

METHOD

Sample and Recruitment

Respondents were recruited from a variety of sources over a six-month period in 1978. Comparison with larger studies (Bell & Weinberg, 1978; Weinberg & Williams, 1974) indicates that we have obtained a suitably varied sample.

A total of 478 men who labeled themselves as homosexual volunteered to participate in the study. The major sample sources are: Sydney gay bars (14%), two nationwide homosexual religious organizations (13%), college and university gay groups (6%), gay social organizations (10%), a homosexual newspaper with a large circulation throughout Australia (27%), friendship circles of respondents, and personal contacts (30%).

The average age in the sample was 32.2 years, with a range from 16 to 74 years. There was a tendency for younger men to volunteer for the research, with 25% aged 25 years or younger, 47% between 26 and 35 years of age, 17% between 36 and 45 years, and 11% aged 46 years or older. In comparison to the younger subjects, the oldest age group was more likely to be recruited through religious organizations (24%), and the national homosexual newspaper (35%).

It should be noted that the youth orientation of the gay world leads to a "relative paucity of truly older gays in most studies" (Harry & De Vall,

1978, p. 208). For instance, Minnigerode's (1976) sample had 14% of respondents over 50 years of age; Kelly (1977) had 16% "older" respondents, while in Jay and Young's (1979) sample of 4,212 gay men, only 9% were over the age of 50 years. Our sample fits this pattern, with 11% in the 46-years-or-more age group.

Most of the respondents were employed, with only 12% either full-time students, unemployed or retired. Ninety percent of those employed were from high-medium status jobs and low-medium status jobs (Congalton, 1969). Among the respondents, 25% had only completed high school, 11% technical or trade training, and 13% had not completed high school. The remaining 51% had some university training, 18% of them at postgraduate level.

Almost all the men classified themselves as predominantly homosexual (97%), and 54% of the respondents said they were exclusively homosexual. Approximately 18% of the men had had psychiatric treatment for their homosexuality, but only 1% were currently having treatment.

QUESTIONNAIRE

An 18-page questionnaire was developed to elicit information in the following areas: demographic variables, psychiatric treatment, social involvement in homosexual and heterosexual circles, same- and opposite-sex relationship histories, homosexual identity, self-esteem, the respondents' perceived acceptance by others of their homosexuality, and age-status norms and perceptions. (Copies of the questionnaire may be obtained by writing to Keith Bennett.)

PROCEDURE

The broad purpose of the study was explained in newspaper articles, during talks at meetings of homosexual organizations, by handouts in gay bars, and in letters to groups outside the Sydney area. Volunteers either wrote, telephoned, or talked in person to one of the authors, after which they were given a copy of the questionnaire. Once the study was described to the individuals, many volunteers distributed questionnaires to people throughout their friendship networks.

Pre-paid, addressed envelopes were provided so respondents could mail back their questionnaires anonymously. This anonymity obviously precluded the exact keeping of return rates since some persons and organizations asked for multiple copies for distribution to friends and members. A calculated return rate is approximately 50%, which compares favorably with other studies of this type.

RESULTS

Perception of Age-Status Norms

Respondents were asked when they believed middle and old age began. We interpreted answers to these questions as *self-perception* of the onset age for the two stages. Respondents then were requested to state the age they thought other homosexuals meant when they talked about someone as being middle-aged and old-aged. The responses to these latter questions were interpreted as perceptions of the age that other homosexuals have of the onset of the two stages, that is, *perception* by others.

The mean ages for self-perception and perception by others are given in Table 1. There are strong differences between self-perception and perception by others for old age (t = 14.95, df = 344, p < .000), with respondents believing that other gays see old age commencing almost nine years earlier than they themselves do. The men also believe other homosexuals see the onset of middle age earlier (t = 5.43, df = 347, p < .000), although the mean difference is less than two years.

TABLE 1

Self-Perception and Perception by Others
Age Onset of Mid and Old Age, in Years

(n = 467)[a]

		How Perceived				
		SELF			OTHER	
TARGET AGE	NO.	MEAN	SD	NO.	MEAN	SD
Middle Age	393	41.2	5.95	454	39.3	6.71
Old Age	349	63.0	7.61	449	54.4	9.36

[a] Number varies because certain respondents failed to answer all questions.

As can be seen in Table 1, most respondents are able to give an age they believe others see as the onset of middle and old age. However, up to one-quarter of the sample cannot or would not give their own definitions of the age-status norms (the response rate for self-perception of middle and old age are 84% and 75%, respectively).

The age of the respondents is related to self-perception of middle age ($r = .16$, $p < .03$) and old age ($r = .23$, $p < .001$), but chronological age is *not* related to perception by others of middle age ($r = .06$), or old age ($r = .04$). Older gay men see the two age categories as beginning later than the younger gay men, but there is no age difference among the respondents in their perception of the age norms other homosexuals hold.

Age Status Labels

The age status labels that the men use for themselves were examined by asking the respondents to describe whether they most often view themselves as "young," "not yet middle-aged," "middle-aged," "past middle-age," "not yet old-aged," or "old-aged." The men also were asked to use these age labels to state how they believe other homosexuals saw them.

The mean results for self-descriptions and perceptions respondents believe others have of them (perception by others) are given in Table 2 by chronological age groupings. There are strong age differences for both self-descriptions ($F = 66.03$, df = 3.457, $p < .000$) and other perception ($F = 133.31$, df = 3,457, $p < .0000$). These differences are reflected in the correlations between respondents' age and self-attributed age status ($r = .54$, $p < .0000$) and perception of age status by others ($r = .67$, $p < .0000$).

While increasing chronological age is associated with older age status categories for both self-description and perception by others, reflection on the mean scores in Table 2 show these to be realistic in terms of the age norms in our society. Interestingly, comparisons between self-description and perception by others within each age group show that, except among men who are 25 years or younger, the respondents describe themselves as younger than they believe other homosexuals perceive them (26-35 years old: $t = 4.24$, df = 213, $p < .000$; 36-45 years: $t = 3.65$, df = 81, $p < .0000$; 46 years or older: $t = 3.26$, df = 47, $p < .002$).

TABLE 2

Means by Age Groups for Age Status Labels

		Condition			
Age in Years		Self-Description		Perception by Others	
	No.	Mean	SD	Mean	SD
25 and under	117	1.18	0.43	1.12	.35
26 - 35	214	1.40	0.59	1.57	.58
36 - 45	82	1.83	0.57	2.05	.59
46 and over	48	2.58	1.10	2.98	.92

Note: Description as young was scored 1, not yet middle-aged = 2, middle-aged = 3, past middle-aged = 4, not yet old-aged = 5, and old-aged = 6.

DISCUSSION

One of the many stereotypes about homosexual males is that they experience a sense of accelerated aging in contrast to their heterosexual counterparts. Evidence from studies exploring the issue of accelerated aging is contradictory. Our own research does not unreservedly support or refute either side of this controversy, but our results do suggest new interpretations about the gay male subculture and its influence on age perception.

The perceptions that the men in this study have of middle age beginning around 41 years and old age at 63 years is not only consistent with studies using samples of individuals who are presumably heterosexual (Neugarten et al., 1965; Atchley, 1977), but they agree closely with Minnigerode's

(1976) finding among homosexual men. Thus, as long as the referent is to *self*-belief and perception, there is no support for the notion of accelerated aging among our respondents.

On the other hand, gay men believe that other homosexual males see middle age as beginning around 39 years and old age at 54 years, findings which are similar to Kelly's (1977; 1980). Respondents in our study hold the view that other homosexual men see the age status categories occurring earlier in the supposedly youth-oriented gay subculture. This is particularly true for the onset of old age.

Contradictions Clarified

We suggest that the discrepancies between Kelly's (1977; 1980) and Minnigerode's (1976) findings may largely be a function of the referent perceptual world. Gay men base their perception on beliefs found in both a dominant heterosexual society (where age status is usually defined by legal and social conventions) and a youth-oriented subculture. Respondents report self-beliefs about the age norms that are similar to those reported in general gerontological literature. We believe the bases of these perceptions are the same as those for the heterosexual world — compulsory retirement, pensionable age, noticeable physical change, and so on. However, when respondents state their perceptions of the age norms held by other gay men, they give a younger criterion for middle age and a strikingly earlier age for the onset of old age.

It is interesting to speculate on the marked differences in the percentages responding to self- and perceptions by others of the age norms. Most respondents were able to specify a chronological age they believed other gay men held for the onset of middle and old age. However, up to a quarter of the men failed to specify their own beliefs of the onset of these age categories. Many wrote such comments as "age is irrelevant," "you're only as old as you feel," and "age is too arbitrary a means of categorization." Our conclusion is that respondents are prepared to see age as a meaningful dimension in the gay community, but a sizeable number do not see chronological age as a useful dimension in their own lives. Many of the men in our sample seem to be saying that "other gays are agist but not me," and they may well organize their social and sexual lives around this perception.

The above comments are strengthened by our findings on the attributions of self-age labels. With the exception of respondents 25 years and under, all age groups saw themselves as younger than they believe others in the gay community saw them.

Overall, our findings suggest new interpretations of the accelerated aging debate arising from the duality and complexity of homosexual life styles and their interaction with age perception.

REFERENCES

Atchley, R.C. (1977). *The social forces in later life.* (2nd Ed). Belmont, CA: Wadsworth.

Bell, A.P. & Weinberg, M.S. (1978). *Homosexualities: A study of diversity among men and women.* New York: Simon and Schuster.

Bengston, V.L., Kasschau, P.L. & Ragan, P.K. (1977). The impact of social structure on aging individuals. In J.E. Birren & K.W. Schaie (Eds.), *Handbook of the psychology of aging.* New York: Van Nostrand Reinhold.

Bennett, K.C. (1979). Age and ageism among Australian male homosexuals. *Australian Psychological Society Annual Conference*, Hobart.

Bennett, K.C. & Thompson, N.L. (1980). Social and psychological functioning of the ageing male homosexual. *British Journal of Psychiatry*, *137*, 361-370.

Berger, R.M. (1982). *Gay and gray. The older homosexual man.* Boston: Alyson Publications.

Congalton, A.A. (1969). *Status and prestige in Australia.* Melbourne: Cheshire.

Fine, G.A. & Kleinman, S. (1979). Rethinking subculture: An interactionist analysis. *American Journal of Sociology*, *85*, 1-20.

Francher, J.S. & Henkin, J. (1973). The menopausal queen: Adjustment to aging and the male homosexual. *American Journal of Orthopsychiatry*, *43*, 670-674.

Friend, R.A. (1980). Gayging: Adjustment and the older gay male. *Alternative Lifestyles*, *3*, 231-248.

Harry, J. & De Vall, W. (1978). Age and sexual culture among homosexually oriented males. *Archives of Sexual Behaviour*, 7(3), 199-209.

Hoffman, M. (1968). *The gay world: Male homosexuality and the social creation of evil.* New York: Bantam Books.

Jay, K. & Young, A. (1979). *The gay report: Lesbians and gay men speak out about sexual experiences and lifestyles.* New York: Summit Books.

Kelly, J.J. (1977). The aging homosexual: Myth and reality. *Gerontologist*, *17*, 328-332.

Kelly, J.J. (1980). Homosexuality and aging. In J. Marmor (Ed.), *Homosexual behaviour. A modern reappraisal.* New York: Basic Books.

Kimmel, D.C. (1978). Adult development and aging: A gay perspective. *Journal of Social Issues*, *34*, 113-30.

Laner, M.R. (1978). Growing older male: Heterosexual and homosexual. *Gerontologist*, *18*, 496-501.

Lee, J.A. (1987). What can homosexual aging studies contribute to theories of aging? *Journal of Homosexuality*, *13*, 43-71.

Minnigerode, F.A. (1976). Age-status labeling in homosexual men. *Journal of Homosexuality*, *1*, 273-276.

Minnigerode, F.A. & Adelman, M. (1978). Elderly homosexual men and women: Report on a pilot study. *The Family Coordinator, 27,* 451-466.

Neugarten, B.L., Moore, J.W. & Lowe, J.C. (1965). Age norms, age constraints, and adult socialization. *American Journal of Sociology, 70,* 710-717.

Weinberg, M.S. & Williams, C.J. (1974). *Male homosexuals. Their problems and adaptations.* London: Oxford University Press.

Lavender and Gray: A Brief Survey of Lesbian and Gay Aging Studies

Margaret Cruikshank, PhD

City College of San Francisco

Until recently, texts and research in gerontology overlooked the gay population. Given a long history of anti-gay bias in the medical and academic communities, this neglect was not entirely a bad thing. Although attitudes toward gay people have become somewhat more tolerant, there is little reflection of this fact in the gerontological literature, even in work published within the last year or two. Pifer's 413-page 1986 anthology, funded by the Carnegie Corporation, *Our Aging Society*, includes not one reference to homosexuals. The same is true of a 1985 standard text, the *Handbook of Aging and the Social Sciences* (Binstork). Georgia Barrow's *Aging, the Individual and Society* (1986) devotes one paragraph to old gay men and one sentence to lesbians.

In addition to ignoring the fact that the elderly population includes gay people, most mainstream gerontologists seem unaware of the small body of work produced by gay gerontologists who have felt increasingly free since the late 70s to pursue their interest in gay subjects. The reference notes of the articles published in this volume attest to the growing literature on gay aging available in a wide range of scholarly journals published since 1970. One wonders how any textbook author could overlook all of these resources. In the future, mainstream researchers should certainly be faulted if they continue to neglect old gay men and lesbians in their survey texts on gerontology. This article reviews the literature and introduces readers to the background for the new studies published here.

Margaret Cruikshank, PhD, teaches English, women's studies, and gay studies at the City College of San Francisco. Correspondence may be addressed to Dr. Margaret Cruikshank, City College of San Francisco, CA 94112.

MEN

One of the most readable works on gay male aging is *Quiet Fire: Memoirs of Older Gay Men* (1985), 17 interviews conducted by Keith Vacha, who works with San Francisco's Mission District elderly. The cover photo itself is consciousness-raising: it shows two old men who are clearly a couple; affection and companionship are expressed rather than eroticism. Vacha wanted to demonstrate the diversity of old gay men. He purposely avoided gay community leaders and well-known people. He astutely notes that the drag-queen image of old gay men, so common in the mass media is like the old "Amos and Andy" image for blacks. *Quiet Fire* aims to: (a) learn about the history of gay people in the 20th century; (b) find role models; and (c) break down the stereotype of the sad and lonely older gay. Given the great emphasis on youth in gay male culture, Vacha wondered how old gay men coped. He concluded that "the discrimination that comes with aging is compounded by the discrimination that comes with being homosexual" (p. 217).

Nevertheless, this book is very positive because the interview subjects accept themselves and their aging, although a few express gerontophobia. The main themes of *Quiet Fire* are: the extreme importance given to sex at all stages of a gay man's life; harassment by their families and police; the importance of military service in hastening or retarding the development of a healthy gay identity; the need to deny their homosexuality in their early lives (especially true of the formerly married men in the sample); the difficulty of achieving a long-term partnership; and frequent use of drugs and alcohol. Vacha does not comment on the internalized homophobia occasionally evident in these interviews, nor does he observe that the 17 men have an unusually high incidence of physical illness. A reader may be struck by the fact that these men lived in a dangerous world because of their emotional/sexual identities—psychological danger, of being fired from jobs, receiving dishonorable discharges from the military, or being rejected by families; and physical danger, not only from random beatings and police brutality, but also from assaults by men they brought home as casual sex partners. Because they have survived dangerous lives, these men seemed unusually buoyant and sure of themselves, in a quiet way.

Published by an academic press, Raymond Berger's *Gay and Gray* (1982) study is more formal than Vacha's and more satisfying to the gerontologist because he raises many issues. Berger's study has 112 subjects and two parts, an interview section and a questionnaire/analysis section. "Like the American child of the conflict in Southeast Asia," Berger begins, "the older homosexual is not wanted by either side—by the gerontologist or the homosexual" (p. 10). Probably this is less true now than in 1982. *Gay and Gray* (1982) aims to refute stereotypes about old gay men, to show their diversity, and to determine their psychological adjustment. The men in this study were, generally speaking, not lonely, unwanted, or isolated. They maintained their earlier level of sexual activity but had fewer partners, which Berger suggests may reflect the increased cautiousness of the old. Their self-acceptance, hard won, was remarkable, given the intense hostility to homosexuality in their lifetime. Significantly, all 112 men "felt they had travelled a long and tortuous road toward self acceptance" (p. 187).

Berger used Neugarten's life satisfaction scale and found that his subjects scored 74.5, higher than Neugarten's subjects. He speculates that "psychological adjustment may increase with age for homosexual men" (p. 76) perhaps because older gays are much less concerned with exposure of their homosexuality.

The subjects saw no difference in aging for heterosexuals and homosexuals. Berger says that an older gay man might find the loss of a long-term partner less traumatic than his heterosexual counterpart because he is less focused on a single partner and tends to be independent of traditional supports such as the family. He has had to be very self-reliant all his life.

The subjects of *Gay and Gray* felt age had brought them new freedom. About half believed that younger gay men felt an aversion to them but those who did socialize with the young had the best adjustment. Most older homosexuals had friends their own age. About 20% had experienced heterosexual marriage. Berger believes fewer future cohorts of old gay men will marry because the pressure to marry has eased somewhat since the 1960s.

Berger notes that gay organizations rarely have older men in leadership positions, a sign of subtle discrimination. More overt forms of discrimination were also recalled; for example, one man frequented a bath house which let men under 21 in free and banned older men on certain nights. One subject said, "We're just not valued."

Berger argues that the problems of old gay men come not from their attitudes, which are positive, but from: (a) institutional policies; (b) legal discrimination; (c) social service agencies' neglect; and (d) medical oversight. Homophobia in nursing homes is a good example of the first, as is the hospital policy of allowing only blood relatives to make decisions in life and death situations, ignoring the longstanding gay partner. An old gay man cannot legally inherit the property of his deceased partner without a will, and bigoted families often successfully contest wills. An example of medical oversight is medical workers failure to realize that an older male patient may be gay and may need treatment for anal fissures resulting from anal penetration.

Gay and Gray (Berger, 1982) differs from *Quiet Fire* (Vacha, 1985) in several ways. There are eight interviews in *Gay and Gray* and 17 in *Quiet Fire*. Berger focused on men over 40; Vacha selected men over 60. Berger's respondents lived in the Midwest; Vacha's lived in California and Arizona. Berger's men seemed much healthier than Vacha's. Finally, the political attitudes of the two groups differed considerably. Many of the men in *Quiet Fire* expressed some dislike of the gay rights movement for being vocal and militant; they thought conciliation was a better approach. Berger's subjects tended to be highly involved in the gay community and politically much more in alignment with it. The differences may affect the findings of the two samples.

An important work which agrees with but also challenges Berger's research is a 48-page essay titled "What Can Gay Aging Studies Contribute to Theories of Aging?" by John Alan Lee (1987). Lee surveys seven sociological theories of aging and concludes that "social exchange, stratification, and conflict" theories are more fruitful for gay aging studies than the disengagement and continuity models.

In 1980, Lee began a four-year study of 47 Canadian gay men over 50. They tended to be less "gay liberationist" in their outlook than Berger's sample. Lee disputes Berger's notion that the various crises old gay men have endured equip them to age well. Instead he argues, "happiness in gay old age is a more likely outcome when a man is fortunate and/or skilled enough to avoid stressful events," i.e., even the stress of coming out. Lee was astonished to see contentment in old age "after a lifetime of deceptions," i.e., by gay men pretending to be heterosexual.

Lee believes that a disproportionate number of older gay men seek partners from Third World countries (not necessarily Asian) where youth is still taught to respect and defer to their elders. From modern British literature we know that it was common for upper-class English homosexuals to seek working-class lovers, often in other countries. A thorough study of the phenomenon Lee mentions would be useful.

A number of Lee's observations are quite different from Vacha's and Berger's. He says that many of the men he interviewed "simply can't stand, or understand, the hardness of the young gay lifestyle, epitomized in music, metal and black leather." His concluding words are striking: "'Liberation' of older gays must come to grips with the historical fact that youth-oriented gay liberation destroyed much that older gays held dear 'in the life.' Out of the closets and into the streets is what many older gays are prepared to do with their garbage, but not with their lifelong identities."

In another article based on his longitudinal study of gay men over 50, (1988) Lee discusses an "age gap in ecological completeness of gay communities, the relative invisibility of older men" which he traces to a generation gap between younger and older gays. For many elders, gay liberation politics "elevate stigma to new and dangerous insights of visibility." Even though it is risky to be closeted, the closet is a source of security, important to older men who fear that the young, by flaunting their sexual preference, will force an end to tolerance by the majority. A characteristic of older gay men is that they resist "master status as homosexuals, for fear that it will swamp their other claims to respect and status." Furthermore, these men avoid labeling themselves as, for example, gay teachers, gay fathers, gay lawyers. A common assumption among lesbian and gay activists has been that such denial of identity would cause considerable psychological strain but in Lee's study that assumption is not proven true. There was no relationship between staying in the closet and life satisfaction.

Of several articles published before Vacha, Berger, and Lee, three are especially noteworthy. In "Age-Status Labeling in Homosexual Men," Fred Minnigerode refutes the popular notion of accelerated aging in gay men (1976). The findings of a study of 241 gay men in Los Angeles between 16 and 79 are summarized in "The Aging Male Homosexual: Myth and Reality," by Jim Kelly (1977). According to Kelly, being gay seems to cause no problem in old age but social stigma may cause problems for aging gays. A study of 478 Australian gay men found that the old gay man is as likely as the young to be involved in the gay community; the old gay man judges himself popular in his community and thus he is as satisfied with his sexual orientation as is the young gay man (Bennett & Thompson, 1980).

WOMEN

Two of the first articles focusing on lesbian aging were "The Older Lesbian" by Del Martin and Phyllis Lyon (1970) and an article of the same title by Matile Poor that appeared in my anthology, *Lesbian Studies* (Cruikshank, 1982). Pioneers of the national and San Francisco gay rights movement, Lyon and Martin coined the phrase "lace curtain lesbians" to refer to those older women who deny being gay even though they are obviously in same-sex relationships. They refer to an unpublished master thesis on aging and lesbianism by Chris Almvig showing that relatively little role playing exists among old lesbians, which is perhaps surprising given the prevalence of butch/femme roles in pre-movement days.

Dr. Poor's article is significant for presenting work from both the humanities and social sciences, and cites the concerns of a group of older lesbians she facilitated: for example, the difficulty of gaining acceptance of their lesbianism from the medical establishment. The problem is well illustrated by a story about two women who fall in love in a nursing home.

The first full-length study of the older lesbian was Mina Meyer's M.A. thesis (1979). Meyer conducted in-depth interviews with 20 women between the ages of 50 and 73, all living on their own rather than in institutions. She found five different responses to aging among this group: (a) they felt fine about it; (b) their attitudes were generally positive but they mentioned health problems; (c) they had a somewhat negative view of aging and were very distressed by health problems; (d) they had a negative view of aging which they associated with death and dying; and (e) they had a political awareness of their situation and understood ageism in their society. Like the male researchers, her subjects were not lonely or isolated. They remained sexually alive.

New typologies are needed to describe and categorize their long-term love relationships, Meyer believes, because the model of heterosexual marriage just does not fit. Contrary to the stereotype that the old are rigid, her subjects showed flexibility in their lives and several were considering innovative, shared-housing arrangements. Meyer used the phrase "late-blooming" lesbian to describe one who had come out in mid life or old age. She found that friendship ties replaced weak kinship ties and concluded that the strong friendships among these lesbians showed good adaptation to aging in that friendships "can enable (them) to survive in an otherwise hostile environment" (p. 135).

None of these women was interested in senior programs. About half had been discriminated against as lesbians. They were well aware of their minority group status; many of them had lawyer-prepared wills, for example, because they knew that their relationships were not legally recognized. Meyer urges that future research record differences between lesbians who have lived through periods in which they were invisible and hid their identities and future cohorts who come out of the closet.

Mina Meyer and Sharon Raphael, two founders of the National Association of Lesbian and Gay Gerontologists, co-authored an article, "The Old Lesbian: Some Observations Ten Years Later" (1988). One development over the past decade is that the word "old," being more direct and honest, is preferred to "older." A concomitant change is the emergence of militant old lesbians "who will no longer allow themselves to be victimized by ageism."

Meyer and Raphael describe the first West Coast Old Lesbian Conference and Celebration held in April 1987 on the campus where they both teach, California State University, Dominquez Hills. The women in Meyer's original study spoke of collective living arrangements which they hoped to create. Ten years later they reported that collective living had not worked out because of economic inequality of residents, lifestyle differences, competition over leadership, and a lack of a workable decision-making process. A final difference between then and now is that today more social organizations and social service agencies attempt to meet the needs of old lesbians and gay men. As before, some lesbians enjoy the company of a mixed group of women and gay men, while others prefer to socialize only with other old lesbians. Closeted lesbians may prefer a mainstream heterosexual setting. Meyer and Raphael have also written "The Older Lesbian: Love Relationships and Friendships" for the anthology *Women-Identified Women* (1984).

Marcy Adelman's 1980 dissertation "Adjustment to Aging and Styles of Being Gay: A Study of Elderly Gay Men and Lesbians" insists that research into homosexuality not trace pathology but instead map development across the life cycle. She found that later life development was not affected by sexual orientation per se, but in many instances was affected by the social stigma attached to gay identity. Like Berger, Adelman found that those who were less satisfied with gay identity had more psychosomatic complaints than those who were experiencing high life satisfaction.

Many of her subjects expressed frustration and anger at the need for secrecy in their lives and for the discrimination they suffered when their identities were disclosed. Disclosure to their families usually meant total rejection. When Adelman examined friendship patterns, she found a correlation between high life satisfaction and heterogeneous friendship patterns rather than exclusively gay patterns.

Adelman's subjects, like Berger's, had reached self-acceptance after lifelong struggle (the old gays of the future will probably be quite different in this respect). Adelman calls for life span longitudinal studies of gay aging and studies that include people of different racial and economic backgrounds, whose accommodations to stigma may be different from those of the subjects studied so far. Adelman makes an excellent point missing in other gay aging studies: Future research should include people who differ in sex-role behavior and appearance. That is, the butch woman and the effeminate man may experience stigma (and aging) differently from those who can pass for heterosexual.

Turning from research to literature, Adelman edited the first collection of autobiographical work by old lesbians, *Long Time Passing* (1987). A pioneer work of lesbian/gay aging, the anthology includes interviews as well as articles. Adelman believes the stories in *Long Time Passing* substantiate the findings of her dissertation: "The most important factor for determining psychological well-being in lesbians in later life is the level of homophobia in society and in ourselves" (p. 11).

The book is made up of 22 articles by a variety of women, including a professional athlete, a doctor, women who served in the Army (including Pat Bond), life-long lesbians, women who came out in mid life, women closely identified with the lesbian community, and women not a part of that politicized world. One essay describes a healing group; another tells of a lover's dying. One of the most effective essays, by Jeanne Adelman, chronicles a love affair beginning when she was 65. The appendix contains legal information, an essay on health, and a description of a San Francisco program, Gay and Lesbian Outreach to Elders or GLOE.

The women represented in *Long Time Passing* describe different coping skills for being gay in a hostile society in the 1920s through the 1950s. They show diversity in their way of handling relationships, some more couple-oriented, others more autonomous. Some couples are sexually active after 20, 30, or 40 years as partners. A major issue for some women is the limit imposed by illness and increasing fragility. One woman writes, for example, "I took a bath all by myself today. You want to know about old age? That's old age" (p. 209). The presence of a supportive community takes on increasing importance as the women age, especially for those to whom the community was not available when they were younger. Adelman's book tends to corroborate Lee's suggestion, in "Invisible Lives of Canada's Gray Gays," that the generation gap is not as pronounced between young and old lesbians as it is between young and old gay men because of the women's movement.

At 81 Monika Kehoe is no doubt the oldest of the researchers on gay/lesbian aging. She received a large grant through the Center for Research and Education in Sexuality (CERES) at San Francisco State University for a study of 100 lesbians over 60, the most ambitious study of that group to date and the only national study. Her book *Lesbians Over Sixty Speak for Themselves* has now been published (Kehoe, 1989). Two chapters based on her research appear in an anthology she edited, *Historical, Literary and Erotic Aspects of Lesbianism* (1986). The first is "Lesbians over 65: A Triply Invisible Minority." Her subjects included few "jocks," although many had considered themselves tomboys in their youth. Forty-one of the 50 subjects in the over-65 group had either good or excellent self-esteem. Celibacy was much more common among them than among the Berger/Vacha/Lee subjects, and only a few used vibrators. Kehoe notes that her study is limited, being confined to white, middle-class, well-educated women, and she also suspects that the reliability of her questionnaire may have been affected by "some respondents' generationally typical resistance to probing of such intimate and personal matters" (p. 141). In her second article, "A Portrait of the Older Lesbian," Kehoe states that an older lesbian is "a very private person . . . reticent about her past as well as her present" (p. 158). I suspect this may be true only of the professional old lesbians. It would be most useful to have a study of working-class old lesbians so that characteristics resulting primarily from age can be separated from class-linked characteristics. Kehoe speculates that old lesbians may be somewhat more youthful than their heterosexual counterparts because they have escaped the expectations laid on wives, mothers and grandmothers. I think physical activity may be just as important — old lesbians may be more physically active than heterosexual women, from lifelong habit, partly because some of them held nontraditional jobs requiring physical labor.

Two autobiographical accounts of ageism by lesbians (as opposed to studies of lesbian aging) have been published: *Look Me In the Eye. Old Women, Aging, and Ageism* by Barbara Macdonald and Cynthia Rich (1983) and Baba Copper's *Over the Hill: Reflections on Ageism Between Women* (1988). In nine angry and eloquent essays, Rich and Macdonald, dissect ageism in mainstream society and in the women's movement. Their book has been very influential. They note that the women's movement has taken up every oppression except the oppression of old women, and they criticize young and middle-aged women for seeing the old as objects and assuming they are "museum pieces" or bearers of culture, interesting only for their past lives and not for their present experiences. Copper discusses "age-passing," the attempt to seem younger than one is, which she views as a way by which women compete and as "an apprenticeship in hatred of women" (Copper, 1988, pp. 73-74). She suggests that women in their 40s and 50s experiencing ageism are frequently the most vicious in their treatment of women older than them. Copper believes that small, thin old women do not receive "the same direct hostility that big motherly women do" (p. 80). All three authors are suspicious of gerontology and gerontologists, including lesbian and gay gerontologists. They believe that the interests of the old conflict with the interest of service providers.

CONCLUSION

Although some studies cited here were published in the 1970s, the field of gay aging is still in its infancy. The longitudinal studies called for by Adelman are obviously needed to develop this field. Considering how unhappy old homosexuals are supposed to be, the evidence in the recent literature of their positive responses to aging and to their emotional/sexual identities is an important discovery. One must cautiously note, however, that the old gay population is still so hidden that those few who come forward to describe their lives are quite likely to be the most robust specimens of their group and are more likely to have a gay political consciousness. That in itself is a source of high self-esteem at any age. Probably most middle-aged and old lesbians and gay men were told at some point in their lives that being gay was disastrous because they were certain to be lonely and pitiable in their old age. This message was a powerful social control that coerced many into marriage. Its persuasiveness came partly from ageism. Now that more positive images are beginning to appear, gay people can develop more realistic expectations of what the future holds, and gerontologists, both mainstream and gay, can better understand the population they serve.

REFERENCES

Adelman, M. (1987). *Long time passing: Lives of older lesbians*. Boston: Alyson.

Adelman, M. (1980). *Adjustment to aging and styles of being gay: A study of elderly gay men and lesbians*. Unpublished doctoral dissertation, Wright Institute.

Barrow, G. (1986). *Aging, the individual and society*. (3rd ed.) St. Paul: Kellogg.

Bennett, K., & Thompson, N. (1980). Social and psychological function of the aging male homosexual. *Journal of Psychiatry, 137*, 361-370.

Berger, R. (1982). *Gay and gray*. Chicago: University of Chicago Press.

Binstock, B. & Shanas, E. (Eds.). *Handbook of aging and the social sciences*. (2nd ed.) New York: Harper & Row.

Copper, B. (1988). *Over the hill: Reflections on ageism between women*. New York: The Crossing Press.

Kehoe, M. (Ed.) (1986). *Lesbians over 65: A triply invisible minority. Historical, literary and erotic aspects of lesbianism*. London: Hawthorn Press.

Kehoe, M. (Ed.) (1986). *A portrait of the older lesbian. Historical literary and erotic aspects of lesbianism*. London: Hawthorn Press.

Kehoe, M. *Lesbians over sixty speak for themselves*. New York: The Haworth Press, 1989. [Also published in *Journal of Homosexuality, 16*, 3/4.]

Kelly, J. (1977). The aging male homosexual: Myth and reality. *The Gerontologist, 17*, 328-332.

Lee, J.A. (1987). What can gay aging studies contribute to theories of aging? *Journal of Homosexuality 13*(4), 43-71.

Lee, J.A. (1988). Invisible lives of Canada's gray gays. In V. Marshall (Ed.), *Aging in Canada*, pp. 138-55. Toronto: Fitzhenry & Whiteside.

Macdonald, B. & Rich, C. (1983). *Look me in the eye. Old women, aging, and ageism*. San Francisco: Spinsters Ink.

Martin, D. & Lyon, P. (1970). The older lesbian. In B. Berzon (Ed.), *Positively gay*. Los Angeles: Media Mix.

Meyer, M. (1979). *The older lesbian*. Unpublished master's thesis, California State University, Dominquez Hills.

Meyer, M. & Raphael, S. (1984). The older lesbian: Love relationships and friendship patterns. In T. Darty & S. Patter (Eds.), *Women-Identified Women*. Palo Alto: Mayfield.

Meyer, M., & Raphael, S. (1988). The old lesbian: Some observations ten years later. In M. Shernoff (Ed.), *Resource book on lesbian and gay health*. New York: National Lesbian and Gay Health Foundation.

Minnigerode, F. (1976). Age-status labeling in homosexual men. *Journal of Homosexuality, 1* (3), 273-276.

Pifer, A., & Bronte, L. (1986). *Our aging society*. New York: Norton.

Poor, M. (1982). The older lesbian. In M. Cruikshank (Ed.), *Lesbian studies*. Old Westbury, NY: Feminist Press.

Vacha, K. (1985). *Quiet fire: Memoirs of older gay men*. Trumansburg, NY: The Crossing Press.

Being There:
A Support Network of Lesbian Women

Beth Dorrell, BA

Half Moon Bay, California

It was a typical San Francisco morning—a little gray, a little cloudy, a little cool, and more fog circling in from the northwest. The three of us sat in the kitchen drinking a cup of fragrant Keemun. We broke into a pound cake rich with currants from the Mexican bakery around the corner, not saying much until the warmth of the tea and cake did their work.

We began to talk about our friend, Benton. (To protect her privacy, her real name is not used.) The stories unfolded one after the other as our memories seemed to spin into a quilt of recollection, Judy Chicago style.

At some point the conversation stopped. We held onto the silence for a few minutes and for a while we cried together, each in our own way—tearfully, inwardly, softly indistinct.

We were three lesbian women, part of a group of seven, who had formed a network of support around an 84-year-old terminally ill lesbian woman. Just as the group seemed to have a life of its own, so the retelling of how it came about and what happened is not any one person's story but that of seven women and, most of all, of Benton, the person at the center of our attention.

For each of the seven members of the group, she had been someone different.

"She was a warrior," said one.

"We were her harem," said another.

"She was the general and we were the troops."

"Benton was the center of the wheel and we were the spokes."

Beth Dorrell is a technical editor and publications consultant in Silicon Valley. During a recent sabbatical, she worked as case manager for a national program for seniors in San Francisco. She is a graduate of Harvard University and has written and edited a number of technical publications. Correspondence may be addressed to Beth Dorrell, 1804 N. Cabrillo Hwy., Half Moon Bay, CA 94019.

"She was a trailblazer."

"I saw her walking down the street one day with her hat and raincoat. She looked like a character out of a 1940s movie with that cigarette sticking out of her mouth. So wonderful."

"Benton and I used to flirt with the waitress together."

"Watching her dance at the tea dances—tiny little steps and proud shoulders—was a wonderful event."

"She needed to hang onto the belief that if she kept going to doctors, she would meet someone who would be able to reverse the failing eyesight, the lung cancer, and all her other medical problems."

"I began to understand for the first time another person's vulnerability, another's illness and needs."

"Even though she finally got to the point where she knew she wasn't going to live forever, she decided she wasn't going to think about it either."

Each of us saw some part of her that she chose to share.

"She had so many facets to her life; there was always something new to find out about her."

Benton had lived on both coasts and in Europe, and her experiences as a lesbian woman during the '20s, '30s, and '40s kept us fascinated. When we met her, she lived in an old-fashioned apartment building in the heart of the city in a neighborhood in flux. It seemed right for her.

The building was the old City—potted palms and a fully liveried doorman at the desk—surrounded by an outside world of cheap hotels and apartments for the elderly poor, the down and out, and newly arriving Vietnamese.

She was ill in the spring of 1984 and had been making the rounds of ophthalmologists and eye surgeons to try and find an answer to her deteriorating eyesight. It was then that the support network began to form around her. Quietly and without any plan of approach, a group of caregivers was created. A few of us knew one or two of the others. Most had not met before.

Ann, a case manager from North of Market Senior Services, received a referral on Benton from Gay and Lesbian Outreach to the Elderly (GLOE). Both agencies represent a growing trend toward direct supportive services. North of Market serves the residents of the inner city and provides case management support as required. GLOE provides active support to the gay and lesbian community with a growing number of activities and volunteers.

Benton had been depicted as isolated, in need of home care, depressed, and slightly difficult. When Ann first saw her, Benton talked and Ann listened. Benton was primarily focused on her physical problems – anticipating cataract surgery and suffering from increasing frailty.

Ann became the first person in the support group and the pivotal information point in the network. The group learned to turn to Ann for advice and counsel and often just to talk things out. With strong support from her agency supervisor, she worked to pull in as many community services as Benton felt were necessary and appropriate. Ann kept well-informed on Benton's medical status, working with doctors, hospital social workers, low-vision clinics, and others to garner as many of the needed community services as possible.

Because Ann knew her way through the maze of services offered (and San Francisco is rich in services for seniors), she was able to give Benton a range of options for professional assistance. Benton began to feel more confident and less isolated. She began to have a greater sense of control over what was happening to her.

As their friendship blossomed, Benton showed Ann a copy of her book, published by a vanity press – a collection of short stories set in the southern U.S. early in the century. The dialogue is painfully authentic and the writing literate, colorful, and stylish.

Throughout her relationship with the group, it was apparent that the book represented a great deal to her; it had been published at her expense when she was in her 70s. Maybe it was her way of saying that, at last, here was something out of a long life to visibly demonstrate her talent. She had published short stories as a young women and been a member of avant garde lesbian/gay groups in Greenwich Village. Many of the people she had known were well-known figures in politics, the arts, journalism.

Ann, as she came to know Benton, went through the same process that each of us would later follow. We listened to her stories, we heard about her life, and we were enchanted.

"Sometimes she didn't seem to know how to deal with us because our lives seemed so placid compared to hers."

The next women to become a part of the network – Eddie and Jo Ann, one a word processor and the other a computer programmer – also began to see Benton as the result of a referral from GLOE. Both were active in GLOE and the lesbian community. Along with Ann, they gave Benton her first taste of what it would be like to know younger lesbian women who were supportive and caring. They were a family within a family, representing stability and togetherness for her. Benton liked what she saw.

At this point Ann called me and asked if I would be willing to ferry Benton back and forth to a few doctor appointments and maybe visit occasionally.

When I met Benton in the lobby of her building, she was sitting in a very deep arm chair surrounded by mirrors and sconces and art deco ornamentation. She stood up, short and with presence, wearing a felt hat, bright tartan jacket, slacks, and high-top leather boots. She put out a cigarette in the huge, old-fashioned ashtray and gave a game imitation of a sprightly walk as she came over to meet me and take my arm.

"Do you mind riding in a pickup truck?" I asked.

"Does it run?" she responded.

I liked her from that moment.

Later, Jonnelle, a corporate computer analyst and former member of a NASA computer team, became a member of the group. She was working on a law degree in the evenings. In a short span of time, Benton inducted her to be her executor and to handle her financial affairs. Jonnelle became a sort of administrator, a channel through which negotiations were conducted with the telephone company, medical providers, the attorney, the bank, and many other groups and individuals.

Fran, a librarian and also a GLOE volunteer, became a member of the network. She later began graduate work in political science, and Benton was keenly interested in her politics. Fran, an activist in lesbian causes, would often talk with Benton about activities in the gay/lesbian community.

"Don't vote for someone just because they're gay or lesbian," Benton warned her.

Marcy, a psychotherapist and author of a number of books and articles about the lesbian community, was the last member to join the group.

"I came to interview Benton for an article in my book and stayed for two years," she said.

Marcy would often visit Benton for long talks. Here Benton was more likely to speak about death and dying, about being Jewish, about the pain of growing up as a lesbian woman in the early part of the century — subjects that she liked to avoid. It was another safe place for Benton within a framework of comradery and caring.

We were an informal group. There was never any clearly defined structure. It was only at the memorial service after her death that everyone met. Ann, when necessary, provided information to each of us about agencies that were involved and what needed to be done.

The support group was a family of choice for Benton — a diverse and scattered group, the opposite of a patriarchal structure. Elisabeth Schussler Fiorenza, the feminist theologian, defines patriarchy as a male pyramid of graded subordinations and exploitations. Adrienne Rich, the poet, has defined the results of this type of structure as "a separation from ourselves."

Within the group, there were no hierarchies, no grabs for power, no grades and levels. There was a diffusion, as each of the women stated in different terms, of ways of caring and connecting.

From the beginning, however, it was clear who was in control of the group. Perhaps it was part of the group's gift to give her this control. Benton developed, or perhaps already possessed, excellent skills for dispensing just so much information, getting what she wanted, and delighting in the fact that she was surrounded by a group of concerned, energetic lesbian women ranging in age from early 30s to late 40s.

She kept her telephone by her easy chair and made periodic calls to each of us. A routine developed. She relied on one person for Mexican dinners, another for a Kosher dinner, and another for a Vietnamese supper at the corner restaurant.

"She was the center of the wheel and we were the spokes."

"She was a grand manipulator. She'd give you just so much information."

If one person was out of town, another was not and would take her for dinner and a walk, a ride out of the city, or to a doctor's appointment.

As we got to know her, she began to ask each of us questions about our lives. She was genuinely concerned about us, what we were doing, our lovers or lack of them, and how we were managing our careers. She began to know each of us well.

Our attitudes toward older women were changing as a result of knowing her.

"I had been dismissing older people all of my life," said Jonnelle. "I became more sensitive, more concerned, less ageist in my thinking."

We developed a routine without any plan as a group of caregivers. In the process, we learned that such an exchange is never a one-way street.

"She validated us in a way; validated us in our own lives."

"Her generation is practically gone — and so she reached out to us."

"She gave each of us some piece of herself."

"She gave me a sense of continuity. There have been lesbians before and will be in the future."

Although the members of the group did not have formal meetings, we became better acquainted over the telephone as we rotated tasks and shared increasing responsibilities. Occasionally some of our paths would cross when we took Benton to a tea dance sponsored by GLOE or met one another going in and out of her condominium.

Each of us, we later discovered, sometimes wondered about the lack of structure of the group. However, we were also highly dubious about changing the delicate mechanism of caregiving that had developed. It was working; leave it alone.

It was in 1985 that Benton learned that she had lung cancer. Her primary physician, a woman internist specializing in geriatric medicine, gave her the results of the tests in a direct and straightforward manner. She cared for Benton throughout her illness and became, in many senses, a member of our network. We relied upon her for information and support; so, of course, did Benton. She made regular home visits and quickly responded when Benton or a member of the group would call with questions and problems. She strongly supported our roles as caregivers and often worked with us to follow through on medical appointments, procedures, and special treatments. In addition, the health maintenance organization of which she was a part sent visiting nurses and provided other services.

Benton did not take the news of lung cancer in a mild and meek manner. She began a serious round of telephoning; she talked with each of us as well as old friends and family at a distance. There was no treatment, other than measures taken to help the discomfort, and the doctor advised her and the group that she had maybe six months to live.

"Her support network was in a sense her hold on life. This kept her going — this wheel that she was operating."

Most of us had never dealt with a devastating illness of someone close; we had only one avenue of approach — to stick with her and learn. She called us more frequently, and we began to experience burnout from time to time. One by one, we dropped out for a week or two, but we always returned.

When one of us felt the need to be away for a while, we talked it over with one or two others and then took our respite. Usually we talked with any group member who was available. There was no one person who fielded all the distress calls that dealt with the individual issues of burnout.

That Benton needed us more often was clear. She did not so much openly deny the seriousness of her illness as ignore it (which is, of course, a form of denial). Each of us sensed that she took care of it in the ways that she could, and we respected that.

"Sometimes when I would visit her, we would just share a companionable silence," said Eddie. "Just putting my hand on her hand and giving her more in an emotional way."

After the first shock had worn off, Benton concentrated again on her failing eyesight. She began another round of ophthalmologists and eye surgeons to find someone who would tell her what she wanted to hear. Often, one of us would take her for a visit to the doctor's office and be with her as yet one more time she would either be given no hope or vague and discomforting information.

Ann tried to give her information about services available for people with limited vision; she rejected almost all of the possibilities. She wanted no part of devices and aids. She would do it her way. We tried encouraging her; this had no effect. We settled for being there.

What seemed the final blow to her frail physical state came early one morning. A bathroom mat slid out from under her when she walked into the bathroom during the night; she fell and lay on the floor, struggling for two hours to reach the telephone.

"I've been reciting the Twenty-Third Psalm before I go to sleep at night," she told me from an impersonal bed in the emergency room. "And look what it got me—a broken hip."

Because the members of the group were all heavily involved with multiple responsibilities—jobs, school, homes to run, organizations—we could not stay overnight with her on a regular basis. We began to talk about what would happen when she came home from the hospital; we began to understand that our group had limitations—we could not do it all.

We had her birthday party, previously planned for a restaurant she had chosen, in the hospital room. She lay propped up in the bed, a slightly angry look on her face that softened as we gathered around her.

She seemed to be saying, why is this happening to me? Can't you do something? Her anger at her increasing frailty and the distress she felt because of it began to overflow when she went from the hospital to an extended care facility and back to the bed in her apartment. More than ever, she wanted one or all of us to provide a solution.

"If she didn't like the answer she got from one of us, she would go to another. She'd keep making the circle until she got the answer she wanted."

Death and dying were not subjects she liked to discuss. When one of us would bring them up and try to soften her denial, she would make it clear that she wanted no part of it. What kind of a doctor is she to give me such distressing information? she asked. She wanted to live; she wanted a future.

As we watched her frailty increase, as we saw her failing, it caused each of us to examine our own lives more closely. How were we living? What kind of old age were we going to have?

Would we, like Benton, end up longing for a consanguineous family that chose not to be there? Could we turn instead to a new family, a network of lesbian women? Was it time to begin building that network and to connect with similar groups? Was what we were doing similar to what other gay/lesbian support groups were doing on an informal basis? Was this what family really meant? Then why not redefine it?

Jo Ann stood by her side, holding her, while she endured the agony of a thoracentesis (lung tap) in the hospital.

"It was so incredibly invasive," she said. But for Benton it was a possibility to sustain life.

Benton returned home from her last visit to the hospital with 24-hour home care. She tortured herself and us with constant inquiries about how she was to pay for all this, what would happen to her condominium, how she would manage.

As the situation deteriorated, we began to talk with one another over the phone. It seemed there was only one solution. She would need to go to a convalescent home. Would she go to one of the best? Finally, she consented; it lasted two weeks. The resources that Ann had placed in motion to find ways to meet the costs of care were stopped.

Benton had left the city on short notice. As had happened so often in the past when she would be a little annoyed with us, she would conjure up old friends from the past to talk on the telephone and blot us out of her life for a few days.

This time, she had made arrangements with two gay men in a nearby city, both of whom were registered nurses. (Benton had an unbelievable backlog, never ending it seemed, of friends from the past who kept popping up.) They were to come and pick her up and take her to their home and care for her.

We knew that they had been caring for Benton's sister, who had Alzheimer's, in their own home for several years. Both of the men had had responsible positions in large hospitals in San Francisco; later they had set up their own home health care business in another city. Some of us had, at an earlier time, suggested to Benton that she might like to consider moving there with her sister to cut down on her expenses.

Nevertheless, we were doubtful. It was all confusing. Jonnelle and I saw her at the convalescent center the day before she left. We took pictures, talked with her, wished her well, and were very unsure about what she was doing. She was, however, in control of her own life again as she felt she had not been in the convalescent home.

After she left, we tried to find consolation in permutations—what could we have done differently? Then, after self-doubt, came anger. Why had she done this? Was she receiving proper care? Was she all right? We tried to reach her but could not because of some confusion about the telephone number. We reassured ourselves that she had, after all, made her own final decision about how and where she was going to die. It might not be her condominium, although she never gave up hope of going back there, but she had made it clear it wasn't going to be a nursing home. We could even smile a little.

After about a week, I heard from her — she sounded good over the telephone, not settled in but doing all right, busy figuring out strategies for getting well and returning to her condominium. She hoped that the personal care of two nurses would speed the recovery she planned on having.

She asked me if I would visit her; I said yes, of course. She asked about other members of the group. She seemed to enjoy hearing about each one, even when I had no particularly new information to share.

And then we heard, a few weeks later, that she had died. We were informed indirectly, and our sadness and grief was compounded because we were not there with her, because we had not had one last chance to say good-bye. At the time, it did not seem to matter that she had beaten the doctor's prediction by over a year.

In the time immediately following her death, her caregivers had, for reasons that were never clear, not informed any of her old or new friends in San Francisco of her death. We went through a period of shock.

We began by handling our grief separately and apart from one another as if the sight of another group member would remind us of our loss. For me, it meant calling the two caregivers and asking for details of those last days of her life. They had gone out to dinner each evening (which Benton always enjoyed), she had begun to use her cane less (a support left over from her last hospital visit), and she enjoyed sitting around with their friends in the evening and engaging in conversation. She had been doing that early on the evening she died.

She had changed the executor in her will to an old friend who lived nearby. (She liked to frequently change her will, but the heirs, her family, always remained the same.) She had also indicated she wanted the simplest possible cremation without ceremony.

The group had yet another level of understanding to process. For her, the options had turned into the one possible thing she could do and remain in some sort of control of her life. Each of us appreciated and admired that, but it was hard to accept. It was only by finally beginning to talk with one another that we could begin to comprehend this and then turn to our grief.

Spontaneously, informally, we put together a memorial service at a reception room in her condominium building. A notice was posted on the bulletin board.

All of the members of the support group, except for one who could not be there, came to the service. Several elderly residents, with hairdos and fashionable clothing just right for 1950, came by to join us. Several old friends attended. We played Edith Piaf records in the background (a request Benton had once made) and recited the Twenty-Third Psalm in her honor. We exchanged reminiscences and joined hands and said the Lord's Prayer, the only prayer she ever admitted to saying. It helped to share our grief but it was not enough.

"I think about her a lot. It's hard for me to realize that she really is dead."

"She had a lot of trouble dying."

"When you work with someone who doesn't feel their emotions, you wind up having them yourself."

With time, each of us began to understand better how the group had worked, how it had sometimes failed, and how it had adjusted as Benton became increasingly fragile; we learned to appreciate one another and to think of ourselves as sharing something special for having known Benton and supported her in the ways that we had. She may have left us, but she would go on being named among us.

"At the end of her life she was more at peace with herself—as a lesbian, as a Jew."

"She gave me a real sense of validation—as a lesbian, as a human being, as a woman."

We had seen Benton change, become more accepting of herself as a lesbian, become proud that she was the center of attention of a group of younger lesbian women.

Some months later as I talked with members of the support network, it was clear that we each identified with Benton in some way. She had affected each of our lives in major ways. I came to see it as a form of transcendence. For us, but perhaps less so for her. It was her gift to each of us.

For herself, she had remained a warrior, as Marcy called her, until the very last. She would not go gently into the good night.

REFERENCES

Fiorenza, E. S. (1984). *Bread Not Stone*. Boston: Beacon Press.
Rich, A. (1978). "Disloyal to Civilization: Feminism, Racism, Gynephobia" in *On Lies, Secrets, and Silence*, p. 307. New York: Norton.

Older Lesbian and Gay People:
A Theory of Successful Aging

Richard A. Friend, PhD

University of Pennsylvania

As a group, older lesbian and gay people are best described as diverse (Kimmel, 1978). The most common unifying elements for this group are the facts that today's older gay and lesbian people have all developed some type of homosexual identity and all grew up in a particular socio-historical period. The popular image of older lesbian and gay people is extremely negative. Older gay men are frequently depicted as lonely, depressed, oversexed, and living a life without the traditional support of family and friends (Kelly, 1977). Older lesbian women are often described as unattractive, unemotional, and lonely (Berger, 1982a). This common negative image conflicts, however, with the descriptions of older gay and lesbian adults from the research literature.

Kelly (1977) argues that the popular negative stereotypes of older gay men are myths that do not accurately reflect the lives of the men he studied. Like Kelly, Berger (1982a, 1982b), Friend (1980), Kimmel (1978), Francher and Henkin (1973), and Weinberg (1970) all report on samples of older gay men who are described as psychologically well adjusted, self-accepting, and adapting well to the aging process. Almvig (1982), Martin and Lyon (1979) and Raphael and Robinson (1980) also describe the ma-

---

Richard A. Friend is on the faculty of the Human Sexuality Education Program at the University of Pennsylvania's Graduate School of Education as well as an Adjunct Assistant Professor at the College of Allied Health Sciences at Thomas Jefferson University.

Correspondence may be addressed to the author at: University of Pennsylvania, Graduate School of Education, Human Sexuality Education Program, 3700 Walnut Street, Philadelphia, PA 19104.

The author would like to acknowledge special thanks to Professor Kenneth D. George for his help and support.

This manuscript was originally accepted for publication in September 1986.

jority of older lesbian women they studied as happy and well adjusted, contrary to popular stereotypes.

It is argued here that these disparate views of older gay and lesbian people reflect two responses to the social construction of homosexuality as a negative identity. Some people internalize the negative discourse of what homosexuality means, while others reconstruct its meaning in positive and affirmative ways. The purpose of this paper is to present a theory of successful aging. According to this theory, by achieving a positive lesbian or gay identity, certain skills, feelings and attitudes are also acquired that function as resources facilitating adjustment to aging.

Using social construction theory, this paper discusses a model of the diverse ways in which older lesbian women and gay men form their individual sexual identity. By highlighting the relationship between the social construction of lesbian and gay identities and the individual psychology of older gay and lesbian people who have worked to make their lives meaningful within the context of a particular socio-historical period of time, a theory of what it means to successfully grow old emerges.

This paper begins with an explanation of social construction theory and presents a model of the relationship between the development of popular ideology and the individual psychology of identity formation. Next, the diverse ways in which older lesbian and gay people have made their lives meaningful and formed their identities are discussed using this model. Finally, a theory of successful aging is offered based on this analysis. Included in this discussion is the potential impact this theory has on the lives of younger lesbian and gay people. Recommendations for future research are also offered.

SOCIAL CONSTRUCTION THEORY AND HOMOSEXUALITY

Social construction theory suggests that sexual functions and feelings have no intrinsic or essential meaning of their own, but are given meaning by the ideological systems developed for their explanation (Foucault, 1978; Weeks, 1977, 1981; Weinberg, 1983; Vance, 1984). This constructionist view contrasts with the more common essentialist view which conceptualizes sex as

> an overpowering force in the individual that shapes not only the personal but the social life as well. It is seen as a driving, instinctual force, whose characteristics are built into the biology of the human animal, which shapes human institutions and whose will must force

its way out, whether in the form of direct sexual expression or, if blocked, in the form of perversion or neurosis. (Weeks, 1981, p. 2)

Foucault (1978) argues that certain knowledge is created through discourse (beliefs, theories, and ideas) which construct our notions of reality and functions as a powerful mechanism of control over individual sexuality. According to this perspective, the great interest of medical authorities during the late 19th and early 20th centuries in describing and documenting sexual behavior functioned to change popular constructions of homosexuality from the notion of sin to sickness (Foucault, 1978; Weeks, 1977; 1981). Weeks (1981) says that while meanings of homosexuality have varied throughout history, it was not until near the turn of the century that a distinction was made between homosexual behavior and homosexual roles and identities.

Homosexual identities fell under the category of what Foucault (1978) called the "perverse adult." Foucault (1978) argues that the construction of an identity known as the "perverse adult" generated control over individual sexuality not through repression, but through the creation of detailed taxonomies and definitions which set up specific notions of what homosexuality meant, and, hence, a limitation on the possibilities of creating individual meaning.

Weeks (1981) says that the notion of a homosexual person or identity (rather than simply homosexual behavior) served two interrelated functions. First, it provided clear definitions of acceptable and unacceptable behavior. In other words, it legitimized heterosexism. Heterosexism is defined as the assumption that everyone is heterosexual, and if they are not, that they should be heterosexual. As a socially constructed belief system, heterosexism facilitates the development of homophobia. Homophobia is a dimension of individual psychology and is defined as the irrational fear and hatred of homosexuality in one's self and in others (Weinberg, 1972). Second, the creation of something known as a homosexual identity facilitated the emergence of a homosexual subculture which allowed some people access to each other and created a system of resistance for challenging heterosexism.

Regarding this latter function, Foucault (1978) describes the reverse discourse of resistance during the turn of the century:

Homosexuality began to speak in its behalf, to demand that its legitimacy or "naturality" be acknowledged, often in the same vocabulary, using the same categories by which it was medically disqualified. (p. 101)

In terms of individual psychology, heterosexism and the socially constructed notion of sickness associated with homosexual identities were resisted by some lesbian and gay people and clearly internalized by many others. Weeks (1981) comments on the relationships between heterosexist discourse and either affirmative resistance or internalized homophobia. He says,

> The striking feature of the 'history of homosexuality' over the past hundred years or so is that the oppressive definition and defensive identities and structures have marched together. Control of sexual variations has inevitably reinforced and reshaped rather than repressed homosexual behaviour. In terms of individual anxiety, induced guilt and suffering, the cost of moral regulation has often been high. But the result has been a complex and socially significant history of resistance and self-definition which historians have hitherto all too easily ignored. (p. 117)

A PROPOSED MODEL FOR IDENTITY FORMATION

Resistance and internalized homophobia are two different responses for managing the heterosexist discourse which constructed the homosexual identity during the turn of the century into the mold of sickness. It is argued that for today's older lesbian and gay adults who grew up close to this particular socio-historical period, resistance or internalized homophobia are the end-points of a continuum of potential cognitive/behavioral responses to heterosexism. Associated with this cognitive/behavioral continuum is a range of potential emotional responses which each action can generate.

In the process of developing an identity as a lesbian or gay person, each individual must make meaning out of the messages they have received about homosexuality. This process of identity formation reflects the relationship between individual psychology and social construction. Given social norms, each person is challenged to interpret these in a way which results in a style of individual meaning for that person. There are a variety of ways in which this can be accomplished. The model presented here suggests that these styles can be described along a set of two continuums.

One continuum represents cognitive/behavioral responses. At one end-point of this continuum is the internalization of the pervasive heterosexist ideologies. This results in the belief that homosexuality is sick and/or otherwise negative. At the other end of the continuum is a cognitive/behavioral response to heterosexism which involves challenging or questioning the validity of these negative messages. As a result, there is a reconstruction of what it means to be lesbian or gay into something positive and affirmative. This affirmative reconstruction is the foundation of the reverse discourse of resistance described by Foucault (1978).

Associated with this cognitive/behavioral continuum is a set of corresponding affective responses. For example, if one end of the cognitive/behavioral continuum is the negative evaluation of homosexuality, the corresponding emotional response to these beliefs is internalized homophobia. Feelings of self-hatred, low self-esteem, and minimal or conditional self-acceptance may result. Associated with the other end of the cognitive/behavioral continuum (a gay or lesbian identity reconstructed as positive) are the feelings of increased self-acceptance, high self-esteem, personal empowerment, and self-affirmation.

The model of cognitive/behavioral and affective continua as processes involved in the development of homosexual identities corresponds with other developmental models regarding lesbian, gay, and bisexual identity formation (Cass, 1979; Coleman, 1981/82; Dank, 1971; Lee, 1977; Minton & McDonald, 1983/84). These models suggest that one early stage of acquiring a homosexual identity involves the internalization of the prevailing norms regarding homosexuality. The last stage, according to Minton and McDonald, involves the realization that social norms can be critically evaluated, and can result in the potential acceptance of and commitment to a positive gay identity. The notion of two continua that is offered here, while consistent with the other developmental models, highlights the significance of, and relationship between cognitive/behavioral and affective processes.

THE IDENTITIES OF OLDER GAY AND LESBIAN PEOPLE

Dawson (1982) estimates that there are currently at least 3.5 million lesbian and gay people over the age of 60. As a group, one factor older gay and lesbian people have in common is living the major part of their lives through historical periods described as actively hostile and oppressive toward homosexuality (Almvig, 1982; Dawson, 1982; Kimmel, 1977, 1978). As indicated earlier, given this socio-historical context, a significant part of the lives of older gay and lesbian people involves managing heterosexism. It is suggested here that there is a range of cognitive/behavioral and emotional responses in this process which characterize at least three distinct groups of older lesbian and gay adults.

Those older gay and lesbian people whose identities conform to the stereotype of being lonely, depressed, and alienated, represent people whose cognitive/behavioral responses to heterosexism are in the direction of extreme internalized homophobia. As a group, they represent one set of end-points on the two continua. This group is referred to here as "Stereotypic Older Lesbian and Gay People" and are the ones identified in the popular myths.

Those older gay and lesbian adults who are described in the research literature as psychologically well-adjusted, vibrant, and adapting well to the aging process represent those whose response to heterosexism is one of reconstructing a positive and affirmative sense of self. They are at the other end of the two continua. This group is referred to as "Affirmative Older Lesbian and Gay People."

The mid-range of these continua reflect men and women who accommodate heterosexism by marginally accepting some aspects of homosexuality but still believing that heterosexuality is inherently better. This group is called "Passing Older Lesbian and Gay People." While some older adults in this middle group may, under certain circumstances label themselves as lesbian or gay, they have a strong investment in either passing as non-gay or non-lesbian, or at least not appearing to be stereotypically lesbian or gay.

These three groups, which represent different places along the two continua reflect three possible styles of identity formation among older lesbian and gay people. Given that this model is based on continua, there are certainly many more styles that are possible. This model is offered to facilitate the conceptualization of a complex process and move toward developing a theory of successful aging. As such, this model is limited by its own linear structure. As Weinberg (1984) suggests, it is not clear whether social identities follow a linear pattern of development. Models constructed in this fashion are problematic because human beings are flexible, creative, and individualistic in their developmental patterns. Linear models tend to ignore human wavering and developmental patterns which occur at rates which are not uniform. As such, this model does not necessarily assume that there are no other developmental sequences that can be adapted and which result in the same or different outcomes as those suggested here.

Stereotypic Older Lesbian and Gay People

Those individuals described as "Stereotypic Older Lesbian and Gay People" conform to the popular negative images as a result of internalizing powerful heterosexist ideology. Dawson (1982) describes their common socio-historical context and those people who internalized the messages. He says,

When today's older gays were young, they faced an unrelieved hostility towards homosexuality that was far more virulent than it is today. They were labeled "sick" by doctors, immoral by clergy, unfit by the military, and "a menace" by police and legislators. If identified as homosexual, they risked the loss of job, home, friends, and family. The need for secrecy caused an isolation which imperiled their most intimate relationships. And the greatest damage was done to those gay people who *believed* what society said about them, and thus lived in corrosive shame and self-loathing. (p. 5)

Kimmel (1977) describes the older gay men in his study who were loners as living lives "of relatively little sexual intimacy. Typically these men had repressed their sexuality and were often fearful that their homosexuality would be discovered" (p. 388). Similarly, Almvig (1982) reports that while lesbianism has gained increased acceptance in recent years, many older lesbian women have led invisible lives of secrecy and personal danger.

The "Stereotypic" group may never associate with openly lesbian and gay people and, therefore, may have never had an opportunity to challenge their own heterosexist belief system. Having internalized extremely negative ideas about themselves, the men and women in this group may also lead lives punctuated by very little intimacy with non-lesbian and non-gay people as well. Isolation of this sort may reflect the assumption that "no one would want to be close with me."

The guilt, anxiety, self-hatred, and low self-esteem which characterize this group of older people may interfere with the process of forming meaningful relationships with others. Emotional distance in interpersonal relationships reflects the extent to which a poor relationship with oneself impacts on relationships with others. Other potential responses to the internalization of extreme homophobia include loneliness, despair, depression, and suicide. Those older lesbian and gay people whose lives are described as reflecting the internalized homophobia end-points of the identity continua, are also the people identified by popular stereotypes.

Passing Older Lesbian and Gay People

The group of people characterized by the mid-range of the continua are the "Passing Older Lesbian and Gay People." They believe the heterosexist sentiments with which they were raised while also acknowledging and marginally accepting their homosexuality. Many manage the conflict that results by marrying heterosexually and/or distancing themselves from anything defined as stereotypically lesbian or gay. Married older gay men in this group may be like Miller's (1979) "Trade Fathers" who engage in sexual encounters with other men but define these behaviors as only "genital urges." Historically, many gay men and lesbian women have married heterosexually assuming this was their only option for some degree of happiness (Martin & Lyon, 1973; Miller, 1979). Many of these older persons who are married may wait for their spouse to die before managing their sexuality in a different way (Kimmel, 1977; Martin & Lyon, 1979).

Not all gay and lesbian people who marry heterosexually are necessarily trying to pass and many are in fact happily married bisexual people. Wolf (1985) reports on 26 married couples in which the husband was bisexual. He describes these marriages as stable and that the partners were satisfied with the quality of their relationships in those marriages where the husband was open and not trying to "pass."

Matteson (1985) reports that more recent marriages involving a bisexual partner are made for positive reasons as opposed to an escape from, or a cover for homosexuality. Matteson compared acknowledged and secretive bisexual marriages and argues that a positive homosexual identity can be developed in the former type of marriages. Matteson says that husbands in acknowledged bisexual marriages "not only accepted their homosexual experience but also affirmed and felt positive about being homosexual" (p. 167). These men have higher levels of self-acceptance in addition to their affirmative homosexual identity, according to Matteson.

It is argued here that "Passing Older Lesbian and Gay People" who are married are more likely to be in secret marriages. Their internalization of the negative messages about homosexuality would prevent them from sharing their sexual orientation with their marital partner, as well as other lesbian and gay people. Given the strength of heterosexist discourse, being secretive and trying to pass is probably more representative of older lesbian and gay people who marry than it is of younger lesbian and gay people. In fact, Matteson (1985) reports that husbands in secret bisexual marriages were older than husbands in acknowledged bisexual marriages.

Married or unmarried, older lesbian and gay adults who try to pass as heterosexual may have some contact with other lesbian and gay people or even form long-term same gender relationships. Much energy is spent, however, in appearing heterosexual. Compartmentalizing the various aspects of their lives is not uncommon among this group. Given marginal or conditional self-acceptance, there is a perceived need to live in two mutually exclusive worlds. This may result in a fragmented sense of self and a lack of authenticity in interpersonal relationships. According to Minton and McDonald (1983/84), "In choosing to hide an essential part of the self, individuals are left with a gnawing feeling that they are really valued for what others expect them to be rather than for who they really are" (p. 102).

The energy of "passing" is reflected in very complicated styles of living which include separate bedrooms, phones, or even housing for the purpose of concealing same-sexed relationships. Martin and Lyon (1979) report on a lesbian couple who wrote:

> We are in our fifties, have been together for 18 years, but have never declared our love for each other in front of a third party. When we shut our doors at night we shut the world out. We have no gay friends that we know of. We are looking for companions, friendship and support, but in the lesbian organizations we've contacted we find only badge-wearing, drum-beating, foot-stomping social reformers. They consider our conservative life 'oppressed,' and we think of their way of life as 'flagrant.' There must be more like us, but how do we meet them? (pp. 140-141)

Emotional issues that are common among this group include heightened levels of anxiety and self-consciousness generated by the possibility of being "found out," conditional self-acceptance, and the absence of emotional supports during crises and times of need. According to Martin and Lyon (1979),

> Other women who had been in lesbian relationships of long standing poured out their grief over the death of a lover. These couples had no gay friends, and the surviving partner felt bereft and alone. True, some of them had straight friends or relatives who knew, but it had never been discussed. (p. 140)

Affirmative Older Lesbian and Gay People

Some older gay and lesbian people live lives of internalized homophobia; still others marginally accept their sexual orientation while accommodating heterosexist sentiments. However, as a social service provider for older lesbian and gay people, Dawson (1982) says while some "have suffered brutal repression for their sexuality and have been growing old in isolation. . . . these people are very much in the minority" (p. 5). Dawson indicates that the largest percentage of older gay and lesbian adults with whom he works are vibrant, active and independent.

"Affirmative Older Lesbian and Gay People" manage heterosexism by reconstructing what it means to be gay or lesbian into something positive, and are reflected in the research literature. According to the literature, the vast majority of older lesbian and gay people studied have managed to attain a high level of self-acceptance and psychological adjustment, even within the hostile and unaccepting historical periods in which they were raised (Almvig, 1982; Berger, 1982a, 1982b; Francher & Henkin, 1973; Friend, 1980; Kelly, 1977; Kimmel, 1977, 1978; Raphael & Robinson, 1980; Weinberg, 1970).

Some of the "Affirmative Older Lesbian and Gay People" presented in the literature may be described as activists engaged in resistance. Foucault (1978) would argue that this resistance is an effort to gain self-empowerment by reconstructing the meaning of a homosexual identity—an attempt to control one's sexuality. These men and women may be engaged in a purposeful attempt to challenge and alter the prevailing and oppressive socio-sexual ideologies and hence their identity reflects this process.

While some may be engaged in resistance as an active attempt for social change, this is likely not true for all of the older lesbian and gay adults in this group. For others, self-acceptance and social integration may not be a conscious socio-political form of resistance. Rather, it may simply illustrate people living lives that comfortably reflect individualistically who they are without struggling to change dominant socio-sexual ideologies. In order to manage the conflicts that being lesbian or gay in a heterosexist environment generates, people in this group may reconstruct the meaning homosexuality has for them individually without being committed to a purposeful attempt for social change.

The disparate views of older lesbian and gay people reflect the endpoints of the continua model described here. The popular image of older gay and lesbian adults as lonely, depressed and isolated reflects the group described here as "Stereotypic Older Lesbian and Gay People." The image of older lesbian and gay adults provided by the research literature describes the group referred to here as "Affirmative Older Lesbian and Gay People." Paradoxically, both are consequences of responses to the social oppression of heterosexism.

At this time it is impossible to assess the extent to which any of these groups are represented in the general population. While a majority of those older lesbian and gay adults described in the literature do not conform to popular negative stereotypes, given sampling bias and limited access to older lesbian and gay people, conclusions about the general population of older lesbian and gay people must be accepted with caution.

Harry (1986) discusses the source-related sampling problems of research on gay men. Specifically, access to research samples is limited primarily to lesbian and gay people who have some degree of involvement in the gay and lesbian communities. Since the oldest and youngest age groups are least likely to be involved in these community resources, Harry (1986) argues that "our studies of homosexuality are largely studies of active gays, those for whom their sexual orientation constitutes a lifestyle" (p. 22). Given limitations of current research, those who internalize heterosexist discourse and whose sexuality may be repressed and/or altered as a result, are not easily accessible for research.

It is argued that the ways in which "Affirmative Older Lesbian and Gay People" reconstruct the meaning of homosexuality also results in growing old successfully. By examining more closely the ways in which they shape their lives and the effects these new ideologies have on events associated with growing old, a theory of successful aging is offered.

A THEORY OF SUCCESSFUL AGING

Even within the hostile and unaccepting historical periods in which they were raised, the vast majority of older lesbian and gay people are described in the research literature as psychologically well adjusted, partially defined as having high levels of self-acceptance and comfort with being lesbian or gay (Almvig, 1982; Berger, 1982a, 1982b; Francher & Henkin, 1973; Friend, 1980; Kelly, 1977; Kimmel, 1977, 1978; Raphael & Robinson, 1980; Weinberg, 1970). It is argued here that these older lesbian and gay adults (labeled here as "Affirmative Lesbian and Gay People") have achieved these high levels of adjustment, in part, as a response to the pervasive negative messages about homosexuality with which they were raised.

In fact, some authors suggest that as a result of managing what it means to be lesbian and gay in a heterosexist world, many lesbian and gay adults develop skills for managing their lives which facilitate their adjustment to the aging process (Francher & Henkin, 1973; Friend, 1980; Kimmel, 1977). A theory of successful aging is presented here to describe these processes.

If the purpose of theory is to explain or predict, the theory of successful aging offered here is valuable in its potential to explain whether or not a particular older lesbian or gay person has aged successfully. Given the individual's particular cognitive/behavioral and affective identity style, one should be able to predict the success of their aging with this theory. Aging can be viewed as falling along a continuum ranging from successful to unsuccessful. This theory argues that those lesbian and gay people who will age successfully are those whose identities are formed in the affirmative direction. Those lesbian and gay people who are in the passing or stereotypic groups of the identity continua will age less successfully according to this theory. This theory examines the process of successful aging which is a result of the reconstruction of homosexuality as something positive within the following contexts: individual psychology; social and interpersonal dimensions; and legal and political advocacy.

Individual Psychology

While sexual orientation appears to be established very early in the life span, it is during adolescence when lesbian and gay people become aware of their sexual feelings and perhaps not until later in life that they begin to manage what these feelings mean (Cass, 1979, 1983/84; Coleman, 1981/82; Martin, 1982). Kimmel (1978) describes this process as a potential crisis, and the extent to which it occurs early in the life span, it is

> one that can involve extensive family disruption, intensive feelings and sometimes alienation from the family—maybe one of the most significant a gay person will face. Once resolved, it may provide a perspective on major life crises and a sense of crisis competence that buffers the person against later crises. (p. 117)

This "crisis competence" is a dimension of individual psychology which is functional in terms of adjusting to aging. An example of crisis competence is reflected in the fact that part of managing issues associated with sexual orientation involves dealing with the potential loss of family and friends. Therefore, some older lesbian and gay people may have already developed psychological skills for dealing with the losses which occur when family and friends move away or die.

Another aspect of individual psychology which facilitates successful aging is challenging, in addition to homosexuality, other socially constructed identities. These identities include gender and old age.

Confronting rigid gender role definitions can be functional to the aging process (Dawson, 1982; Francher & Henkin, 1973; Friend, 1980, 1984). Given the prevalence of traditional gender role definitions, many older people today may have a limited number of skills for managing daily living. Rigid gender role definitions may mean that a recently widowed heterosexual woman may have to learn to read the electric meter, repair household appliances, or even balance the checkbook. A widowed heterosexual man may have to learn how to do laundry or cook.

If part of reconstructing the meaning of homosexuality as something positive involves confronting the somewhat arbitrary ways in which sexual feelings get defined as "appropriate" or "inappropriate," then this same analysis easily applies to the arbitrary construction of traditional gender role definitions. As a result, throughout their lives older lesbian and gay adults have had the potential for greater freedom to learn skills which may be considered non-traditional.

Greater flexibility in gender role definitions may allow older gay and lesbian people to have developed ways of taking care of themselves that feel comfortable and appropriate. These skills may be less developed among heterosexual women and men who may be used to having or expecting a husband or wife to care for them.

Challenging the arbitrary social construction of gender roles may be more threatening to the sexual identities of older heterosexual people than older lesbian and gay adults. Having addressed the issues of gender roles and sexual orientation earlier in life, many older lesbian and gay people may feel more comfortable when it comes to engaging in non-traditional gender role definitions.

In our culture what it means to be an older person is also the result of a particular set of socially constructed beliefs and attitudes. Attitudes about aging and older people generally are negative, and views of older women are frequently more negative than those of older men (Bennett & Eckman, 1973; Francher, 1962; Green, 1981; Palmore, 1971; Sontag, 1975).

Ageism, which refers to this set of negative attitudes, describes the overt discrimination which occurs based simply on age (Schaie & Geiwitz, 1982). Ageism also generates "gerontophobia," the irrational fear of aging and the elderly (J. Turner, personal communication, May, 1985). Ageist assumptions include the beliefs that the elderly are all unproductive, senile, incompetent, overly dependent, asexual and unattractive. Given that these stereotypes and myths are the foundation for many people's attitudes regarding older people and the aging process, ageism and gerontophobia can be challenged and reconstructed in positive and affirmative ways in much the same way as homosexuality and gender.

Access to diverse models of what it means to be an older person is essential to this process of challenging stereotypes. These models include older people who are active, productive, sexual and self-determining individuals. A diversity of styles of adjusting to aging provides evidence that stereotypical images are arbitrarily constructed and have the potential for change.

Older gay and lesbian people who have had experience in reconstructing the arbitrary definitions of what homosexuality and gender mean are also more likely to be able to transfer these affirmative processes to their identities as older people.

Crisis competence, flexibility in gender role, and reconstructing the personal meanings of homosexuality and aging so they are positive have powerful effects on the individual psychology of older lesbian and gay people. At a cognitive level there is the adoption of a set of beliefs that affirm personal worth. At a behavioral level, adaptive skills which promote both daily living and a sense of competence and empowerment are developed. As previously suggested, these cognitive and behavioral dimensions impact positively on emotional factors such as self-acceptance and self-esteem. According to this theory of successful aging, these factors of individual psychology function to promote adjustment to the aging process in the ways described.

Those lesbian and gay people who are either passing or have internalized negative and stereotypic messages are less likely to have developed the type of crisis competence and gender role flexibility than "Affirmative Older Lesbian and Gay People" have developed. If crisis competence as an aspect of individual psychology is based on resolving potential losses and conflicts, it is not clear whether the "passing" and "stereotypic" groups have indeed come to this stage of resolution. Additionally, by definition, "passing" and "stereotypic" older lesbian and gay people have not reconstructed the negative social constructions of homosexuality. Therefore, they may be less likely to have challenged the arbitrary constructions of gender and old age as well.

Social and Interpersonal Dimensions

Reconstructing the meaning of homosexuality as positive involves social and interpersonal dimensions as well as individual psychological process. Family, friends, and community can all be sources of affirming homosexuality as positive in a way that facilitates successful aging.

Dawson (1982) reports that many adults grow old believing that their children or extended family will provide for them in their old age. With greater longevity and current changes in family patterns, this type of family support for the elderly is not insured. Dawson (1982) reports that "gay people have been less likely to assume that their families would provide for them in old age" (p. 6) and are more likely to have carefully planned for their own future security. Through considering real or imagined loss of family support earlier in life, older gay and lesbian people may be better prepared for the realities of old age.

Another potential resource in adjusting to old age is the re-definition of family which occurs for many lesbian and gay people. Francher and Henkin (1973) report in their study that for older gay men who lost family support, this support was replaced with a strong network of friendships. Bell and Weinberg (1978) describe these friendship circles as a "surrogate family." Almvig (1982) says, "'family' for the older lesbian can be made up of a current lover, past lovers and friends, besides her own blood-line family" (p. 148).

Likewise, rather than simply replacing lost family support with the support of friends, Friend (1980) reports that in his sample there was an overall gain of *reinforcing* family supports with those of friends. According to Friend, many gay men expected to lose the support of family when they came out, but this did not happen. He concludes that, "This in turn facilitates adjustment for older gay men and gives them a broad network on which to rely in times of instrumental or socio-emotional need" (Friend, 1980, p. 244).

The resources provided by all of these family arrangements can also be strengthened by the presence of an empowering community. In many places, the lesbian and gay communities offer many opportunities for cultural, social, political, and religious activity and support that are open to older people. In larger urban areas, there may even be intergenerational organizations like the New York based Senior Action in a Gay Environment (SAGE) which provides a variety of social and support services specifically for older lesbian and gay adults.

Intergenerational associations in groups such as SAGE are important in that "Affirmative Older Lesbian and Gay People" can serve as role models for younger gay and lesbian people. It has been argued that the negative and stereotypic images of older lesbian and gay adults have functioned as a form of social control to keep younger lesbian and gay people from "choosing" an openly lesbian or gay lifestyle or developing greater self-acceptance (Friend, 1980, 1984; Kimmel, 1978). Kimmel (1978) writes:

> Since development of a positive identity involves a sense of the future course of that identity, the lack of information about gay adult development has allowed the stigma of homosexuality to intertwine with the stereotypes about aging in our society. Thus, highly negative views of gay aging have been produced, leading to even greater difficulty in the development of a positive gay identity among young homosexuals. Fears about aging as a gay person have been used to dissuade young people from accepting their homosexuality, further hindering self-acceptance. (p. 114)

These intergenerational associations can be powerful sources of socio-emotional support and strength for both the younger and the older people involved. For the older people, they may also provide a sense of generativeness, or guiding the next generation (Erikson, 1963). For the younger people they can also provide a sense of hope for the future, a model for achieving one's goals and a clear sense of the possibilities associated with developing a positive lesbian or gay identity.

The "stereotypic" group, given their alienation from others, are least likely to develop any type of surrogate family system. Likewise, their low self-esteem may also preclude careful and thoughtful financial and emotional planning for their own future. Those who are "passing" and invested in being perceived as heterosexual will have fewer non-heterosexual family arrangements and non-heterosexual community involvements. Heterosexually married, the older lesbian or gay adult faces the same financial and emotional uncertainties as the older heterosexual person where support is not insured.

Legal and Political Advocacy

In the process of achieving an affirmative lesbian or gay identity, many older people have developed advocacy skills for managing heterosexism and ageism in a direct fashion. Others familiarize themselves with advocacy organizations which provide them additional resources for insuring their rights. For example, the difficulties of managing terminal or chronic illness may be magnified by the policies of intensive care units which exclude everyone except next of kin (Kimmel, 1978; Martin & Lyon, 1979). The attitudes of nursing staff and physicians may create an unaccepting atmosphere (Anderson, 1981; Lief, 1973) and the expression of affection between lovers and/or same-sex friends may be discouraged (Weinberg, 1982). An openly lesbian or gay relationship may be used by family members as evidence of senility in contesting a will. Being acknowledged as next of kin or as legal spouse can be complicated when writing wills, making funeral arrangements, or participating in other aspects of the mourning process. All of these issues require some knowledge of the legal and health care systems and can be managed by either addressing them in advance of a crisis or having another person act as a legal or social advocate. Older lesbian and gay people who have a comprehensive support system which includes family, friends and community are more likely to have the resources for managing these issues.

In addition to health care, areas where the elderly face discrimination include housing, employment, and traditional social service systems. As a result of crisis competency, supportive friends, family, and community, as well as positions of advocacy, "Affirmative Older Lesbian and Gay People" may have certain resources for ensuring their rights that many other older people have not developed.

Older lesbian and gay people described as "stereotypic" or "passing" are not only unlikely to seek out or participate in legal and political advocacy, they are unlikely to perceive the need for this type of action. Advocacy is based on the belief of supporting and insuring human rights. Self-hatred, low self-esteem, and the general "I'm not worth it" attitude of the "stereotypic" group is in conflict with the assumptions of advocacy. Persons in the "passing" group would actually distance themselves from any form of advocacy that might be lesbian or gay identified.

The model presented here suggests that developing an affirmative identity as a gay or lesbian person involves restructuring the meaning of homosexuality as something positive. As a result of this process, certain attitudes, skills and emotional resources are gained that function to promote successful aging according to this theory. These resources include: individual psychological processes, social and interpersonal dimensions, and legal and political advocacy.

This theory of successful aging has clear value for mental health practitioners, policy makers, as well as researchers. This theory's ability to predict successful aging provides specific areas for assessment in health care and program planning. By more clearly explaining and describing the diverse ways in which lesbian and gay people age, and the relationship between successful aging and identity formation, greater focus is provided for future research.

RECOMMENDATIONS AND CONCLUSIONS

Based on the proposed model and theory, several recommendations for future research emerge. The model of identity formation along two corresponding continua presented here contends that those who positively reconstruct the meaning of homosexuality develop resources which promote successful aging. The theory of successful aging described here delineates the specific areas in which these resources are developed.

Additional research is needed in order to verify and refine the theory presented here. Research that examines the degree to which the factors within each area outlined by the theory contribute individually and collectively to adjustment to the aging process is necessary. Experimental research of this type would not only help to validate the theory, but provide necessary information regarding a significant segment of the older adult population.

The model of identity formation contends that "stereotypic" and "passing" older lesbian and gay adults are least represented in the research literature and additional information regarding these groups is necessary. As such, research that examines special problems, needs and potential resources of these groups, as well as information regarding how to safely identify them within their current contexts is very important. Research that examines attitudes regarding aging among younger lesbian and gay people who have contact with older gay and lesbian people who may or may not serve as role models is necessary.

Cohort analyses that examine the management of heterosexism by older gay and lesbian adults versus younger gay and lesbian people are also needed. The age groups could be further broken down into the three groups described here which represent different places on the identity continuums. The type of research that examines differences between groups of older and younger lesbian and gay people as a result of aging or as a result of living in different socio-historical periods would not only provide valuable information about the lives of these women and men, but also about the transhistorical and context-specific qualities of heterosexism. Given the recent Supreme Court ruling (*Bowers v. Hardwick*, 1986) which upheld the State of Georgia's sodomy law, and the ever-growing fears about AIDS, understanding the extent to which these events are unique or transhistorical would be useful for developing strategies to challenge their potentially oppressive outcomes.

A history of managing heterosexism is a significant factor which has influenced the ways in which the identities of older lesbian and gay people have been constructed. Some of these people have internalized these negative ideologies; others have accommodated to them, while still others have shaped their lives around a reconstructed set of positive and affirmative beliefs. The power of older gay and lesbian adults to challenge the negative messages about homosexuality and to create new meanings of affirmation and happiness provides an important lesson. Not only are these older lesbian and gay adults potentially significant role models for younger lesbian and gay people, but they may also offer valuable insights for all people regarding what it means to grow old in ways which promote independence, self-determination, and a sense of engaging in life.

REFERENCES

Almvig, C. (1982). *The invisible minority: Aging and lesbianism.* New York: Utica College of Syracuse University.

Anderson, C.L. (1981). The effect of a workshop on attitudes of female nursing students toward male homosexuality. *Journal of Homosexuality, 7,* 57-70.

Bell, A.P. & Weinberg, M.S. (1978). *Homosexualities.* New York: Simon and Schuster.

Bennett, R. & Eckman, J. (1973). Attitudes toward aging: A critical review of recent literature and implications for future research. In C. Eisdorf and M.

Powell Lawton (Eds.), *The psychology of adult development and aging*. Washington, DC: American Psychological Association.

Berger, R.M. (1980). Psychological adaptation of the older homosexual male. *Journal of Homosexuality*, *5*, 161-175.

Berger, R.M. (1982a). The unseen minority: Older gays and lesbians. *Social Work*, *27*, 236-242.

Berger, R.M. (1982b). *Gay and gray*. Urbana: University of Illinois Press.

Bowers v. Hardwick, No. 85-140 S. Ct. (1986).

Cass, V.C. (1979). Homosexual Identity Formation: A theoretical model. *Journal of Homosexuality*, *4*, 219-235.

Cass, V.C. (1983/1984). Homosexual Identity: A concept in need of definition. *Journal of Homosexuality*, *9*, (2/3), 105-126.

Coleman, E. (1981/1982). Developmental stages of the coming out process. *Journal of Homosexuality*, *7*, (2/3), 31-43.

Dank, B.M. (1971). Coming out in the gay world. *Psychiatry*, *34*, 180-197.

Dawson, K. (1982, November). Serving the older gay community. *SEICUS Report*, 5-6.

Erikson, E. (1963). *Childhood and Society*. New York: W.W. Norton and Co.

Foucault, M. (1978). *The history of sexuality*, volume 1: *An introduction*. New York: Vintage Books.

Francher, S.J. (1962). American values and the disenfranchisement of the aged. *Eastern Anthropologist*, *22*, 29-36.

Francher, S.J. & Henkin, J. (1973). The menopausal queen. *American Journal of Orthopsychiatry*, *43*, 670-674.

Friend, R.A. (1980). GAYging: Adjustment and the older gay male. *Alternative Lifestyles*, *3*, 231-248.

Friend, R.A. (1984, June). *A theory of accelerated aging among lesbians and gay men*. Paper presented to the combined annual meeting of American Association of Sex Educators, Counselors and Therapists and The Society for the Scientific Study of Sex, Boston, MA.

Green, S.K. (1981). Attitudes and perceptions about the elderly: Current and future perspectives. *Aging and Human Development*, *13*, 95-115.

Harry, J. (1986). Sampling gay men. *The Journal of Sex Research*, *22* (1), 21-34.

Kelly, J. (1977). The aging male homosexual: Myth and reality. *The Gerontologist*, *17*, 328-332.

Kimmel, D.C. (1977). Psychotherapy and the older gay man. *Psychotherapy: Theory, Research and Practice*, *14*, 386-393.

Kimmel, D.C. (1978). Adult development and aging: A gay perspective. *Journal of Social Issues*, *34*, 113-130.

Lee, J.A. (1977). Going public: A study in the sociology of homosexual liberation. *Journal of Homosexuality*, *3*, 49-78.

Lief, H.I. (1973). Obstacles to the ideal and complete sex education of the medical student and physician. In J. Money & J. Zuben (Eds.), *Contemporary sexual behavior: Critical issues in the 1970's*. Baltimore: The Johns Hopkins University Press, 441-453.

Martin, D. (1982). Learning to hide: The socialization of the gay adolescent. *Adolescent Psychiatry, 10*, 52-65.

Martin, D. & Lyon, P. (1973). Lesbian mothers. *Ms., 2*, 78-82.

Martin, D. & Lyon, P. (1979). The older lesbian. In B. Berzon & R. Leighton (Eds.), *Positively gay*. Millbrae, CA: Celestial Arts.

Matteson, D.R. (1985). Bisexual men in marriage: Is a positive homosexual identity and stable marriage possible? *Journal of Homosexuality, 11* (1/2), 149-171.

Miller, B. (1979). Unpromised paternity: Life-styles of gay fathers. In M.P. Levine (Ed.), *Gay men: The sociology of male homosexuality*. New York: Harper and Row.

Minton, H.L & McDonald, G.J. (1983/1984). Homosexual identity formation as a developmental process. *Journal of Homosexuality, 9*, 91-104.

Palmore, E. (1971). Attitudes toward aging as shown by humor. *The Gerontologist, 11*, 181-187.

Raphael, S.M. & Robinson, M.K. (1980). The older lesbian. *Alternative Lifestyles, 3*, 207-229.

Schaie, K.W. & Geiwitz, J. (1982). *Adult development and aging*. Boston: Little, Brown & Company.

Sontag, S. (1975). The double standard of aging. In *No longer young: The older woman in America*. Proceedings of the 26th Annual Conference on Aging, The University of Michigan, Wayne State University, pp. 31-39.

Turner, J. (1985, May). Personal Communication.

Weeks, J. (1977). *Coming out: Homosexual politics in Britain, from the nineteenth century to the present*. London: Quartet.

Weeks, J. (1981). *Sex, Politics and Society*. London: Longman Group.

Weinberg, G. (1972). *Society and the healthy homosexual*. New York: St. Martin's.

Weinberg, J.S. (1982). *Sexuality: Human needs and nursing practice*. Philadelphia: W.B. Saunders Company.

Weinberg, M.S. (1970). The male homosexual: Age-related variations in social and psychological characteristics. *Social Problems, 17*, 527-537.

Weinberg, T.S. (1983). *Gay men, gay selves: The social construction of homosexual identities*. New York: Irvington.

Weinberg, T.S. (1984). Biology, ideology, and the reification of developmental stages in the study of homosexual identities. *Journal of Homosexuality, 10*, 77-85.

Wolf, T.J. (1985). Marriages of bisexual men. *Journal of Homosexuality, 11* (1/2), 135-148.

Vance, C.S. (1984). Pleasure and danger: Toward a politics of sexuality. In C.S. Vance (Ed.), *Pleasure and danger: Exploring female sexuality*. Boston: Routledge and Kegan Paul.

Natives and Settlers:
An Ethnographic Note on Early Interaction of Older Homosexual Men with Younger Gay Liberationists

John Grube, MA, AOCA

The Ontario College of Art

A flood of studies of "gay community" over the past decade has not only made this a "buzz topic" (Murray, 1984, p. 60) in social science, but has given the impression that a stable and elaborate gay community is a post-Stonewall (post-1969) phenomenon. Not so. Homosexuals prior to Stonewall were not merely atomistic individuals in search of others of their kind. They had a historical culture, whether "underworld" or not, with points of entry, established territories, initiation procedures, annual festivities, and "circles" with leaders ("queens") (Hooker, 1961; Leznoff & Westley, 1963; Simon & Gagnon, 1967). To make a distinction important to this paper, I refer to the pre-Stonewall gay world as the *traditional gay community*. The more institutionally complete post-Stonewall community with openly declared leaders (Lee, 1977, 1978; Murray, 1979) will be termed the *organized gay community*.

An important yet often neglected feature of the *traditional gay community* was its ideology about the patterns of adaptation in which members of the subculture might resolve the tensions between their stigmatized status and the world at large. These patterns varied from becoming a "flaming

John Grube teaches English and Creative Writing at the Ontario College of Art.

Correspondence may be addressed to the author at: Ontario College of Art, Department of Liberal Arts Studies, 100 McCaul St., Toronto, Ontario, Canada M5T 1W1.

The author would like to thank Dr. Stephen O. Murray and Professors Richard J. Hoffman, John Alan Lee and Victor Marshall for their helpful criticisms of earlier versions of this article.

119

queen" or "flaunting" homosexual (Crisp, 1969) to leading a double life in which one's public status was entirely heterosexual (married, with children), while one's private sexual outlet was known only to a very few.

One of the first sociological studies of the *traditional gay community* (Leznoff & Westley, 1963) simplified these patterns into *overt* and *covert* homosexual roles. Barry Dank (1971, 1972) published the first psychosociological studies of the processes by which a new recruit to the gay world made his choice between alternative patterns of "coming out" and marrying (or not). These decision-making processes may be usefully compared with those facing an immigrant to a "new world." Decisions must be made about how much of a former culture to retain, how much of the new setting to assimilate. But host environments rarely offer a single route to accommodation, and forerunners among the immigrant group often provide models for different kinds of accommodation (Gordon, 1961). A young person "coming out" as a homosexual likewise has to decide among models of adaptation to the heterosexual culture, and this process has been made more complex by the multiplication of such models since Stonewall.

There were few models of the "public and respectable" gay individual before 1969, for this role was largely restricted to the brave, famous and independently well-off (e.g., André Gide). Even less common was the model of "spokesperson" of an openly homosexual organization (e.g., Magnus Hirschfeld). For most homosexuals the choice was clear. If they wanted success and high status in the dominant culture defined as heterosexual reality (Adam, 1978), they had to hide their homosexual activity in a secret culture (Warren, 1977). In other words, they learned to accommodate to the prevailing heterosexual world. Let us think of them as similar to the indigenous people or "natives" before white settlers arrive.

By contrast the gay liberationists were like settlers who arrive, ignore the indigenous population, and set out to transform the landscape, in this case using as a model an existing pattern of heterosexual leftwing political activism. Many of the early gay activists adopted not only the leftist faith in the possibility of social change, but also much of their value system and lifestyle.

Adopters of each route have often left the others to go their own way, while occasionally applying epithets to the other choice ("closet queens" vs. "boat rockers" and "militants"). The alternative choice of patterns of accommodation has sometimes erupted into open conflict over the "politically correct strategy" to take in surviving as a homosexual.

The evidence is certainly not conclusive yet, but there does appear to be a greater likelihood of older homosexuals, whose earlier socialization was in the *traditional gay culture*, to be less ready to assimilate to the *organized gay community* and its ideology than young homosexuals born after 1960. Early in the conflict of natives versus settlers, some older gay men ventured from the native into the settler camp to become gay liberationists, but soon found the *organized gay community* offered no welcome for older homosexuals (e.g., Schaffer, 1973; cf. also Lee, 1987).

Certain observers suggest there is now a condition of "mutual avoidance" between older and younger homosexuals. For example, Berger (1982, p. 161) notes that "public gay institutions . . . are frequented mostly by younger gays" while "older gays rely on social networks (sometimes one or two friends), dinner parties, and other 'private' mechanisms." I shall argue that a more insightful understanding of the difficulties of gay aging in the immensely significant period of homosexual history following Stonewall can be furthered by an analysis of gay experience in terms of the different models of accommodation by "natives" and "settlers."

METHODOLOGY

During the period 1983-1987, 35 gay men were interviewed as part of a larger project, Project Foolscap, dedicated to recovering the oral history of earlier gay life in Toronto. The main concern of this project is to recover memories concerning the early development of the modern gay community, including the adaptation of members of the *traditional gay community* to the new gay liberation.

Respondents ranged in age from 40 to 92 and almost all had spent their adult lives in Toronto. An unstructured private interview of each man was conducted, lasting about four hours, covering a list of key topics which included initiation into the "gay community" as defined at that time; interaction with the police or with psychiatric therapy; interpersonal relationships; perceptions of gay social structure (ranging from "the only one in the world" experience to membership in extended circles); first contact with gay liberationist individuals and ideas; membership, if any, in post-Stonewall organizations; and personal experience of contact and conflict between the new gay "radicals" and the *traditional gay community*. All quotations in this paper, unless otherwise specified, are taken from transcripts of these interviews.

From these interviews emerged central themes that are the topic of this paper: (a) A distinction had to be made between the *traditional gay community* and the modern, *organized gay community*. (b) The *organized gay community* is largely modeled on heterosexual institutions with a gay "United Appeal," gay business council, gay counselling service, and so forth. (c) The basic structural unit of the *traditional gay community* appeared to be the mentor-protégé pair (Grube, 1986). (d) Older gay men socialized into the *traditional gay community* understand and perceive the nature of gay relationships and community quite differently from the new gay liberationists. The two conceptual models frequently come into conflict.

Rather than attempt a survey approach at this still early stage in the research of Project Foolscap, I have chosen three men to represent three distinctive patterns of adaptation among the 35 men interviewed. First, I briefly review the socialization of older gay men as "natives" into the *traditional gay community*. Then I briefly review the influence of nongay, leftist radicalism in the 1960s leading to a gay ideology of accommodation as "settlers" and its early conflict with the established accommodation pattern. Then I present the three men as examples of adaptation to the conflict between the adaptation patterns.

SOCIALIZATION
INTO THE TRADITIONAL GAY COMMUNITY

All dominated groups experience intense pressure to assimilate and the history of *traditional gay communities* is a history of accommodative survival (Adam, 1978; Bérubé, 1981; Boswell, 1980; Cory, 1951; and many others). Maurice Leznoff's pioneering study of Montreal's *traditional gay community* of the early 1950s (Leznoff & Westley, 1963) perceptively noted the strong pressures to assimilate to heterosexual society; that is, to "pass." Open homosexuals existed but these men either worked in occupations with "traditionally accepted homosexual linkages in the popular image" such as artists, interior decorators or hairdressers, or they worked in low-status occupations such as bellhops. Leznoff and Westley (1963) quote an upwardly mobile informant, Robert, who had just become the manager of an appliance store and who felt he had to cut himself off from his openly gay friends if he was to assimilate into the heterosexual and heterosexist corporate structure:

> My promotions have made me more conscious of the gang I hang around with. You see, for the first time in my life I have a job that I would really like to keep and where I can have a pretty secure future. I realize that if word were to get around that I am gay I would probably lose my job. I don't see why that should be, because I know that I'm the same person gay or not. But that's the way it

works. I don't want to hang around with Robert any more or any of the people who are like Robert. I don't mind seeing them once in a while at somebody's house, but I won't be seen with them on the street any more.

Robert was, in Leznoff's words, "an overt queen" and this was in the 1950s. If he really did assimilate to the role models the appliance company executives provided, he may well have risen to the top of the corporate structure, gaining in the process not only monetary rewards but the esteem of his straight colleagues.

The same pressure to assimilate was still reported to me by older gay people in Toronto in 1987. For example, Del, a man of 55 socialized into the *traditional gay community*,

> Quite a few of my very close gay friends are still very closeted, they hold excellent jobs that are very highly paid and they have parties, house parties . . . and some of them, like the ones who are the wealthiest, they hire models or call-girls, whatever you want, just to go along as escorts to company parties, as a camouflage.

It is startling to realize that for many Toronto homosexuals, especially older men such as Del's business friends, very little has changed since Leznoff and Westley's investigation 35 years ago. There are the discreet little house-parties, the ruses with employers, the continued attempts to 'pass' or accommodate to the existing (heterosexual) social landscape.

LIBERATION: SETTLERS TRANSFORMING THE LANDSCAPE

The American origins of a "liberated" gay community are now well-documented (e.g., Marotta, 1981; D'Emilio, 1983), as are its European ancestors (e.g., Lauritsen & Thorstad, 1974; Steakley, 1975; Adam, 1987). Work on the origins of Canadian gay liberation has also been published (Kinsman, 1987). Although there is good reason to believe in the "survival of domination" (Adam, 1978) of a heterosexist reality, to date little attention has been paid to the social pressures felt by liberation activists to accommodate to the heterosexual definition of reality. While proposing to transform the social landscape, many of the new "radicals" actually adopted existing (in this case, leftist political) heterosexual models of social change.

Many young gay activists were deeply imbued with the values of the

New Left. This is no longer a controversial point with most scholars, but if it is less than obvious, then compare, for example, the New Left essays in Long (1972), with the gay liberationist essays in McCaffrey (1972), and Humphreys (1972). Many of the early radical gay liberationists angrily rejected the covert life of the *traditional gay community* and tried to 'reform' it along heterosexual lines. There is irony here that the "liberators" of homosexuals also had their images shaped by a heterosexual politics.

It is often overlooked today that the beginning of organized gay liberation was signaled by a revolt of the natives of the *traditional gay community* — the so-called Stonewall riot. But with the progress of gay liberation, the "settlers" (or activists) steadily distanced themselves from the "natives." Marotta's careful micro-historical study of the warring gay liberation factions in New York City in the early 1970s shows a pattern that was replicated in Toronto and, no doubt, in many other locations.

Most vocal and visible is the radical faction. Marotta (1981, p. 147) describes the founders' of the New York Gay Liberation Front point of view: "The radicals who ran GLF, believing the Movement their community, worked to establish GLF as a homosexual division in the radical vanguard." The Movement was straight, active, macho. Therefore, any gay liberation movement that was basically one of its divisions would also have to be straight, active, macho — as far as gay men really can assimilate to this model.

Although Marotta does not say so, when there were chants at demonstrations, they were often modeled on football yells ("two, four, six, eight, gay is twice as good as straight"), football being one of the most macho sports in North America. It followed, of course, that these gay radicals would see the *traditional gay community* — so different from the *organized gay community* they wished to construct — in terms of disapproved stereotypes. As Marotta (1981) points out:

> When they discussed what it was like to be gay, radical male GLFers rapidly agreed that they found gay life unpleasant and unsatisfying. This led them to conclude that male homosexuals who wanted to be fulfilled sexually had to abandon traditional styles of promiscuity and to avoid subcultural institutions like bars, bathhouses, and pornographic bookstores. What they neglected to consider was that some homosexuals found participation in the gay male subculture genuinely fulfilling. Instead of arguing "each to his own," the radical males tended to generalize their personal prefer-

ences and to condemn traditional gay male patterns as "unlibera-
ted." (p. 105)

This led to one GLF manifesto assertion that "GLF must demand the
complete negation of the use of gay bars, tea rooms, trucks, baths, streets,
and other traditional cruising institutions" (Marotta, p. 121). In other
words, they proposed abolition of many of the long-established social
institutions of the *traditional gay community*, which was admittedly much
less "institutionally complete" (Lee, 1978; Murray, 1979) but had nevertheless survived since any one could remember. Rather like the first American pioneers who saw themselves as establishing a New World blithely
overlooking the existence of a long-established native community, the
new gay liberationists on occasion treated the "natives" as backward abo-
rigines or as passive lepers hiding in ghettos (Humphreys, 1972, p. 14;
Hunter, 1972).

By contrast, the group Marotta calls cultural reformists decided to celebrate the gay community they found and endow it with cultural institutions. The Gay Activists' Alliance did this as a conscious political act
(Marotta, 1981):

> GAA's Firehouse, as it continued to be known, rapidly became
> the base for gay cultural enterprises of unprecedented scope and va-
> riety. New committees explored gay themes in literature, theater,
> film, art, and music. . . . By institutionalizing the cultural reformist
> approach to gay liberation, GAA took a giant step in the direction of
> legitimizing homosexual interests and promoting the idea that enjoy-
> ing traditional gay pastimes was not only moral and salutary, but
> political. As more and more homosexuals, often without appreciat-
> ing the political outlook most responsible for legitimizing and en-
> couraging their activities, followed the lead of the first cultural
> reformers, there was a surfacing of the gay subculture and a prolifera-
> tion of identifiably gay bars, discos, restaurants, bathhouses, book-
> stores, sex shops, artistic enterprises, publishing ventures, hotels,
> community centers, and neighbourhoods. (p. 193)

Political analysts of the dynamics of leftist social change, especially
Marcuse (1976), have often warned of the power of the dominant culture,
especially of its economic and commercial institutions, to "co-opt" social
change through "repressive desublimation." In some respects, the new
organized gay communities are a clear example of the ironic extent to
which radical efforts to liberate homosexuals have led to the very "mim-

icry of straight society" that the radical liberationists condemned (e.g., Wittman, 1972, p. 161).

THREE EXAMPLES OF ACCOMMODATION

Many gay men in Toronto, especially those socialized before Stonewall have made very little accommodation to the *organized gay community*. They continue in their private circles. It is almost startling today, considering the widespread media and public awareness of gay life, to meet young men from small towns somewhat distant from Toronto who arrive in the city and have little or no knowledge of the *organized gay community* or of the *traditional gay community*, often spending many months before making their first contact. Neither the older gay man who has made no effort at accommodation nor the naive younger man of today are discussed here. Instead, the three men below are chosen to shed light on the experiences of those who made some accommodation to the dynamics created by the two patterns of accommodation.

KEN

Ken has been a dedicated Toronto radical leader since the early 1970s. Like many individuals born and educated in Toronto, he went to the U.S. for graduate study, to Cornell, in 1968. It was there he realized for sure that he was gay, and began going to Mory's in his off hours:

> It was a weird, weird bar because it was not only for people at the two universities and townies but it was also a gay bar, a black bar, and a drug-addict bar, I mean it was, like, everything that Republican Ithaca reviled, gathered in that bar, and so it was rather an interesting institution. At one point the owner tried to throw the gay people out, didn't want them there, and the bar was seized by gay people a few nights later.

Ken took part in that operation, and was deeply influenced by the Cornell atmosphere:

> You have to understand that the campus within weeks after I arrived there was in chaos, because the black students, armed, had taken over the student center . . . generally there was a loosening of all those props that sort of, you know, guide you in what you think of as acceptable behaviour . . . there were certain (gay) events that

were directly inspired by what had been going on in connection with the racial question.

At Cornell he came into marginal contact with some queen-and-entourage formations of the *traditional gay community* (Leznoff & Westley, 1963), formed an unfavorable impression of them, and so continued to be influenced socially and politically by the basically straight behaviour and values of those men leading the campaigns against the U.S. involvement in Vietnam and in favour of black liberation. Gay radicals such as Ken looked up to such men — the gravitational pull of assimilation operates almost imperceptibly.

Back in Toronto some years later, Ken and his radical friends took up the fitness craze and ran into a group of gay men already entrenched at the local YMCA. How did he and his radical gay friends relate to these men socialized in the pre-Stonewall era? Ken is remarkably candid: "We were like the settlers arriving among the Indians, you know, they just didn't exist for us, we were bringing social organization with us." This perspective is worth pondering, because it underlies much of the *organized gay community's* thinking. In this view the *traditional gay community* before Stonewall had no structure and does not merit serious study or respect — except for a few illustrious predecessors who were gay radicals before their time. Just as the white men arrived among 'primitive,' therefore expendable, Indians, so the young gay radicals of the early 1970s occupied gay spaces reported by early observers (e.g., Cory, 1951) without consulting the indigenous inhabitants. The old YMCA was classic gay space, but Ken reported:

> We only realized, gradually realized, that there already was an existing gay network, within the Y, there was this layer of older men in particular who you'd see were always looking at you with squinty eyes, and would never speak to you or anything, obviously because for one they were terrified and two they were afraid we were going to blow it for them all, and later on too I discovered that in fact there was this guy called Al, who was one of the instructors there who was in fact one of these queen-bees, and the center of a social circle and peoples' careers rose and fell on whether they got invited to his dinner parties or not, and he didn't like us very much, and of course his whole world had been swept aside, in a sense, or this other center suddenly appeared full-blown in his midst you know, and he had no purchase on it and of course we were totally unaware of any of this . . . that little group of men who looked at you through slitty eyes, very few of them ever came over into the group that I belonged to.

Some did. Yeah, there got to be a breaking down of the boundaries there but there was always this residue, this hard-core residue of what I take to be self-hating gay men who resented us for, like, disturbing their little grotto for one thing, and probably for not being available for another. And also for carrying on our little sexual thing right there, you know, right in the showers, and so on and so forth, whereas they were very furtive about it, we were scandalously, and from their point of view, dangerously, more open.

In the end the Toronto YMCA, like many others, started aggressively marketing family memberships to upwardly-mobile straights in its brand new building and is no longer primary gay space. Ken has a record of 15 years' work in Toronto as a full-time gay radical helping to construct the *organized gay community* he and his friends would like to see. Their vision is not one that includes the "natives," those gay men socialized before 1969. Here is a potential problem for gays who are aging and whose "whole world had been swept aside," as Ken put it. There is little space for the "natives" in the radical vision.

MICHAEL

Elements in Michael's life story shed light on the "born-again" gay radical without leadership aspirations. Michael was born, grew up, and was educated in English-speaking Montreal. He experienced the usual pressures to conform. The assimilationist pressures were so strong at McGill University that, although he couldn't make the football team, or even be an official cheerleader, he felt the need to associate himself with the football cult:

> I spent most of my . . . second year at McGill as a cheer-leader, for the football team, of all bizarre things . . . I wasn't an official one, you had to be a sort of fraternity boy to be in that . . . so I was, like, freelance cheerleader, which nobody asked for, and nobody particularly wanted, and so I went there, and I'd get myself drunk . . . and I'd go and make a fool of myself.

His unwillingness to accept a gay identity was so great that he voluntarily underwent aversion therapy: "It was like an act of faith in a way, a sort of desperate faith, I mean faith doesn't involve thinking through things, faith involves saying 'I give myself to this.'"

Shortly after breaking off his therapy in 1972 he went on a trip to

Europe and North Africa. In Athens he had the "conversion" experience
that was to lead him into radical gay liberation:

> One of the things that happened was in Athens, there happened to
> be the first of the student demonstrations against the colonels, and
> terrible police smashing of this and beating up of students and I saw
> all that, and it was the first time in my life, this is after lots of
> Vietnam demonstrations and so on here but I never, it was as if those
> things were outside my world. It was the first time, and suddenly,
> amazing, on that one day, it was as if a veil was removed from me,
> and suddenly I saw the world completely in the reverse from every-
> thing I had done before that, totally in political terms, without any
> theory, I had no Marxist theory, but everything I looked at from then
> on was to do with power and wealth and control, and powerlessness
> and revolution and struggle.

On his return to Toronto, where he had moved, he phoned the Community Homophile Association of Toronto hotline, and began to understand
about bathhouses, dances, sexual encounters. Shortly afterwards he discovered that Gay Alliance Toward Equality, a radical gay organization
was more to his liking:

> I was becoming involved in a quite militant way with gay libera-
> tion, so I was, I was very quickly becoming intolerant of people who
> were sort of downtown bar, very puritanical in a way . . . anyway
> my political coming-out far outpaced my sexual coming-out. Far. I
> was desperately fumbling around sexually, but meanwhile taking
> this extremely militant stance, and being right, like, at the edge of
> things . . . everything was for gay liberation, I mean it was total, for
> me it was like a full-time job.

Michael took up gay journalism, the first activity at which he was an
unqualified success. His monthly column was:

> . . . essentially whatever I was thinking about when I wrote it, what-
> ever I was doing and saying, and which is why I think I was so
> popular, it was like a very direct expression of gay liberation, no
> theory, just practice, and anger one month, funny another month,
> bitchy another month, whatever was going came out in the column,
> and at the same time for GATE we were producing materials and we
> were organizing educationals, as we called them which were meet-
> ings where there'd be speakers, and movies and so on.

This was unpaid, voluntary work, but for Michael and many others it helped organize their life and give it meaning.

Michael's contact with the "natives" of the *traditional gay community* was almost non-existent and he felt "extremely angry with people who wouldn't come out." He does recall vividly one contact with a "native":

> I'd been to a party and I remember this person, this well-dressed, well-coiffed, well-turned-out person, with a good job, lots of money and privilege and so on, the party was like that, it was a high-rise apartment block, people with lots of money and comfort, I got into an argument with this person about gay liberation, he being one of many people then who probably still I suppose would say 'oh you people rocking the boat, you, you're the ones who cause our problems, if you'd just keep quiet we'd be all right,' and I remember screaming at him, shouting at him that it was people like him, chains, something about chains, people like him they had their chains in their head, and I wrote this column then, immediately afterwards . . . saying how I wanted to drag these people by their Vidal Sassooned hair out of the closet, and kicking and screaming force them to, and I was damned if I was going to put myself on the front line for other people. It always did make me angry, that, I mean distributing literature in bars and having people refuse it.

Although Michael felt fulfilled in many ways by his discovery of gay liberation, he began to feel that the movement was narrowing the ground on which it stood to "the right of gay men to their bath-houses, when it should have been part of a vast, world-wide struggle of all progressive forces." As he now says:

> I realized only a couple of years ago that in fact my gay liberation had not been a sexual liberation, in fact it had been a justice struggle, because I never achieved sexual liberation for myself through it, and that's one of the reasons in fact that I eventually abandoned it, I was never a sexual liberationist, I was always a human rights fighter, that was very different.

He sadly realized in the end that he didn't have "what real revolutionaries have, which is a very long vision, you work and you work and you work," so he abandoned gay journalism and moved into a variety of other progressive causes.

KEN AND MICHAEL CONTRASTED

Ken absorbed directly the values and attitudes of the straight movement men who led the antiwar campaign at Cornell. He also has integrity and a fine mind which has given him self-assurance and staying power, something he has needed to remain a radical gay leader for 15 years. At 40 he is even beginning to mellow in his relations with members of the *traditional gay community*. Michael, by contrast, came into the *organized gay community* already constructed by Ken and his friends. For the first time he felt welcome in a group, for the first time his writing skills were properly utilized, gay liberation had started with a "conversion" experience ("it was as if a veil was removed from me") and his life now had meaning and direction. But he picked up negative attitudes toward the *traditional gay community*, the "natives," from his new mentors who themselves had absorbed these attitudes from straight movement men. The accommodation of Ken, an original "settler," was to the straight left. The accommodation of Michael was to the world these "settlers" had constructed. He lacked Ken's Marxist belief-system, and he lacked roots in the tribal rituals of the *traditional gay community*. So he had nothing to fall back on. As a result the effect of his secular "conversion" began to wear off and he ceased to be a gay activist at all.

GEORGE

The man Michael met and disliked (in the party anecdote above) is probably still giving downtown Toronto parties and telling all gay activists he meets — radical or reformist — not to rock the boat. If anyone is going to bring him over into the *organized gay community* it is probably the reformist George.

George was born into a working-class Toronto family 63 years ago, started work in a factory at 16, helped organize a radical union there, was fired for his union organizing at another job, came into contact with the arts through Communists (the Labor Arts Guild), and through them with the Toronto gay community of the mid-1940s. Although George had been cruising parks, cans, and moviehouses since early adolescence, and had been servicing his high-school jock peers sexually, it took Communist Party members interested in bringing along working-class youths to get him into the Toronto gay community and to arrange an acting scholarship at a prestigious institution.

As George says of this 1943-46 era: "I came to the conclusion that everybody in the arts was homosexual and leftist because that was the world I was presented with.'' He was never able to commit himself to any party, then or later, but this early experience with Marxist dialecticians made it possible to understand the mind-set of the gay radicals, the "settlers," such as Ken and his friends whom he encountered in the 1970s. George remembers fun, stimulating parties in the 1940s "in lofts at Bathurst and Queen and draughty dusty rehearsal studios," with actors, writers, puppeteers and visual artists; in fact, he experienced the *traditional gay community* in all its rich variety.

George was also close to the one Toronto figure who tried to promote a Canadian homophile movement as early as 1948 (Champagne, 1986). This man, Jim Egan, was a well-known and respected member of the *traditional gay community*, gave parties where homosexual rights ideas were canvassed, kept in touch with the homophile movement in other countries, and published on such subjects under his own name in the popular press. The closest he got to starting a homophile movement in Toronto was the founding of a small weekly discussion group at a gay club, whose activities were written up favorably in the mainstream press (Katz, 1964). It was in this context that George's reformist political ideas were formed.

In the fall of 1969 the first local above-ground gay organization was formed at the University of Toronto with George present. The political context had changed dramatically. Demonstrations and sit-ins were the order of the day, Marxist theory had become fashionable again for the first time since the 1940s. However, as George says, "soon we were having these splits . . . along the militant lines, political action, take to the streets, attack, versus the back-stage approach," the gay radicals versus the reformists who were mostly former homophiles. George therefore spearheaded the formation of a community group:

> In the Fall of '70-'71 it became apparent that we needed a community group, that many people in the community wouldn't come to the university, though it was an intellectual group, they were uncomfortable, and my thrust had been towards helping people to come to terms with their homosexuality, and the beginning of organization along the lines of social services work. Where can I get a doctor? Where can I get a lawyer?

The conflict between George and the radicals soon surfaced again, and it was partly a matter of age and socialization. George was what Ken thought of as a "native," having deep roots in the *traditional gay community*, an early inoculation against Marxism, and social service concerns for

his community. The radicals, or "settlers," came with straight left socialization. George describes the community organization he helped found as:

> . . . a discussion group, we were a help group, a self-help group.
> And leaning towards social services. I was very concerned about
> people being arrested and I set up the first organization going to
> courts, and monitoring courts, and since my bent was that way, and
> I was—the leader, quote—I felt there was room for the political
> arm, but it wasn't long before those that were into radical politics
> were fed up with this namby-pamby approach as they saw it of help-
> ing people, that we had to attack the institutions of our oppression,
> and we had to get out of the closets and into the streets, and we had
> to protest and storm the barricades, and build barricades of our own,
> with which we could defend ourselves.

The radicals soon left and started their own organizations. As George
recognized, specialist gay organizations arose to deal with the social service needs of the gay community. He himself made a good run for alder-
man in 1980, became an investor in the gay bath-bar scene, helped start
the local chapter of the Lambda Business Council, and in spite of strong
and sustained radical attempts to damage his credibility, he still remains
the unofficial mayor of gay Toronto as he enjoys his seventh decade.

CONCLUSION

It has become almost conventional wisdom among gay liberationists
(at least the many holding a social constructionist view) to question the
existence of a gay community before 1969. It has also become somewhat
commonplace to question, if not blame, the extent to which traditional
homosexuals hid themselves, accommodated to the prevailing heterosexist ideology through marriage and other forms of the double life, and
otherwise declined to challenge heterosexist domination.

But if traditional homosexuals are to be questioned for their accommodation to the heterosexual world they survived in, then it is equally just to
question the accommodation of gay liberationists. In many ways, modern
gay communities in large North American centers have become mirror
images of their heterosexual counterparts, with their entertainment institutions, financial institutions, business councils, United Appeal, and even
their own telephone directories.

In the traditional or "native" gay community, with basic structural
units such as the mentor/protégé couple (Grube, 1986), the queen-and-

entourage formation (Leznoff & Westley, 1963), and the party and dinner circles, communities were formed in which older men had privileges and duties. Older men introduced young men, for example, to their social circle, sometimes in exchange for sex, often for the glamorous social company of youth. As a man grew older in these "native" communities, he was able to command a modest respect as long as he (1) had some money and (2) reasonable health.

This is not true of the post-1969 *organized gay community*, which lacks an effective equivalent of the mentor/protégé tradition, so useful in training new leaders. It lacks attractive social institutions dedicated to the needs of homosexuals as they age; the difficulties of organizing sustainable institutions for older gays are well-known (Berger, 1982; Dawson, 1982; Lee, 1987). Older men socialized in the *traditional gay community* have reason to feel "aversion" (Berger, 1982: p. 167) to the new "liberated" community; they may well have reason to reject a liberationist movement which has, in two decades, ironically led to a gay version of heterosexual reality, and one in which they are not especially welcome.

No one in his right mind would want to go back to the oppression and underground communities of the pre-Stonewall era. We owe a great debt to the dynamic energy of the radicals and the institution-building of the reformists. But the time has come to take a second look at the *traditional gay community* into which men who are now middle-aged or elderly were first socialized. Their experience can offer much in the way of survival techniques, the training of new leaders, the transmission of culture, as well as provide an honorable and welcome place in the community for homosexuals as they grow old. After all, even attractive young radicals do age.

REFERENCES

Adam, B.D. (1978). *The survival of domination*. New York: Elsevier.
Adam, B.D. (1987). *The rise of a gay and lesbian movement*. Boston: Twayne.
Bérubé, A. (1981, Oct. 15). Marching to a different drummer. *Advocate*.
Berger, R. (1982). *Gay and gray*. Urbana, IL: University of Illinois Press.
Boswell, J. (1980). *Christianity, social tolerance and homosexuality*. Chicago: University of Chicago Press.
Champagne, R. (1986). Canada's pioneer gay activist: Jim Egan. *Rites*, 3 (7), 12-14.
Cory, D. W. (1951). *The homosexual in America*. New York: Greenberg.
Crisp, Q. (1968). *The naked civil servant*. London: Jonathan Cape.
Dank, B. Coming out in the gay world. *Psychiatry* (34): pp. 180-197.

Dank, B. (1972). Why homosexuals marry women. *Medical aspects of human sexuality* (6): pp. 12-23.

Dawson, K. (1982, November). Serving the gay community. *Sex Information and Education Council of the United States Report*, 11 (2).

D'Emilio, J. (1983). *Sexual politics, sexual communities*. Chicago: University of Chicago Press.

Gordon, M. (1961). Assimilation in America: Theory and reality. *Daedalus*, (90), pp. 363-365.

Goffman, E. (1963). *Stigma*. New York: Prentice Hall.

Grube, J. (1986). Queens and flaming virgins: Towards a sense of gay community. *Rites*, 2 (9), 14-17.

Hoffman, M. (1961). *The gay world*. New York: Basic Books.

Hooker, E. (1961). The homosexual community. *Proceedings of the 16th International Congress of Applied Psychology*.

Humphreys, L. (1972). *Out of the closets*. Englewood Cliffs: Prentice Hall.

Hunter, J. F. (1972). *The gay insiders*. New York: Stonehill.

Katz, S. (1964, Feb 22/March 7). The homosexual next door. *Maclean's*.

Kinsman, G. (1987). *The regulation of desire, sexuality in Canada*. Montreal: Black Rose Books.

Lauritsen, J. & Thorstad, D. (1974). *The early homosexual rights movement (1864-1935)*. New York: Times Change Press.

Lee, J. A. (1977). Going Public. *Journal of Homosexuality*, 3 (1), 49-78.

Lee, J. A. (1978). *Getting sex*. Toronto: General Publishing.

Lee, J. A. (1987). What can homosexual aging studies contribute to theories of aging? *Journal of Homosexuality*, 13 (4), 43-71.

Leznoff, M. & Westley, W. A. (1963). The homosexual community, in Hendrik Ruitenbeck (Ed.) *The problem of homosexuality in modern society*. New York: E. P. Dutton.

Long, P. (1972). *The new left*. Boston: Porter Sargent.

Marcuse, H. (1986). *Eros and civilization*. London: Panther Books.

Marotta, T. (1981). *The politics of homosexuality*. Boston: Houghton Mifflin.

McCaffrey, J. (1972). *The homosexual dialectic*. New York: Prentice Hall.

Murray, S. O. (1979). Institutional elaboration of a quasi-ethnic community. *International Review of Modern Sociology*, (9): pp. 165-178.

Murray, S. O. (1984). *Social theories, homosexual realities*. New York: Gay Academic Union of New York.

Schaffer, R. (1973). Will you still need me when I'm 64? *The gay liberation book*. San Francisco: Ramparts Press.

Simon, W. & Gagnon, J. (1967). Homosexuality, the formulation of a sociological perspective. *Journal of health and social behaviour*, (8): pp. 177-85.

Steakley, J. (1975). *The homosexual emancipation movement in Germany*. New York: Arno Press.

Warren, C. (1977). *Identity and community in the gay world*. New York: Wiley.

Weeks, J. (1977). *Coming out*. London: Quartet.

Wittman, C. (1972). *A gay manifesto*. In McCaffrey, 1972.

Loneliness and the Aging Homosexual: Is Pet Therapy an Answer?

Monika Kehoe, PhD

San Francisco State University

Loneliness is not only a matter of being alone. Solitude need not be equated with loneliness; the latter can be experienced in a crowd. Loneliness is, rather, a deep awareness of isolation from other caring persons. It is, of course, not exclusively a condition of the old; it can occur at any age and is more likely the result of loss — desolation — rather than isolation. The National Center for Health Statistics tells us that, of the 26.3 million Americans over the age of 65 who are not in hospitals or nursing homes, almost a third (8 million) live alone. According to the current estimate, 10% are homosexual.

Among these are some lesbian and gay elders[1] who are especially vulnerable to the loss of a partner.[2] Because of disapproval and distancing by their relatives, they are often left with no meaningful human contacts. Having been closeted as a couple, the surviving member may have no close heterosexual friends in the community and know few other homosexuals. S/he may be inhibited or hindered in seeking new relationships, not only by the general resistance of the aged to reaching out but also by lack of opportunity. The negative stereotypes of old age may cause other persons to turn away from any attempt the elder may make to draw closer. The deprivation of human companionship can be especially distressing at holiday time for those alone who are bombarded with TV programs that celebrate traditional family gatherings and stress the necessity of "togetherness" for good cheer.

Monika Kehoe is a teacher in the Gerontology Institute and a Research Associate in the Center for Research and Education in Sexuality, San Francisco State University. Dr. Kehoe has published 35 articles and six books, the most recent being *Lesbians Over 60 Speak for Themselves* (The Haworth Press, 1989).

137

THE MODERN NATURE OF LONELINESS

What, then, is the nature of this affliction and what are the kinds of human loneliness as identified in our time? What events have contributed to make it a serious subject of contemporary psycho-social research and of general professional concern?[3]

Beginning with the industrial revolution in the West, and the consequent urbanization and change in family structure, social patterns of estrangement and alienation have become a familiar element of modern life. An awareness of loneliness is now a basic component of human self-consciousness. We often feel alone inside our individual bubble of self.

Human consciousness exists reflexively, and the lonely, in order to fill the void of their desolation, traditionally created a caring God as the perfect companion. In the last half of the 20th century, space exploration and the vision of an infinite universe, along with a turning away from the traditional concept of deity as the omnipresent and caring "other," leave us apprehensive and intrinsically isolated on our blue-marble planet. The explosion of technology, with our lives directed by the computer and menaced by a Star Wars bureaucracy, brings us to the edge of recognition of our irredeemable insignificance and impotence. We are no longer the center of the universe or even of an extended, loving and supportive family.

Although physical aloneness may be a contributing factor, loneliness is more a state of mind, a genre of forlornness, a feeling of abandonment where one is separated from others by barriers or handicaps. It has been claimed that loneliness is a psychological drive, independent of physiological factors and even of environmental elements. Its contradictory is belonging. Loneliness is the reality, friendship its escape.[4]

Our present concern over "identity crises," as well as the popularity of cults and groups of born-again Christians, relates specifically to this urge to belong. We are born alone and die alone. Meanwhile, we must keep ourselves attached and occupied to escape the boredom which is often our perception of loneliness.

Obviously, old women, as the survivors in our culture, will experience loneliness more than men. In 1980, there were five times as many widows as widowers over 65.[5] Many of these have had family support systems[6] to rely on while lesbians in their 60s, 70s and beyond, who have not had children or whose children have repudiated them, are often without relief. Suddenly left alone, by the loss of a partner, they may find themselves in a state of life-threatening depression. In the report of my study of lesbians over 60, I have noted:

Although loneliness and isolation are prime causes of deep distress and frequently of suicide among the elderly, we can only speculate how many of the more than a million American women over sixty who identify as lesbians do kill themselves. Life-style is not indicated on death certificates and families, who tend to "take over" at these times, are reluctant to admit or recognize the relationship the deceased may have had with her "roommate."[7]

PET THERAPY – ONE POSSIBLE REMEDY

What then are the remedies for this sometimes fatal condition which respondents to the study indicated was their most serious problem, namely, loneliness? Manifestly, greater rapport with others, more friends, more social life, more joining groups, and, in serious cases, counseling and/or psychotherapy. But the desolate woman in her 70s may not have the energy to initiate efforts toward any of these. All sorts of barriers to such human contact may intervene to induce what might be described as a state of paralysis. In such a case, a loving, non-judgmental pet may supply the necessary "other-ego" needed for companionship.[8]

But, of course, some people are not animal lovers. Indeed, there are those who abhor pets. My own observation[9] of the strong reaction of some of the elderly in the nursing homes I visit for the SPCA has persuaded me that not all residents welcome the introduction of pets into their living environment. It may be of some cultural interest that there seems to be much less appreciation of the pet program among the minority elderly, particularly Asians. Nevertheless, the majority of the clients are enthusiastic supporters and, according to staff reports, look forward eagerly to the animal visits.

Friendship with a cat, dog, or bird requires little of the nurturing often demanded by human relationships. Animals offer unconditional love that promotes a person's emotional well-being. Students of the human-pet bond report: "providing elderly people in retirement homes with a pet has significantly eliminated frequent episodes of depression."[10]

Lest this suggestion seem to trivialize the condition of those elderly alone and depressed, let it be said that Pet-Assisted Therapy as a treatment for the depression brought on by loneliness is receiving more and more attention lately in the gerontological journals and in medical research. An article in the *Gerontologist* carries a list of 14 references to the subject dating from 1979. This current professional concern has trickled down even to the popular weeklies. The Science Section of the September 1, 1986, issue of *Newsweek* carries the title, "Freud Should Have Tried

Barking," and is subtitled, "Man's Best Friend Can Also Be His Best Therapist." This article reports on the previous week's Boston Conference at which 150 researchers informed the 850 attendees on the subject of "pets' ability to heal body and soul." The writers point out that "some 1,100 programs in hospitals use pets as therapists." Again, my own observation of the effects on many patients in nursing homes (70% of whom are female), when they are able to cuddle a small, furry animal, has convinced me of the mood-elevation that can result from even such limited contact.

Those trained to care for the elderly know that very old people, living alone or in nursing homes, are often starved for intimacy and touching. Some, barricaded in wheel chairs, cut off from human communication by deafness and/or impaired vision, exist in a state of situational and chronic isolation in which they are almost totally withdrawn from social contact. I have watched such a person revive and smile as she rubbed noses with a cooperative chinchilla.

Animals can have a surprisingly restorative effect on the depressed and lonely, many of whom have been hurt by words. As the authors of *Between Pets and People* tell us, "Animals do not use words, and patients can safely approach them when they cannot approach people."[12] The pace and mechanization of the modern city where many of the elderly reside in hotels and high-rise apartments, cut off from nature without even a tree in sight and with only a houseplant to talk to, may preclude the possibility of their having pets. But, for those who are allowed to share their home with a loving dog, cat, or other cuddly animal, such a companion can satisfy a deep emotional need and relieve much of the stress brought on by being trapped alone in a concrete, urban environment. A small animal is a living thing that can be held, stroked and hugged.[13]

For one of the most vulnerable segments of our society, aged homosexuals who are alone and lonely, a pet that demands care and attention and, in return gives affection and loyalty, may be the most effective tonic to ward off depression. Especially for those women (73%) in our study (mentioned previously) who had no children—the majority (52%) of whom never wanted any—pets are one practical solution for a solitary old age. Elderly lesbians who have been victims of homophobia much of their lives, having read and/or listened for years to the obloquy heaped upon their kind, can relate to pets especially well because of the animals' wordless and attentive capacity to make them feel safe, needed and worthy.

Considerable research has already been conducted on the therapeutic role of pets in connection with the geriatric population in general.[14] Animal Assisted Therapy in relation to the specific homosexual segment of the aging population still offers an open field, and a challenging one, for investigation.[15]

It is regrettable that the questionnaire in my study of lesbians over 60 neglected to ask about pet ownership or the role animals play in the individual respondent's total life satisfaction. Now that gerontological studies have established that loneliness is such a pervasive problem for the elderly, and pet therapy has been discovered to be such a boon to their spirits, researchers who study the social and psychological adjustment of homosexuals in their advanced years will undoubtedly investigate the significant place animals have in providing love and companionship.

NOTES

1. "Elders," "the aged," "old age," "old," "the aging," as used throughout this article, refer to those whose chronological age is over 60.
2. According to a recent San Francisco Shanti information service estimate, the AIDS epidemic has affected few (from 3 to 5%) gay males over 60. But no hard data is available on this age group. However, some have lost younger lovers to the disease.
3. The Nov/Dec 1986 issue of the American Society on Aging *Connection* focused on the topic, "Loneliness and the Older Adult."
4. See Mijuskovic, B., *Contingent Immaterialism*, Amsterdam: Gruner Publishing Co. (Chap. VIII, "Loneliness: An Interdisciplinary Approach"), p. 182.
5. Starr-Weiner Report, New York, McGraw Hill, 1981, p. 182.
6. According to Robert N. Butler, MD, in his *Why Survive: Being Old in America* (New York: Harper & Row, 1975), half of all Americans are widows by 65.
7. Kehoe, Monika, PhD, *Lesbians Over Sixty Speak for Themselves*, New York, The Haworth Press, 1989.
8. For further treatment of this idea, see Alan Beck, ScD, and Aaron Katcher, MD, *Between Pets and People: The Importance of Animal Companionship*, New York, G.P. Putnam's Sons, 1983.
9. The author is a volunteer in the Animal-Assisted Therapy Program sponsored by the San Francisco SPCA. In Feb. 1987, this agency began a new project to take animals to visit AIDS patients in their own homes.
10. Fox, Michael, "Interactions Between People and Their Pets" in Bruce Fogle, ed., *Interrelations Between People and Pets*, Springfield, IL, Charles Thomas Publisher, 1981, p. 30.
11. Goldmeier, John, "Pets and People: Another Research Note," *Gerontologist*, vol. 26, #2, Apr. 1986.
12. Beck, Alan, ScD, and Aaron Katcher, MD, op. cit., p. 159.
13. Ashley Montague in his important book, *Touching* (New York, Harper

and Row, 1971), had an appendix in which he deals with "Touch and Age." In this afterthought, he points out that the male in our society is programmed to be a non-tactile creature. As a result, in old age, his needs for touching as intimacy are increased because his main expression through sex is reduced (p. 321).

14. See, also, Odean Cusack and Elaine Smith, *Pets and the Elderly: The Therapeutic Bond*, New York, The Haworth Press, 1984.

15. Unfortunately, it is almost impossible to identify lesbians or gay men in nursing homes where they are so carefully closeted in fear of staff discrimination, loss of privilege or of government support. This is one of the strong arguments for the establishment of special retirement and nursing home facilities for homosexuals as there are for other minority groups such as Jews.

REFERENCES

Beck, A. & Katcher, A. (1983). *Between pets and people: The importance of animal companionship*. New York: G. P. Putnam.

Butler, R. N. (1975). *Why survive: Being old in America*. New York: Harper & Row.

Cusak, O. & Smith, E. (1984). *Pets and the elderly: The therapeutic bond*. New York: The Haworth Press.

Fox, M. (1981). Interactions between people and their pets. In B. Fogle (Ed.), *Interrelations between people and pets*. Springfield: Charles Thomas.

Goldmeier, J. (1986, April). Pets and People: Another research note. *Gerontologist 26* (2).

Kehoe, M. (1989). *Lesbians over sixty speak for themselves*. New York: The Haworth Press.

Mijuskovic, B. (1978). *Contingent immaterialism*. Amsterdam: Gruner Publishing.

Montague, A. (1971). *Touching*. New York: Harper & Row.

Starr-Weiner Report (1981). New York: McGraw Hill.

Can We Talk?
Can We *Really* Talk?
Communication as a Key Factor
in the Maturing Homosexual Couple

John Alan Lee, PhD

Scarborough College, University of Toronto

THE PROBLEMS AND POSSIBILITIES
FOR MATURING HOMOSEXUAL COUPLES

Despite revolutionary changes in sexual behavior, marriage and family life in recent decades, the living arrangement most widely desired among the old remains that of sharing one's space with a loving partner (Brecher, 1984; Stone & Fletcher, 1987). While divorce is now a familiar life passage, most people remarry, and though widowhood is now one of life's "expectable events" (Matthews, 1987), even aged widows and widowers often prefer recoupling to the completion of life alone.

True, there is a greater preference (and opportunity) among young adults today for the single life than in previous decades. For example, in Toronto one-fifth of all households are now single occupancy (Statistics Canada, 1981). Yet the marriage rate remains high, and there is no evidence that the majority of adults, when they age, prefer life alone to life with an intimate partner whose sharing, in Bacon's words, helps to double the joys and halve the sorrows.

Lesbians and gay men cannot help being affected by these prevailing heterosexual values. Though many elect to continue their satisfying single

John Alan Lee is Professor of Sociology, Scarborough College, University of Toronto.

The author is especially grateful to Dr. Brian Miller of Los Angeles, for his comments on use of the communication instrument reported here, with his psychotherapy clients.

143

life into old age, studies indicate that aged homosexuals are more likely to report a high level of satisfaction with life if they are happily coupled (Berger, 1982, p. 175; Lee, 1987, p. 146). Aging homosexuals have some positive (and increasingly celebrated) role models, such as Gertrude Stein and Alice B. Toklas, Christopher Isherwood and Don Bachardy. But they must also cope with heterosexist images which suggest that maturing homosexual partners are no happier than two scorpions trapped in a bottle. For example, Richard Burton and Rex Harrison in *The Staircase* portray an aging gay couple who can no longer survive without each other but have forgotten how to love each other.

The very notion that homosexuals can become a happy *couple* growing old together is new to our language: "The word *couple* usually refers to a male-female relationship" (McWhirter and Mattison, 1984, p. xiii). One widely recognized difficulty for the aging homosexual couple is the gay community's lack of support (Berger, 1982; Blumstein and Schwartz, 1983, p. 322; Lee, 1987b). Blumstein and Schwartz ask (1983, p. 323) "What would give institutional status to gay relationships?" Such status is possible, because their findings indicate that the similarities in structure of homosexual and heterosexual coupling are much more significant than the differences. They conclude that the gay community need not have the same rules of marriage as nongays, but there must be "some *predictable elements* so that couples could agree on their *obligations*" (p. 325, my emphasis).

Blumstein and Schwartz discuss legal status and ceremony for the gay couple, although they are not convinced that a solution lies in that direction. My own conviction is that an institutional status for couples in the gay community will draw its strength not from external, formal or legal status, but from internal dynamics. *Predictable elements* come from within the relationship, when there is *a clear and mutual understanding of obligations*.

EVERYONE AGREES ON THE IMPORTANCE OF "TALKING IT OUT"

A plethora of books and magazine articles indicates that today's older heterosexual couple does not expect marriage to remain happy into old age without active effort by each partner. For example, Book-of-the-Month Club Selections in 1987 devoted four pages to the topic; we are even offered the insights of former President Carter and his wife Rosalynn on ways to make "the remaining years" satisfying (Carter & Carter, 1987). The days when aging couples stayed together because there were no alternatives are gone forever. A common theme in all recent aging literature is the importance of *communication* to the enduring couple. Brecher, in a study of 1500 respondents born before 1928, when referring to such factors as health, income, education, and religion, concludes that "Of the 15 nonsexual factors reviewed, only one appears to be strongly associated with marital happiness: the quality of communications between spouses" (Brecher, 1984, p. 141).

In their landmark study of American couples, drawing on a huge sample (3,574 married couples, 642 cohabiting couples, 957 gay male couples and 772 lesbian couples) Blumstein and Schwartz (1983) repeatedly note the vital role of communication. Of an enduring gay couple they observe quite simply: "The secret of their success? Both agree that it is being able to talk things out" (p. 507).

TWO TECHNIQUES FOR REALLY TALKING IN MATURING HOMOSEXUAL COUPLES

The Blumstein and Schwartz Questionnaire

My lover and I had the good fortune to be recruited into the Blumstein and Schwartz study just months after we met 12 years ago. We each completed the detailed questionnaire separately, as instructed, but before we mailed them, we decided to make copies, and exchange them. The resulting discussions condensed years of "getting to know you" into months, and persuaded us of the vital role of *real talk* in building enduring gay intimacy.

Real talk is defined here as talk about the fundamental contractual relations between the partners: *The obligations which make a relationship's future more predictable* and thus give it the stability essential if gay couples are to survive into happy old age together. At one time it was common practice to openly negotiate the contract between bride and groom with the aid of a marriage broker (as illustrated in *Marriage a la mode*, a famous series of paintings by the 18th-century English artist, William Hogarth). But the notion of marrying for romantic love, rather than by social arrangement, suppressed consciousness of the contract (Lee, 1973, 1975). This social change affected gay couples as much as nongay (Lee, 1976). The key to the efficacy of the Blumstein and Schwartz questions in provoking *real talk* is that the respondents are *made aware* of the contract which is always implicit in pairing relationships (Bernard, 1972; Blau, 1964; Libby & Whitehurst, 1973; Van Deusen, 1974).

The items of a coupling contract range from the trifling (but still the stuff of argument) such as who will do the shopping and housecleaning, to the explosive, such as sexual fidelity when one's partner is out of town. Over the years, my lover and I found that repeated use of portions of the Blumstein and Schwartz questionnaire helped us unravel communication "knots" (Laing, 1970). We have shared our experience with gay groups, such as *Gays and Lesbians Aging* (GALA) of Toronto (Lee, 1989). Use of the Blumstein and Schwartz questionnaire to provoke *real talk* in gay couples having problems, has been successfully tested in professional psychotherapy (Miller, 1988).

McWhirter and Mattison (1984) have reported persuasive data on the "stages" through which gay male couples pass. More recently the same authors (Mattison and McWhirter, 1987) have argued the importance of resolving "stage discrepancies" through therapeutic communication. Clearly, the time is ripe to make known more widely the value of the Blumstein and Schwartz questionnaire in helping couples to communicate. However, users should be cautioned: *Real talk* can open a "can of worms" which requires professional help to resolve. Both my lover and I have benefitted from the guidance of professional psychotherapy when the knots proved too difficult or painful to unravel. Professional help is especially useful when (as is often the case) problems predate the couple's first encounter.

THE USE OF METAPERSPECTIVE

Our society does not encourage high levels of self-disclosure, even to intimate friends. We are reluctant to hand other people weapons and show them where to stab, by allowing them to know our sensitivities, deepfelt but hidden needs, and vulnerabilities. This is especially so for males. Yet psychologists have demonstrated the benefits of self-disclosure (e.g., Jourard, 1964, 1971). R. D. Laing (1970) has examined the knots people tie themselves into through failure to disclose the true self and communicate effectively with others, even in relationships of great intimacy. His *metaperspective method* (Laing et al., 1966) is a sadly underused tool — perhaps because metaperspectives are presented as a method of research, not as a therapy. Moreover, he provides a complex scoring system few ordinary mortals are likely to adopt, and the number of his questions (60) is excessive for most therapy.

A simplified version of Laing's metaperspective method is workable, requires no scoring, and moves the couple readily into communication. It can be used with the aid of a professional therapist or by the couple unassisted, after a little experience. A simple example would be an obvious discomfort between partners following some event:

> You've just returned home from a movie, or the evening's guests have just departed, or you've just had sex. You say something strongly positive or negative about the event. Your partner just grunts, indicating a lack of agreement, but also an unwillingness to talk about it. How can this knot be untied before it leads to conflict?

Bach and Wyden's (1971) rules are worth applying at this point — rules such as timing your communications fairly and productively. (Bach and Wyden is recommended reading for all lesbian and gay couples who hope to age happily together.) Applying one of their rules, you suggest to your partner the next morning, that perhaps s/he didn't share your feelings about the movie/guests/sex or whatever, last night. Can we make a date to *really talk* about it?

When that time comes, Laing's metaperspective method is brought into play. Each of you privately writes down a few statements about the event — for example, the visit by guests: What I liked about them. What I disliked about them. What I would do differently next time.

Laing calls these statements *perspectives*. They are direct, and from my own point of view. But my partner also has a point of view, and is busy writing it down. When we exchange, imagine my surprise to find that while I really enjoyed a guest's table talk, my partner really hated it, but was too polite to say so.

Exchanges of this kind can be useful, but Laing considers them merely exchanges of perspective, or points of view. But how good is your ability to put yourself in your partner's shoes, and see things from your partner's standpoint? Laing calls this *metaperspective*. Thus, before you exchange your comments, you answer a second set of questions:

> What do I think my partner liked about the visit? What do I think he disliked? What do I think my partner would do differently?

These questions measure your ability to get into your partner's head, and see events from an intimate's point of view. It's a sure sign of knotted communication when you think your partner liked something, and learn after the exchange, that this person you thought you knew so intimately, *disliked* most what you thought s/he liked most.

But Laing doesn't stop there. He takes the perspective one step further. Before exchanging, each partner answers a third set of questions:

What do I think my partner will think I liked best? Liked least?

Questions of this kind go beyond my ability to see things from my partner's point of view instead of my own by standing in my partner's shoes. These questions ask me to be really intimate: To get into my partner's head, behind those beautiful eyes, and see *me*. Laing argues that only if I can see myself *as my intimate other sees me*, can I grow maturely in effective relationship with that other. The argument is hardly novel and was made effectively by Martin Buber's *I and thou* (1958), but Laing's methodology allows practical application.

Laing's three levels of communication can produce enough material for an hour's discussion, even with the use of one or two questions at each level, on a single event or topic. There's really no need to multiply the questions, as Laing does, to the point of weary repetition. It's also unwise to deal with too many events or topics in one session of *real talk*. Obviously, the Blumstein and Schwartz questions can be combined with the Laing method, or each can be used separately.

That loving partner you coupled with a few years ago is not the same person now, and neither are you. It is healthy for a couple to stop from time to time for a review: Where have we come from, how are we doing now, where do we want to go from here? This review can perform the same supportive functions as scrap books, slide collections, photo albums, souveniers, etc., by developing ritual celebration of accomplished relationship. The review can serve as a kind of enriching 'anniversary.'

Real talk reviews can also help to identify repeated patterns of hidden problems—those pernicious "life scripts" (Berne, 1964) which are so taken for granted that they are difficult to locate and analyze, much less alter. Those scripts are the wallpaper you've stopped noticing on the walls of your relationship—walls which you eventually want to take down (Frost, 1964, p. 33).

USING THE BLUMSTEIN-SCHWARTZ QUESTIONS

Professors Blumstein and Schwartz have graciously given permission for the reproduction of their questions here. Much of their 38-page Couples Survey is irrelevant to marital self-therapy; it is concerned with the numerous demographic variables correlated in *The American Couple*. Below, I present and discuss the questions found most useful for real talk. **(Note: these items are copyright by Blumstein and Schwartz and may not be reproduced except for personal use with a partner.)**

Each partner first answers the questions independently of the other. Then the two sets should be combined in a folder and left around the house for a few days, so that each has time to read and compare both sets. Each partner may wish to make a few notes — an "agenda" for their session of *real talk*. Ample time, convenient to both partners, must be set aside for this session and it should proceed only if both are feeling ready at the time.

Being optimistic, aging gay/lesbian couples can expect to use *real talk* many times over the years, so photocopy the questions below and leave the original clean. You need at least two copies to start — one for each partner. There is no need to use all the questions at any session nor to stick to the existing questions. You may want to add a few of your own. My lover and I have, and these are indicated. Also, as you grow older together, and more able to communicate and predict the obligations of each, some items may no longer need discussion; but one should never assume that anything is settled forever in a relationship of people who continue to grow and change.

INSTRUCTIONS FOR RESPONDING

Each section of the survey contains a group of statements on the left. To the right of each statement is a scale from 1 to 9. Above the numbers are indicators of their meaning. For example, in section A, number 1 means that the statement is about something EXTREMELY IMPORTANT, while number 9 says the statement is NOT AT ALL IMPORTANT.

Answer each statement in terms of your own personal opinion and preferences. There are no "rights and wrongs" here, and you will only defeat the purpose of *real talk* if you try to answer the way you think your partner would *like* you to answer.

Circle the number indicating your position on the scale, for each statement. For example, in 1: Ideal Relationship, a circle around 1 beside statement d: "that we both have the same hobbies and interests" would mean that it is extremely important to your happiness in the relationship for you and your partner to be involved in the same hobbies and interests. A circle around 9 would mean this is not important at all; you're quite happy to let your partner pursue one hobby while you pursue something else quite different.

INSTRUCTIONS FOR ADDING METAPERSPECTIVE

The Blumstein and Schwartz questions can be combined with Laing's metaperspective technique, but it is best not to try this until you and your partner are experienced (perhaps three or four sessions of *real talk*). To use the Laing method, make FOUR copies of the questions, since each partner needs two copies. Label one copy "my view" and answer according to your own feelings. Label the second copy "my partner's view" and answer *according to the way you think your partner will be answering his or her first copy*. Your partner, of course, carries out the same two tasks.

Thus, the folder to be studied for the upcoming *real talk* session will contain four sets of responses: (a) Partner A's own view of the questions being discussed. (b) Partner B's own view of the questions being discussed. (c) Partner B's *predictions* of Partner A's own view. (d) Partner A's predictions of Partner B's own view. As noted above, this method allows you to see how well you can truly "understand" (stand in the place of, and see from the viewpoint of) your partner.

Since each question generates twice the data to talk about, fewer questions can be handled in a session of *real talk* when using the Laing method. For example, in Section 5 of the survey: *Satisfaction with the relationship*, you might circle number 1 for item e — how the house is kept — but on your second copy, predict that your partner will be very DISsatisfied, by circling number 9. After all, your partner seems to be constantly bitching about the dust or the dishes! In the talk session, you may be astonished to discover that your partner is *satisfied*, but thinks you are the unhappy one. Perhaps each of you has been bitching for years about something that doesn't really bother either of you that much! The bitching, then, may serve some other purpose quite unrelated to a tidy home. Now you may be on the track to uncovering something valuable, but long hidden not only from your partner, but from yourself.

CONCLUSION: SOME COMMENTS
ON POSSIBLE OUTCOMES OF REAL TALK

None of the following comments intend to suggest that you can be your own therapist, much less your lover's. If *real talk* reveals problems too difficult to unravel, consult a professional therapist.

1. Ideal Relationship

Our culture bombards us with contrasting examples of the ideal in beauty, character and even basic values (Rokeach, 1968). It is unlikely that you and your partner have chosen identical ideals. When answers are compared with those of the partner, each may wish to seriously reconsider some ideals. Research indicates that enduring couples move toward greater agreement on basic values.

There's not much either partner can do about the social background they came from (item 1) but a lot can be done to change one's social culture now. Some ideals adopted years ago (for example, as a son or daughter, or a newly hired employee, attempting to "pass" as straight) may now merit serious reconsideration if they are becoming stumbling blocks to a more mature partnership as you and your lover age.

2. Qualities of the Ideal Partner

Men and women can change their bodies a certain amount to please a partner—shaving hair or growing it, for example, or gaining or losing weight. Partners can also change their personalities to some extent. However, lovers should be cautious in trying to remake a partner, for often we are originally attracted because the partner is unlike us in important ways—and complements us, rather than duplicating.

3. Opinions

As with ideals, enduring intimacy tends to be correlated with increasing agreement in opinions, but the life of an aging couple may be enriched by disagreement on certain topics, which remain the subject of interesting (but non-confrontational) arguments for many years. The goal of *real talk* is not to eliminate these sources of entertainment in old age, but to deal with basic conflicts that keep resurfacing again and again over the years. For example, it may be difficult for someone who finally decides to "go public" to avoid dragging their partner out of a comfortable closet (item j). This is one of the classic problems in building gay community institutions to serve aging homosexuals (Lee, 1988).

4. Lifestyle

We know that opinions vary, but it's surprising how each partner's perception of "facts" may vary too. For example, each may be quite convinced of the "fact" that he or she does most of the shopping or is putting more time or money into the relationship. Unlike differences of opinion and ideals, it is possible to resolve many differences of fact by the simple expedient of counting. If there are problems because each partner thinks the other is not doing enough work, it may be useful to assign "points" to each household task (based, for example, on the time required, or time plus difficulty or inconvenience). There's no reason to consider such solutions silly or childish—most major corporations do it, under fancy titles like "time and motion study" and "job evaluation."

5. Satisfaction with the Relationship

I have adapted the Blumstein and Schwartz questions so that those which are most applicable early in a relationship—even the first few months—are in the first sections here. As the years pass, many of these questions are settled, or compromises reached. Older couples have often learned to live quite happily with partners who, ironically enough, are not the "ideal type" (for example, not the type the partner prefers when looking around the bar, or at porn videos).

With section 5, the questions get closer to the core of a relationship that will endure through midlife and into old age. This requires that satisfaction should *increase* with time for *both* partners. Nongay couples can rely on a lot of social support systems to keep them together, but homosexual partners must often fend off social pressures that would split them apart.

If partners store their response sheets after each *real talk* session, and compare them *following* the next session, special attention can be paid to topics where satisfaction has declined. This is especially valuable if there is a long time gap between sessions. Declines in satisfaction, or widening gaps in responses to questions, indicate areas where the relationship is not wearing well with age. As item m. indicates, this is a section where metaperspective is especially useful.

6. Taking Initiatives in the Relationship

With these questions you can readily move more deeply into the effort to achieve metaperspective. As couples age together, early preferences tend to set into *boring habits*. Sometimes one partner silently resents having to "take all the initiatives" (for example, to start sex, or plan a holiday), yet the other partner is feeling exactly the same thing. Alternatively, your partner may wish s/he was allowed once in a while to take the initiative, if only you wouldn't jump in first all the time! One partner may have to learn to hold back a little because the other takes more time to act, not because of less love or commitment, but because of a more cautious or serious nature. This section can produce explosive revelations of feelings long kept hidden for fear of the partner's reaction, so gentleness is called for.

7. Power in the Relationship

The advice to be gentle is even more relevant here. Power is something most of us are deliberately encouraged to leave to others — to our parents, as children; then to teachers, to our employers, to the bureaucrats and the military-industrial complex. There's a stronger taboo on openly discussing power relationships than even that about talking sex — yet we are less aware of the taboo (Lee, 1979).

Few couples, gay or nongay, have carefully analyzed and understood the power dynamics of their relationship. Bach and Wyden's (1971) rules of fair fighting between "intimate enemies" are especially useful here. Fortunately, aging does seem to lead to a more philosophical approach in many couples. Eventually both decide that the things they fought each other to control, were vainglorious anyway. The Quaker saying seems to grow truer in the aging couple: "It is better to lose an argument than a friend."

8. Sharing the Relationship

People very often stick with their partners "for better or worse" because worse would be *much worse* if you were alone. As a middle-aging homosexual, I gain great hope from watching an aged gay couple solicitously attend to each other's needs. It is more moving than the same behavior in a nongay married couple because I know that today's aged gays and lesbians are survivors of yesterday's struggle with heterosexist hatred. Somehow they have found a way through to deep trust, commitment, and sharing.

This doesn't necessarily mean that all is peace and quiet, with every major difference settled. Mutually happy aging lesbian and gay couples are not necessarily those who eventually answer all these *real talk* questions in perfect agreement or complement with their partners. Blumstein and Schwartz (1983, p. 448) describe a middle-aged lesbian couple who appear to have reached an optimum of "communication, honesty and emotional warmth." But they also describe another couple (1983, p. 455) who have been together for 16 years in a "high conflict relationship that has survived despite emotional tumult." Indeed, the authors conclude that this couple live and love together because they enjoy arguing with each other.

The point is, both couples share the same secret of homosexual love enduring into old age: *They really talk to each other*.

REFERENCES

Adelman, M. (1986). *Long time passing*. Boston: Alyson.
Bach, G. R. & Wyden, P. (1971). *The intimate enemy*. New York: Avon.
Bernard, J. (1972). *The future of marriage*. Cleveland: World Publishing.
Berne, E. (1964). *Games people play*. New York: Grove Press.
Blau, P.M. (1971). *Exchange and power in social life*. New York: Wiley.
Blumstein, P. & Schwartz, P. (1983). *American couples*. New York: William Morrow.
Brecher, E. M. (1984). *Love, sex and aging*. Boston: Little Brown.
Butler, R. N. (1977). Successful aging and the role of life review, in S.H. Zarit, (Ed.), *Readings in aging and death*. New York: Harper and Row.
Buber, M. (1958). *I and thou*. New York: Scribners.
Carter, J. and Carter, R. (1987). *Everything to gain: Making the most of the rest of your life*. New York: Morrow.
Frost, R. (1964). *The poetry of Robert Frost*. New York: Holt Rinehart.
Jourard, S. (1964). *The transparent self*. New York: Van Norstrand.
Jourard, S. (1971). *Self disclosure*. New York: Wiley.
Laing, R. D., Phillipson, H. & Lee, A.R. (1966). *Interpersonal perception*. New York: Harper and Row.
Laing, R. D. (1970). *Knots*. New York: Random House.
Lee, J.A. (1973). *Colours of love*. Toronto: New Press.
Lee, J.A. (1975). The romantic heresy. *Canadian Review of Sociology and Anthropology*, 12, (4, part 2), 514-28.
Lee, J. A. (1976). Forbidden colors of love: Patterns of gay love and gay liberation. *Journal of Homosexuality*, *1* (4), 401-17.
Lee, J.A. (1979). The social organization of sexual risk, *Alternative lifestyles*, 2 (1), 69-100.
Lee, J.A. (1987). The invisible lives of Canada's gray gays, pp 138-155 in V. Marshall, (Ed.), *Aging in Canada*. Toronto: Fitzhenry and Whitside.
Lee, J.A. (1987b). What can homosexual aging studies contribute to theories of aging? *Journal of Homosexuality*, *13* (4), 43-71.
Lee, J.A. (1989). Invisible men: Canada's aging homosexuals. Can they be assimilated into Canada's "Liberated" Gay Communities? *Canadian Journal on Aging*, *8* (1), 79-97.
Libby, R. and R. Whitehurst (1973). *Renovating marriage*. Danville: Consensus Press.
Matthews, A. M. (1987). Widowhood as an expectable life event, in V. Marshall, (Ed.), *Aging in Canada*. Toronto: Fitzhenry and Whiteside.
Mattison, A., and McWhirter, D. (1987). Stage discrepancy in male couples. *Journal of Homosexuality*, *14* (1/2), 89-100.

McWhirter, D. P., & Mattison, A. M. (1984). *The male couple*. Toronto: Prentice-Hall.

Miller, B. (1988). (Psychotherapist, Los Angeles). Private communication with the author.

O'Neill, G. and O'Neill, N. (1974). *Open Marriage*. New York: Avon.

Rokeach, M. (1968). Beliefs, attitudes and values. San Francisco: Jossey Bass.

Stone, L.O. and Fletcher, S. (1987). The hypothesis of age patterns in living arrangements, in V. Marshall, (Ed.), *Aging in Canada*. Toronto: Fitzhenry and Whiteside.

Vacha, K. (1986). *Quiet fire, memoirs of older gay men*. Trumansburg, N.Y.: Crossing Press.

Van Deusen, E. (1974). *Contract cohabitation*. New York: Grove Press.

The Blumstein and Schwartz Survey Adapted

The order of questions and sometimes the title of sections are the present author's, not Blumstein and Schwartz's. Where I have added a question useful in my 12-year relationship, it is indicated with an *. Remember, you are free to add or drop questions.

1. Ideal relationship

In an *ideal* relationship how important to you would each of the following be? Describe the kind of relationship you would like to have, whether this describes your current relationship or not.

		Extremely Important								*Not at all Important*
a.	That we can confide all of our personal feelings to each other	1	2	3	4	5	6	7	8	9
b.	That our relationship is permanent	1	2	3	4	5	6	7	8	9
c.	That my partner is well liked by my friends	1	2	3	4	5	6	7	8	9
d.	That we both have the same hobbies and interests	1	2	3	4	5	6	7	8	9
e.	That we both have the same feelings about women's issues	1	2	3	4	5	6	7	8	9
f.	That our relationship does not interfere with other important parts of my life	1	2	3	4	5	6	7	8	9
g.	That I have someone to grow old with	1	2	3	4	5	6	7	8	9
h.	That my partner is sexually faithful to me	1	2	3	4	5	6	7	8	9
i.	That I am sexually faithful to my partner	1	2	3	4	5	6	7	8	9
j.	That my partner provides me with financial security	1	2	3	4	5	6	7	8	9

k. That I find my partner sexually
    compatible 1 2 3 4 5 6 7 8 9

l. That we both have the same so-
    cial class background 1 2 3 4 5 6 7 8 9

m. That I am well liked by my
    partner's friends 1 2 3 4 5 6 7 8 9

n. That we both have the same
    feelings about gay liberation
    (e.g., marching on Gay Pride
    Day) 1 2 3 4 5 6 7 8 9

o. That my partner can pass as
    straight when we are among
    straight people 1 2 3 4 5 6 7 8 9

2. Qualities of an ideal partner

How much of each quality would you want in an *ideal* partner? Describe
the partner you would like to have, whether this describes your present
partner or not.

		Extremely								*Not at all*
a.	Forceful	1	2	3	4	5	6	7	8	9
b.	Sexy-looking	1	2	3	4	5	6	7	8	9
c.	Affectionate	1	2	3	4	5	6	7	8	9
d.	Aggressive	1	2	3	4	5	6	7	8	9
e.	Romantic	1	2	3	4	5	6	7	8	9
f.	"Movie star" good-looking	1	2	3	4	5	6	7	8	9
g.	Understanding of others	1	2	3	4	5	6	7	8	9
h.	Ambitious	1	2	3	4	5	6	7	8	9
i.	Compassionate	1	2	3	4	5	6	7	8	9
j.	Muscular build	1	2	3	4	5	6	7	8	9
k.	Accomplished in her/his cho-sen field	1	2	3	4	5	6	7	8	9

Extremely   *Not at all*

l. Expresses tender feelings eas-
    ily...................... 1 2 3 4 5 6 7 8 9

m. Shy....................... 1 2 3 4 5 6 7 8 9

n. Athletic 1 2 3 4 5 6 7 8 9

o. Outgoing 1 2 3 4 5 6 7 8 9

p. Self-sufficient 1 2 3 4 5 6 7 8 9

3. Opinions

The following are general statements about lesbian or gay couples who live together, but not necessarily about your relationship. How much do you agree or disagree with each statement?

Strongly Agree   *Strongly Disagree*

a. If both partners work full-time,
    both of their career plans
    should be considered equally in
    determining where they will
    live 1 2 3 4 5 6 7 8 9

b. The two partners should share
    the responsibility for earning a
    living for the household 1 2 3 4 5 6 7 8 9

c. The two partners should pool
    all their property and financial
    assets 1 2 3 4 5 6 7 8 9

d. A member of a couple together
    a long time should not accept a
    job s/he wants in a distant city,
    if it means ending the relation-
    ship..................... 1 2 3 4 5 6 7 8 9

e. Couples should try to make
    their relationship last a lifetime 1 2 3 4 5 6 7 8 9

f. There are times when I am with
    my friends and I do not want
    my partner along 1   2   3   4   5   6   7   8   9

g. It is important to me that my
    partner spend some time wit-
    hout me 1   2   3   4   5   6   7   8   9

h. Partners who really love each
    other don't want to have sex
    with anyone but the partner... 1   2   3   4   5   6   7   8   9

i. In these days of AIDS, part-
    ners should not have even
    "safe sex" with anyone else.. 1   2   3   4   5   6   7   8   9

j. Partners should agree, before
    either tells anyone, other than
    friends, that we're homosexual 1   2   3   4   5   6   7   8   9

4. Lifestyle

Certain household tasks are necessary to keep things running smoothly.
Rate each of the following tasks according to who does most of the work,
in your opinion. Then answer the general question at the end of the list.

		I do this all of the time				*We do this equally*				*He does this all of the time*	*Neither of us does this*
a.	Repairing things around the house	1	2	3	4	5	6	7	8	9	X
b.	Doing the dishes	1	2	3	4	5	6	7	8	9	X
c.	Cooking breakfast	1	2	3	4	5	6	7	8	9	X
d.	Cooking the evening meal....	1	2	3	4	5	6	7	8	9	X
e.	Vacuuming the carpets	1	2	3	4	5	6	7	8	9	X
f.	Doing the laundry	1	2	3	4	5	6	7	8	9	X
g.	Making arrangements to have repairs done around the house.	1	2	3	4	5	6	7	8	9	X

	I do this all of the time				We do this equally				He does this all of the time	Neither of us does this
h. Making complaints to the land-lord/lady..................	1	2	3	4	5	6	7	8	9	X
i. Cleaning the bathroom	1	2	3	4	5	6	7	8	9	X
j. Caring for pets.............	1	2	3	4	5	6	7	8	9	X
k. Taking out the trash.........	1	2	3	4	5	6	7	8	9	X
l. Doing the grocery shopping ..	1	2	3	4	5	6	7	8	9	X
m. Taking care of the lawn......	1	2	3	4	5	6	7	8	9	X
n. Ironing my clothes..........	1	2	3	4	5	6	7	8	9	X
o. Mixing drinks for company...	1	2	3	4	5	6	7	8	9	X
p. Driving the car when we are going somewhere in town to-gether....................	1	2	3	4	5	6	7	8	9	X

	Much more than fair share				Exactly a fair share				Much less than a fair share
q. Considering the chores done in your household, do you feel your partner is doing his/her "fair share"?..............	1	2	3	4	5	6	7	8	9

5. Satisfaction with the present relationship

Part 1: How satisfied are you with each of the following parts of your relationship?

	Extremely Satisfied								Not at all Satisfied	Does not Apply to our Situation
a. Our moral and religious beliefs and practices	1	2	3	4	5	6	7	8	9	
b. How my partner's job affects our relationship	1	2	3	4	5	6	7	8	9	X

c. How we communicate....... 1 2 3 4 5 6 7 8 9
d. How my job affects our relationship .... 1 2 3 4 5 6 7 8 9 X
e. How the house is kept....... 1 2 3 4 5 6 7 8 9
f. The amount of influence I have over the decisions we make .. 1 2 3 4 5 6 7 8 9
g. Our social life 1 2 3 4 5 6 7 8 9
h. The amount of money coming in 1 2 3 4 5 6 7 8 9
i. How we express affection for each other................. 1 2 3 4 5 6 7 8 9
j. How we manage our finances. 1 2 3 4 5 6 7 8 9
k. Our sex-life 1 2 3 4 5 6 7 8 9
l. How satisfied are you with your relationship in general?.. 1 2 3 4 5 6 7 8 9
m. How would your partner rate her/his satisfaction with your relationship in general? 1 2 3 4 5 6 7 8 9

Part 2: How bothered would you be if your partner behaved in each of the following ways?

Extremely Bothered ... *Not at all Bothered*

a. Cried when emotionally upset. 1 2 3 4 5 6 7 8 9
b. Initiated sex 1 2 3 4 5 6 7 8 9
c. Avoided making decisions ... 1 2 3 4 5 6 7 8 9
d. Waited for me to initiate sex.. 1 2 3 4 5 6 7 8 9
e. Had a very close (non-sexual) friendship with a man 1 2 3 4 5 6 7 8 9
f. Had a very close (non-sexual) friendship with a woman..... 1 2 3 4 5 6 7 8 9

g. Was more sexually attractive to
    other people than I am....... **1** 2 3 4 5 6 7 8 **9**

Extremely Bothered ... *Not at all Bothered*

h. Earned much more money than
    I did 1 2 3 4 5 6 7 8 9

i. Had sex with someone else... 1 2 3 4 5 6 7 8 9

j. Had a meaningful affair with
    someone else 1 2 3 4 5 6 7 8 9

Part 3: Rate your satisfaction with the relationship today, with each of the times listed in the past , if applicable.

Much better ... *The same* ... *Much worse*

a. Our relationship today, com-
    pared with three months ago.. 1 2 3 4 5 6 7 8 9

b. Our relationship today, com-
    pared with one year ago 1 2 3 4 5 6 7 8 9

c. Our relationship today, com-
    pared with three years ago ... 1 2 3 4 5 6 7 8 9

Part 4: Spending time together.

a. On the average, how many
    evenings a week do both you
    and your partner spend at
    home?.................... 1   2   3   4   5   6   7

b. During a typical week, how
    many days do you and your
    partner have dinner together? . 1   2   3   4   5   6   7

Much more ... *Neither more nor less* ... *Much less*

c. Would you prefer to spend
    more or less time with your
    partner? 1   2   3   4   5   6   7   8   9

Part 5: Thinking about the alternatives to this relationship.

a. How often during the past year have you seriously considered ending this relationship? . . . . .

        Never   Once   Two or three times   More than 3 times

b. How often do you think your partner has seriously considered breaking up, in the past year? . . . .

        Never   Once   Two or three times   More than 3 times

c. If you did decide to end the relationship, which partner's life would be more disrupted? . . . .

    Mine much more   *Both equally*   *Her/His much more*

    1   2   3   4   5   6   7   8   9

Part 6: Possible futures

1. How likely is it that you and your partner will still be together ...(CIRCLE ONE ANSWER ON EACH LINE.)

    Extremely Likely   *Extremely Unlikely*

a. Six months from now? 1   2   3   4   5   6   7   8   9

b. One year from now? 1   2   3   4   5   6   7   8   9

c. Five years from now? 1   2   3   4   5   6   7   8   9

d. Twenty years from now? 1   2   3   4   5   6   7   8   9

2. If something were to happen to your partner and you were forced to live without him/her, how difficult would it be for you to do each of the following?

    Extremely Difficult   *Not at all Difficult*

a. Do household tasks (such as cleaning, laundry, and managing the household) 1   2   3   4   5   6   7   8   9

		Extremely Difficult							Not at all Difficult
b.	Find another partner	1	2	3	4	5	6	7	8	9
c.	Cook appetizing meals	1	2	3	4	5	6	7	8	9
d.	Maintain my present standard of living	1	2	3	4	5	6	7	8	9
e.	Make household repairs (such as plumbing or electrical repairs)	1	2	3	4	5	6	7	8	9
f.	Find or continue employment .	1	2	3	4	5	6	7	8	9
g.	Avoid loneliness	1	2	3	4	5	6	7	8	9

6. Taking initiatives in the relationship

Rate each of the following according to how often *your partner* does it.

		Always							Never
a.	Makes sure our household runs smoothly	1	2	3	4	5	6	7	8	9
b.	Confides his/her innermost thoughts and feelings to me ..	1	2	3	4	5	6	7	8	9
c.	Tries to bring me out of it when I am restless, bored, or depressed	1	2	3	4	5	6	7	8	9
d.	Sees himself/herself as the decision-maker in our relationship......................	1	2	3	4	5	6	7	8	9
e.	Knows what I am feeling even when I do not say anything...	1	2	3	4	5	6	7	8	9
f.	Tells me what s/he likes most about me	1	2	3	4	5	6	7	8	9

g. Suggests a workable solution
   when we face a dilemma..... 1 2 3 4 5 6 7 8 9

h. Acts very affectionately to-
   ward me.................. 1 2 3 4 5 6 7 8 9

i. Tells me his/her feelings about
   the future of our relationship.. 1 2 3 4 5 6 7 8 9

j. When we argue, apologizes for
   behavior even when s/he thinks
   s/he is right 1 2 3 4 5 6 7 8 9

7. Power in the relationship.

For each of the different decisions listed below, indicate first, on the left, who usually has the most influence over the decision. Then on the right, indicate whether you think this particular decision is a major or minor one in your relationship.

Who Usually Has Most Influence?

Scale (left): I have all. (1) 2 3 4 — We have equal influence (5) 6 7 8 — S/he has all (9) — X We never make this decision

Major or Minor Decision?

Scale (right): Very Major (1) 2 3 4 5 6 7 8 Very Minor (9)

	Who Usually Has Most Influence?	Major or Minor Decision?
a. What groceries to buy	1 2 3 4 5 6 7 8 9 X	1 2 3 4 5 6 7 8 9
b. How to decorate our home	1 2 3 4 5 6 7 8 9 X	1 2 3 4 5 6 7 8 9
c. Where to go on a vacation	1 2 3 4 5 6 7 8 9 X	1 2 3 4 5 6 7 8 9
d. When to go out to eat	1 2 3 4 5 6 7 8 9 X	1 2 3 4 5 6 7 8 9
e. Whether to move to another city, state, or country	1 2 3 4 5 6 7 8 9 X	1 2 3 4 5 6 7 8 9
f. Where to go out for an evening	1 2 3 4 5 6 7 8 9 X	1 2 3 4 5 6 7 8 9
g. Whom to invite to our home	1 2 3 4 5 6 7 8 9 X	1 2 3 4 5 6 7 8 9
h. How much money to spend on groceries	1 2 3 4 5 6 7 8 9 X	1 2 3 4 5 6 7 8 9
i. How much money to spend on entertainment	1 2 3 4 5 6 7 8 9 X	1 2 3 4 5 6 7 8 9
j. How much money to spend on my own clothes	1 2 3 4 5 6 7 8 9 X	1 2 3 4 5 6 7 8 9
k. How much money to spend on furniture and home furnishings	1 2 3 4 5 6 7 8 9 X	1 2 3 4 5 6 7 8 9

8. Sharing the relationship

Part A: Who is more likely to do each of the following—you or your partner? Be honest!

I do this much more   _We do this equally_   _S/he does this much more_

a. Pay the other compliments ... 1   2   3   4   5   6   7   8   9

b. Say that one sees the other's point of view when we are having an argument............ 1   2   3   4   5   6   7   8   9

c. Do favors for the other, even when they are not asked for .. 1   2   3   4   5   6   7   8   9

d. Begin to talk about what is troubling our relationship when there is tension between us 1   2   3   4   5   6   7   8   9

e. Give the other a spontaneous hug or kiss when something good or exciting has occurred . 1   2   3   4   5   6   7   8   9

f. See oneself as running the show in our relationship 1   2   3   4   5   6   7   8   9

g. Offer advice when the other is faced with a problem........ 1   2   3   4   5   6   7   8   9

h. Sense that the other is disturbed about something...... 1   2   3   4   5   6   7   8   9

i. Give in to the other's wishes when one of us wants to do something the other does not want to do 1   2   3   4   5   6   7   8   9

j. Take on a problem in a rational rather than emotional way.... 1   2   3   4   5   6   7   8   9

k. Contribute the most in reaching a solution when we face a dilemma.................. 1   2   3   4   5   6   7   8   9

		I do this much more				We do this equally				S/he does this much more

l. Criticize the other's judgment. 1　2　3　4　5　6　7　8　9

m. Keep one's feelings to oneself 1　2　3　4　5　6　7　8　9

n. Let the other know one would
   like to have sex .... 1　2　3　4　5　6　7　8　9

o. Refuse to have sex.......... 1　2　3　4　5　6　7　8　9

p. Initiate sexual relations ...... 1　2　3　4　5　6　7　8　9

Part B.

		I much more				Both equally				S/he much more

1. In general, who has more say
   about important decisions affecting your relationship, you
   or your partner? .... 1　2　3　4　5　6　7　8　9

2. Who do you think *should* have
   the final say about important
   decisions affecting your relationship, you or your partner?. 1　2　3　4　5　6　7　8　9

3. Who is more committed to the
   relationship, you or your partner? .... 1　2　3　4　5　6　7　8　9

4. Who has altered habits and
   ways of doing things more to
   please the other, you or your
   partner? .... 1　2　3　4　5　6　7　8　9

Sexual Attitudes and Behavior
in Midlife and Aging Homosexual Males

Mark Pope, EdD

Career Decisions, San Francisco

Richard Schulz, PhD

University of Pittsburgh

INTRODUCTION

Even though research has been done on gay people, little has been done on the aging gay male. This article discusses some of the findings of a study of 87 homosexual males between the ages of 40 and 77 in the Chicago metropolitan area. Using a self-report questionnaire, data were gathered on the sexual attitudes and behavior of this group.

The stereotype of the aging gay male is being changed (Kelly, 1977). Kelly's study stated the societal myths of the aging gay man include the following: That he no longer goes to bars, having lost his physical attractiveness and his sexual appeal to the young men he craves. He is oversexed, but his sex life is very unsatisfactory. He has been unable to form a lasting relationship with a sexual partner, and he is seldom sexually active anymore. When he does have sex, it is usually in a "tearoom" (public toilet). He has disengaged from the gay world and his acquaintances in it. He is retreating further and further into the "closet" — fearful of disclo-

Mark Pope is President of Career Decisions (A Career Counseling and Consulting Firm) and Adjunct Professor at the University of San Francisco, Golden Gate University, and at John F. Kennedy University as well as Clinical Supervisor in Stanford University's Counseling and Health Psychology Program.

Richard Schulz is Professor and Director of the Gerontology Program at the University of Pittsburgh's Western Psychiatric Institute.

Correspondence may be addressed to Mark Pope, EdD, Career Decisions, P.O. Box 1734, San Francisco, CA 94101-1734.

sure of his "perversion." Most of his associations now are increasingly with heterosexuals. He is labeled "an old queen," as he has become quite effeminate.

Kelly, in this pioneering study, stated that the aging gay men in this study bear little resemblance to this stereotyped composite image. The sex life of the older gay man was, characteristically, quite satisfactory, and he desired sexual contact with adult men, especially those near his own age. The subjects were not, however, currently involved in a gay liaison, defined in Kelly's study as an emotional and sexual relationship of one year's duration or longer. The number of persons in liaisons increased with age. After an apex (in the 46 to 55 year old category), partnerships decreased to almost none. Two reasons for this decline often mentioned by older gays were the death of the loved one and the rejection of the notion of having a single lifelong lover.

Kleinberg (1977) stated that the aging gay male was better off than his heterosexual counterpart. Attributing this to having lived through the "long closeted life," the gay males in this study were survivors of the widowhood, loneliness, and loss of social place which are many times terminal grief for the heterosexually-oriented person.

All of the gay males in the Kimmel (1977) study were sexually active and their sexual relationships continued to be an important part of their life. Several respondents reported that sex was less important now than when they were younger, but several indicated that sex was more satisfying for them now. Kimmel's subjects also pointed out some of the advantages in aging for the gay male: more awareness of one's responsibility for self; non-reliance on family or children; more "continuity of life" (not having to cope with children leaving home); no limiting "male"/"female" roles in performing necessary tasks of life such as cooking, shopping, managing finances; having lived alone before, living alone is now not an ego shattering experience; and having a friendship network on which to rely for social and sexual companionship and support.

Berger (1982) administered a questionnaire to 112 gay males from 41 to 77 years old and then selected 10 subjects for an extensive interview. This comprehensive study also reported data on sexual activity and satisfaction of the subjects. Berger stated that the reported level of sexual activity was quite high for this sample, and that almost 75 percent of the questionnaire sample were satisfied with their sex lives.

None of the above-cited studies, however, included data by consistent age cohort. Berger (1982) did not categorize the subjects into age categories when presenting the data on sexual activity or sexual satisfaction. Kelly (1977) used varying age categories in reporting the data, using a 50 to 65 age bracket for sexual satisfaction and a 46 to 55 age bracket for number of gay partnerships (coupling). Kelly also did not provide any tabular data for these categories. Neither Kimmel (1977) nor Kleinberg (1977) had large enough samples (less than 15 each) to make cohort analysis meaningful.

METHOD

Historically, there has been no gay reference group in the research literature which took into account the racial, socio-economic, or age parameters of the American gay subculture. Because of the unique character of this subculture, that is, ability to conceal sexual orientation, fear of reprisals in various life situations, et cetera, effective population sampling techniques have not been utilized. Almost all studies to date of noninstitutionalized gay men have used gay organizations (Evans, 1969; Hooker, 1956), gay bars (Myrick, 1974), friendship networks (Loney, 1972), gay newspaper advertising (Laner, 1978; Lee, 1976), or a combination of these methods (Berger, 1982; Kelly, 1977; Minnigerode, 1976; Saghir & Robins, 1973; Weinberg & Williams, 1974). Further, some of the above referenced studies had very small samples. For instance, the Kleinberg (1977) and Kimmel (1977) studies only considered 5 and 14 subjects, respectively.

The data in this study were collected through questionnaires mailed to 235 members of Maturity, a social group for gay men 40 years of age or older (see Appendix A). Maturity was the only organized group of this type in the metropolitan Chicago area at the time. Also, Maturity provided an opportunity to contact a large aging gay male population.

The decision to use the questionnaire format for data collection was made on the basis of the Pfeiffer et al. researchers. Pfeiffer et al. (1968) conducted a similar study using interviews. Four years later, Pfeiffer et al. (1972) did a follow-up study, but used questionnaires instead of the interview. In the latter study, increased response rates were noted.

The questionnaire used here was accompanied by a letter from the co-chair of the National Caucus of Gay and Lesbian Counselors (now Association for Gay, Lesbian, and Bisexual Issues in Counseling), a group of mental health counselors in the American Personnel and Guidance Association (now American Association for Counseling and Development). In the recent past the policy of mental health professional organizations such as the American Psychological Association, the American Association for Counseling and Development, and, especially, the American Psychiatric Association was that a homosexually-oriented individual was inherently "mentally ill." Although these organizations have repudiated these policies, it was felt that there might continue to be a virulent distrust of this type of psychological research, that somehow this research might be "used against" gay people. By accompanying the questionnaire with this letter, inviting the subjects to participate in this study, it was felt that many of these fears could be assuaged and increased response would be the outcome.

RESULTS

Some interesting descriptive data were garnered through the questionnaires. Of the 235 questionnaires which were mailed, 101 were returned. Fourteen of the returned questionnaires were from gay males under 40 years of age and were not used in this analysis. The ages of the respondents ranged from 40 to 77 years. Thirty-seven (43%) of the respondents were between the ages of 40 and 49, 29 (33%) were in the 50 to 59 age cohort, and 21 (24%) were in the 60-plus age category. While the mean income level for the total group fell in the $15,000 to 20,000 per year category, 44% of the 60-plus age group earned less than $10,000 per year. Sixty-three percent of the respondents rented their residence and 33% owned their house or apartment. It was also an overwhelmingly urban group with 73% residing in cities with over 100,000 population, 15% in suburban areas, 15% in small cities, and only one percent in rural areas. No information was gathered on the racial makeup of the group. Because of the difference in the income level of the 60-plus age group, there may be some psychological dissonance inherent in their economic situation as they see many of the younger gay men living much better than they do.

Reported Current Frequency of Sex

In the 40 to 49 age group, 54% of the respondents reported that they had sex more than once per week, 34% of the 50 to 59 age group respondents reported similarly, while only 5% of the 60-plus age category reported sex more than once per week. This latter group, however, did report 38% having sex once-per-week. Each of these percentages is the statistical mode for their cohort (see Table 1).

Percentage of Respondents Remaining Sexually Active

Ninety-one percent of the total respondents reported that they were still sexually active. Ninety-seven percent of the 40 to 49 age category were active currently, 86% of both the 50 to 59 and 60-plus categories reported that they had not stopped sexual activity. Twenty percent of the 60-plus age group, however, did not report a specific frequency. They instead

Table 1

Current Frequency of Sexual Relations in Percentages for Gay Men (N=87)

Age Group (years)	Number	None	Once Per Month	Once Per Two Weeks	Once Per Week	More Than Once Per Week	Other But Active
40 - 49	37	3	3	8	27	54	5
50 - 59	29	14	10	7	14	34	7
60+	21	14	9	14	38	5	20

considered themselves "active," but declined to categorize themselves in the once-per-month to more-than-once-per-week groups (see Table 1).

Reported Current Level of Sexual Feelings (Interest)

There did seem to be a decline in sexual interest with age; however, over 45% of the respondents in each of the age groups reported currently having strong sexual feelings. In all age categories over 90% of all respondents reported a moderate or strong sexual interest. There was a tendency for the 40 to 49 age group to report a strong interest (62%) while the 60-plus age group reported a weaker interest percentage (48%); nevertheless, even in this latter group, this represented the statistical mode. Still, in the over 60 group, almost half of those responding indicated a moderate degree of sexual interest (see Table 2).

Percentage of Respondents Reporting Continued Sexual Feelings (Interest)

All of the respondents reported having a current interest in sex; five percent of the 40 to 49 group reported a weak interest, while only 10% of the 60-plus category responded similarly (see Table 2).

Table 2

Current Level of Sexual Interest in Percentages for Gay Men (N=87)

Age Group (years)	Number	None	Weak	Moderate	Strong
40 - 49	37	0	5	33	62
*50 - 59	29	0	0	38	52
60+	21	0	9	43	48

*Percentages do not equal 100 here as two respondents marked two choices and one respondent did not answer.

Change in Level of Reported Enjoyment of Sex

Sixty-nine percent of the respondents reported no change in their enjoyment of sex from their younger years to the present, 13% reported an increase, and 16% a decrease. The age of the respondents had no effect on this measure.

DISCUSSION

This is one of the few studies of older gay men to utilize this large a sample. Most of the previous studies have used less than 15 subjects, with the notable exceptions of Berger (1982), Minnigerode (1976), and Weinberg and Williams (1974). Because of the sampling methodology, however, the findings of this study cannot be applied as representative of all aging gay males. This sample of 87 men can, however, provide additional information on the older gay male in modern American society.

It is obvious, however, that these older gay men have maintained both their interest in sex as well as their ability to function sexually. Similar findings have been reported by both Kelly (1977) and Berger (1982). This may be a function of the predominant male sexual attitudes in current American society as well as the particular institutions in the gay male subculture, for example, bars and baths, which both foster these attitudes and provide a testing ground for their concomitant behavior.

Vacha (1985) specifically dedicated his book to the "survivors of an era beset by greater persecution than present." From several of the written comments returned with the completed questionnaires, the older gay men in this study who did provide comments have also developed coping mechanisms which have allowed them to function in their particular environments. These older gay men, who have functioned for almost all of their years in a more homosexually-oppressive society than today's younger gay generations, have adapted to the specific mores of the society in which they found themselves. From several of the written comments returned with the completed questionnaires, these coping mechanisms were not acquired easily.

The method of acquisition of these coping mechanisms is not within the scope of this study; however, further research using these age categories might yield data on these areas. One possible approach might be to do a study using younger gay men, younger heterosexually-oriented men, and same age-categoried midlife and aging heterosexually-oriented men as additional comparison groups. Using these groups would allow an examination of the type and nature of the coping mechanisms to see if there are differences on the basis of age and sexual orientation. For purposes of this study, it is sufficient to note that the older gay males in this sample seem to have both the desire and the ability to function in sexual situations.

Also, neither sexual "activity" nor sexual "relations" were operationally defined for the respondents before responding to the survey. It was left to the individual to interpret the questions. For purposes of this analysis, these two phrases have been defined as equivalent. It, however, is noted that a relatively large percent (20%) of the 60-plus age group in the gay male sample refused to categorize themselves as to frequency of sexual "relations," but indicated that they continued to remain "active." The questionnaire specifically asked about sexual "relations." Asking about sexual "activity" may have elicited a different response as "relations" may seem to exclude masturbation or any self-erotic behavior. Future studies should include self-erotic behavior as a separate category in order to analyze the contribution of this category to sexual "activity."

Further, the data for this study were gathered during 1978, before Acquired Immune Deficiency Syndrome (AIDS) became a national health issue. It is beyond the scope of this study to assess the direct effect of AIDS on this population.

This study should be seen as the beginning of a more generalized study of older gay male sexuality. Other areas must be explored in a comprehensive study. Especially in the aging male and female who for many reasons are relatively isolated, a classification of self-erotic behavior or masturbation may take on added prominence. Unless specific information is asked about this form of sexual activity, there may be a bias on the part of most respondents to omit this classification. Also, using consistent age cohorts in future research will enable cohort comparisons to be made much more easily.

The current study of 87 midlife and aging gay males' sexual behavior and attitudes is a unique study which paves the way for additional studies of this often misunderstood area of human sexuality.

REFERENCES

Berger, R. M. (1982). *Gay and gray: The older homosexual man*. Boston: Alyson Publications.

Evans, R. B. (1969). Childhood parental relationships of homosexual men. *Journal of Consulting and Clinical Psychology, 33*, 129-135.

Hooker, E. (1956). A preliminary analysis of group behavior of homosexuals. *Journal of Psychology, 42*, 217-225.

Kelly, J. (1977). The aging male homosexual. *The Gerontologist, 17*, 328-332.

Kimmel, D. C. (1977, November). Patterns of aging among gay men. *Christopher Street*, pp. 28-31.

Kleinberg, S. (1977, November). Those dying generations: Harry and his friends. *Christopher Street*, pp. 7-26.

Laner, M. R. (1978). Growing older male: Heterosexual and homosexual. *The Gerontologist, 18*, 496-501.

Lee, J. A. (1976). Patterns of gay love and gay liberation. *Journal of Homosexuality, 1*(4), 401-418.

Loney, J. (1972). Background factors, sexual experiences, and attitudes toward treatment in two "normal" homosexual samples. *Journal of Consulting and Clinical Psychology, 38*, 57-65.

Minnigerode, F. A. (1976). Age-status labeling in homosexual men. *Journal of Homosexuality, 1*, 273-276.

Myrick, F. (1974). Attitudinal differences between heterosexually and homosexually oriented males and between covert and overt male homosexuals. *Journal of Abnormal Psychology, 83*, 81-86.

Pfeiffer, E., Verwoerdt, A., & Davis, G. C. (1972). Sexual behavior in middle life. *American Journal of Psychiatry, 128*, 1262-1267.

Pfeiffer, E., Verwoerdt, A., & Wang, H-S. (1968). Sexual behavior in aged men and women. *Archives of General Psychiatry, 19*, 753-758.

Saghir, M. T. & Robins, E. (1973). *Male and female homosexuality*. Baltimore: Williams & Wilkins.

Vacha, K. (1985). *Quiet fire: Memoirs of older gay men*. Trumansburg, NY: The Crossing Press.

Weinberg, M. S., & Williams, C. J. (1974). *Male homosexuals*. New York: Oxford University Press.

Appendix A

Questionnaire

1. If you were to rate your enjoyment of sex in your younger years, would you rate this as:
   ( ) None   ( ) Mild   ( ) Very much

2. Please classify your sexual feelings in your younger years:
   ( ) None   ( ) Weak   ( ) Moderate   ( ) Strong

3. How much do you enjoy sexual relations at the present time?
   ( ) None   ( ) Mild   ( ) Very much

4. How would you rate your sexual feelings at the present time?
   ( ) None   ( ) Weak   ( ) Moderate   ( ) Strong

5. What is your present frequency of sexual relations?
   ( ) None   ( ) Once per week
   ( ) Once per month   ( ) More than once per week
   ( ) Once every two weeks ( ) Other, but active

6. If your sexual relations have stopped, when did this occur?
   ( ) Not stopped   ( ) 6-10 years ago
   ( ) One year ago or less ( ) 11-20 years ago
   ( ) 2-5 years ago   ( ) 20 years ago or more

Social Exchanges Between Older and Younger Gay Male Partners

Richard Steinman, MSW, PhD

University of Southern Maine

The often noted tendency for heterosexual women to couple with partners at least slightly older than themselves appears to be a cross-cultural phenomenon (Presser 1975). In contrast, the literature (Symons 1979, Momeni 1976, Patel-Gira 1974) reports a trend, also defying cultural boundaries, for men of all ages to exclude older people from candidacy for conjugal relationships.

The tendency of many middle-aged and older men – in North America as elsewhere – to replace age-peer wives with younger partners is well known (Cain 1982). This appears to have ancient roots. It is possible, in fact, that the institution of polygyny evolved, at least in part, in order to supply affluent, mature men with legitimate access to a recurring stream of young wives, even as the husband and his first wife advanced into old age. There is no reciprocal trend to speak of amongst wives.

Bias against older prospective partners is reported by some to be endemic within gay male culture, whereas no comparable trend is reported amongst lesbians (Symons 1979). From an exhaustive review of the literature, Symons concludes that there is a strong tendency for men, of whatever sexual orientation, to prefer younger partners. In the absence of women's countervailing tendencies, this trend may be even more pronounced among gay males than heterosexual couples. A 1975 nonprobability survey of 243 participants in Detroit gay bars and homophile organi-

Richard Steinman is Professor Emeritus of Social Welfare at the University of Southern Maine.

Correspondence can be sent to the author at the Department of Social Work, University of Southern Maine, 96 Falmouth Street, Portland, ME 04103.

The author acknowledges, with appreciation, the collaboration of Margaret Yeakel, DSW, and B. Erik Bergström, MS, in preparing this report, and the comments of Alice Lieberman, MSW, PhD.

zations found that a majority of men 18-24 years old reported preferring older partners, but that "above age 25 this choice sharply declines . . . [Above age 34] there occurs a sharp increase in choosing someone younger and the percentage so choosing seems to stabilize at 50%" amongst all older men (Harry & DuVall, 1978, p. 204). These data appear to support Symons' hypothesis.

The phenomenon of partnerships among gay men of substantially divergent ages raises some interesting questions. What significance, if any, do younger men attach to their partner's position in life? What values, if any, does each attach to the other's age?

Stimulated by curiosity about such questions and by a general interest in the extent to which the relations of gay couples in relatively enduring partnerships were similar to, or differed from, such relationships among other conjugal couples, the author set out to explore the significance of an age differential for such partnerships. The primary intent was to illumine the social exchanges operative between partners, and the degree to which they perceived those exchanges to be balanced or imbalanced.

THEORETICAL UNDERPINNING

To guide the exploration, we drew on the work of five social theorists — Blau (1967) and Homans (1950), social exchange theorists, and the equity theorists, Walster, Walster, and Berscheid (1978). Homans has elaborated the concept of social exchange as the central process in enduring human associations. This concept derived originally from economics. Along with social theorists of many disciplines, including anthropology, political science, social psychology, and sociology, Homans has used it to call attention to the fact that ongoing human interactions involve both benefits and costs for the parties involved in them. Such benefits and costs operate as valences of varying degrees, both attracting individuals to, and repelling them from, engagement in the exchange.

In his "Excursus on Love," Blau (1967) comments that "The aim of both [partners] in courtship is to furnish sufficient rewards to seduce the other but not enough to deflate their value, yet the line defined by these two conditions is often imperceptible" (p. 81).

Forces are generated in the process of exchange toward establishing and maintaining a balance in the "benefit-cost ratio" such that the benefits of continuing engagement are experienced as outweighing the costs. The power of each party to influence the other toward continued engagement exists to the extent that each experiences the other as providing resources, or access to resources, that benefit the self and that outweigh the costs of securing them. Such resources may be intrinsic, in the form of personal attributes or characteristics, or extrinsic, in the form of material possessions, influence or services. Thus, according to Homans, (1950):

> Persons that give much to others try to get much from them, and persons that get much from others are under pressure to give much to them. This process tends to work out, at equilibrium, to a balance in the exchange.

If a relationship is to continue, each partner must strive to reciprocate the benefits provided by the other. Walster et al. (1978) have contributed the concept of equity as an important dynamic in maintaining relationships.

> So long as individuals perceive they can maximize their outcomes (whether material or psychic) by behaving equitably, they will do so. If they can maximize their outcomes to their advantage by behaving inequitably, they will do so. When exchanges become inequitable, those receiving less usually become distressed. The more inequitable the relationship in their disfavor, the more distress they feel. They attempt to eliminate their distress by restoring equity or terminating the exchange.

In an age-stratified relationship, the youthful persona of the younger partner may be offered in exchange for certain benefits from the older partner. It is well established, for example, that couples judge each other in regard to degree of physical attractiveness (Berman et al. 1981; Coombs 1979; Sigall & Landy 1973). Berscheid et al. (1973) argue that beautiful women and handsome men can use their attributes to attract and keep partners who contribute more than their share in other spheres. For example, the aesthetically "inferior" partner might contribute more than his share of money, affection, or kindness and considerateness. And Marx (1978) has commented that:

> That for which I can pay—that am I. Thus, what I am and am capable of is by no means determined by my individuality. I am ugly, but I can buy for myself the most beautiful of women. Therefore I am not ugly, for the effect of ugliness—its deterrent power—is nullified by money. (p. 103)

This research began with the hypothesis that, among age-stratified gay male couples, the "exchange benefits" provided by the older man would be heavily weighted in the direction of extrinsic resources such as material possessions, money and services, together with the prestige or other kind of power with which they tend to be associated. Benefits made available by the younger man were expected to be weighted in the direction of intrinsic attributes such as physical attractiveness, sexual appeal, other personal attributes and considerations, and status acquired from having a young lover. Therefore the central hypothesis in the substudy here reported was:

> Older gay male partners tend to exchange greater extrinsic resources in return for presumed greater sex appeal, and other intrinsic rewards, from their younger partners.

METHOD

Sampling

Between 1983-1985, data were gathered in several regions of the United States from 280 women and men in relationships with someone significantly younger or older than themselves. These respondents were divided into four sub-groups, three of which were comprised, respectively, of lesbian couples, heterosexual couples with older men, and heterosexual couples with older women. The fourth cohort was comprised of the 46 gay male couples who are the subjects of this report.

In addition to their fitting into one of the above-named cohorts, couples were selected according to the following criteria:

- The initial phase of their relationship was of at least three months' duration.
- They were lifelong or longterm residents of the United States.
- The gap in their ages was at least 10, later changed to eight years.

Initially, 10 years was selected as the minimum age gap based on Blood's (1972, p. 526) observation that "Older partners in heterosexual relationships tend to be dominant in decision-making [if] the age difference [is] fairly large, e.g., 10 years or more" (as cited in Harry, 1983, p. 219). Since the dynamics of dominance is one major issue which impinges upon the degree of equity in relationships, 10 years was initially settled upon as the minimum age gap for this study. Despite an extensive literature search, Blood's report was the only one found which addressed this issue. However, it proved to be so difficult to win the participation of older women—younger men couples that several of the latter were accepted into the study with only an eight-year age difference. Consequently the same minimum was adopted for the other three sub-samples of the study as well.

Snowball sampling was particularly well suited to the sub-sample of gay couples since they are relatively hidden from view on two counts: sexual orientation and age discrepancy. Data were gathered from identified couples who were then encouraged to inform the researcher of "other appropriate persons" to seek out (Grinnell 1981, p. 88).

Schedules and Data-Gathering

Respondents furnished both qualitative and quantitative data. Each provided demographic and related information by means of a self-administered, pre-coded questionnaire. Each participant responded to a structured interview schedule of 27 open-ended questions in a private interview which averaged about 100 minutes in length. The interviews were transcribed and subjected to three rounds of coding and content analysis.

Limitations of the Sampling Method

While the sample was not randomly selected, the sampling method was well suited to the exploratory nature of our inquiry. Two major limitations of the design adopted should be noted. Ideally, this study should have been conducted with comparison groups made up of couples with no significant age differences. As a result of finite resources, this was not possible. Due to the nonprobability sample, it may not be assumed that the data are representative of gay male age-divergent couples in general.

DESCRIPTION OF THE SAMPLE

As previously indicated, this report concerns a sub-sample of gay male couples from whom data were obtained as part of a larger study. For the purposes of this report I refer to this group as the sample.

Data on Couples

Demography

Data were obtained on age, ethnicity, race, education, employment, income and religion (current and during childhood) of each respondent.

Age Discrepancy

The duration of each relationship, and the gap in partner ages, was obtained from 46 gay male couples (92 individuals). The age discrepancy between partners ranged from 8 to 40 years, with a median age gap of 14 years (see Table I for details). The increase in mean age discrepancy between younger and older partners in each of these four cohorts correlates with the decreasing mean age of the younger partners, but not with that of the older partners.

Duration of Relationship

The median duration for the 46 relationships was four years, but the range in duration is substantial, from (less than) one to 37 years. See Table II for details.

Table III cross-tabulates size of age gap and duration of relationship. There is a modest inverse association between size of age gap and duration of relationship: the larger the age gap, the shorter the relationship. Couples with age discrepancies of 11 years or less were more than twice as likely to have relationships which had endured at least four years, when compared to couples with greater age gaps.

Figure I provides a graphic representation of the amount of each couple's age discrepancy relative to the age of each partner. The couples are ordered in accordance with the age of the younger partners. Each of the 46 horizontal bars in this Figure simultaneously represents the age discrepancy within a gay male couple, and the age of each partner.

The extreme left point of each bar indicates the age of the younger partner while the age of each older partner is indicated by the extreme right point of the bar.

To illustrate the reading of this Figure, the tenth bar from the top represents partners who were 23 and 63 years old at the time they were interviewed — the largest age discrepancy in the study (40 years), whereas a short bar halfway down, as well as the fourth bar from the bottom, each represent the shortest age gap in the study (eight years) — the partners being 31 and 39 years old, and 46 and 54 years old, respectively.

Data on Individual Respondents

The following is a description of the sample of *individual respondents*.

Age. Table I divides the sample into four roughly equal sub-groups according to the age difference between partners. Within each, it displays the range in age of younger and older partners.

TABLE I. Age Discrepancies of 46 Gay Male Couples
Size of Discrepancy Between Younger and Older Partners' Ages

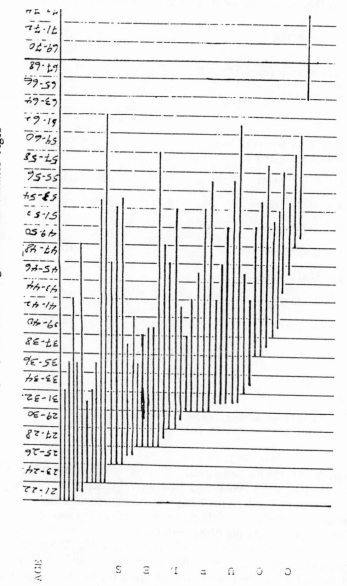

Each bar represents a couple. For each bar, the extreme left point indicates the age of the younger partner, and the extreme right point the age of the older partner.

TABLE II. Duration of Relationships (Percentaged vertically) (Median = 4 years)

Duration	f	%
Less than 1 years (3 months and 8 months, respectively)	2	4.3
One year	5	10.9
More than one year and less than 2 years	4	8.7
2 - 2-1/2 years	7	15.2
3 - 3-3/4 years	3	6.5
4 - 4-3/4 years	3	6.5
5 - 5-1/2 years	5	10.9
6 - 6-3/4 years	5	10.9
7 - 8-1/2 years	5	10.9
11 - 37 years*	7	15.2
T O T A L S	46	100.0%

*Durations of one, each: 11 years, 16 years, 17 years, 23 years, 26 years, 31 years, and 37 years.

Ethnicity. Of the 92 participants, 88 percent (81) were white. Of the remainder, two were Asian and two were black, with 7 falling into "other" categories. All of the latter were younger partners.

Educational Attainment. A higher level of education was more likely to have been achieved by the older partner, and the higher the educational degree, the more likely this was to be true. See Table IV for details.

Employment. More than one-fifth of the sample had been in their current position for less than two years; one-fifth for two to five years; one-fifth, 6 to 11 years; and one-fifth, 12 to 18 years. The remaining fifth had been in their current posts for 19 to 40 years.

There were striking contrasts between the occupational distribution of

TABLE III. Couples' Age Gaps, and Duration of Relationships (Total N = 46 couples) (Percentaged Vertically)

Couples' Age Gaps	Duration of Relationships	
	3 months - 3-3/4 yrs.	4 - 37 years
8 - 11 years	13.6 (3)	29.2 (7)
12 - 13 years	27.3 (6)	20.8 (5)
14 - 20 years	27.3 (6)	25.0 (6)
22 - 40 years	31.8 (7)	25.0 (6)
T O T A L S	100.0 (22)	100.0 (24)

younger and older partners. Professionals comprised virtually three times as many older partners (43.5 percent, N = 20) as younger ones (15.2 percent, N = 7). The same proportions applied to managers: nine older partners (19.6 percent) compared to three younger partners (6.5 percent). Opposite trends were discerned in the technician/semi-professional category. Almost a quarter of younger partners (N = 11) made up this group in contrast to 6.5 percent of older partners (N = 3). Even more pointedly, the laborer/operative/craftsman category and the students were entirely younger partners. See Table V for further details.

Subjects' annual incomes ranged from less than $7,000 to more than $100,000 *at the time the intimate phase of the relationship commenced.* In order to detect whether disparate incomes between older and younger partners might have played a part in the formation of their relationships, respondents were asked to report their respective incomes.

Income, All Individuals (right-hand column in Table VI). The median income for the sample was $12,500. Fifty-four percent earned under $15,000, with half (more than a quarter of the sample [N = 24]) earning below $7,000. Almost another quarter (N = 22) earned between $15,000

FIGURE 1. Discrepancy Between Partners' Ages, for Each of 46 Couples

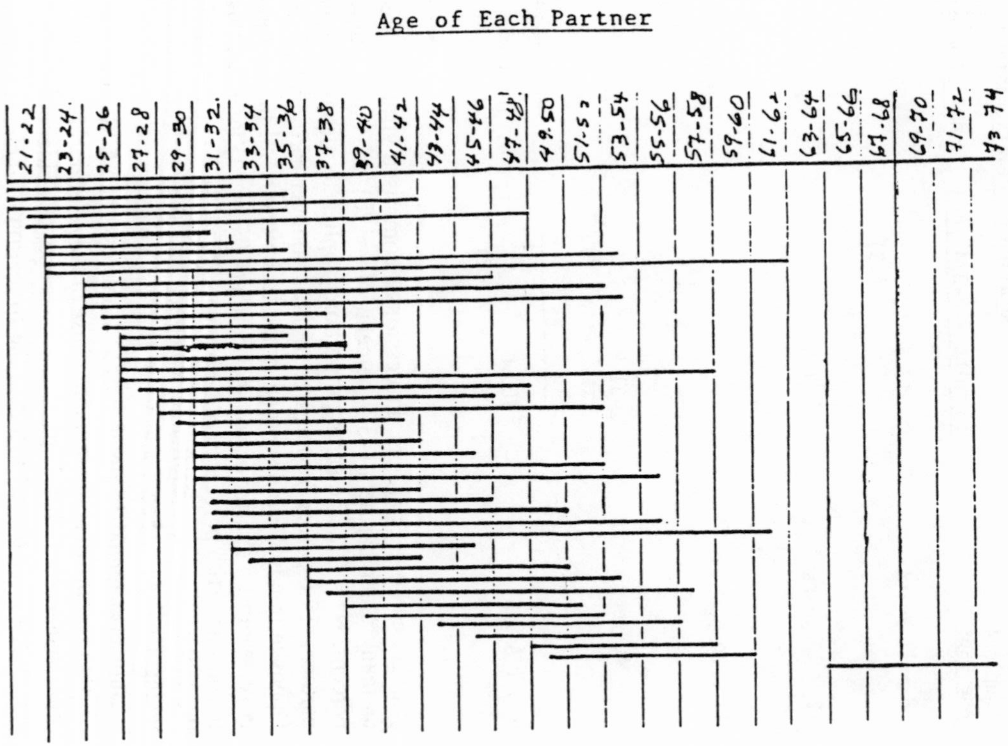

Age of Each Partner

21-22 23-24 25-26 27-28 29-30 31-32 33-34 35-36 37-38 39-40 41-42 43-44 45-46 47-48 49-50 51-52 53-54 55-56 57-58 59-60 61-62 63-64 65-66 67-68 69-70 71-72 73-74

TABLE IV. Highest Level of Education (Percentaged Vertically)

	Respondents' Highest Level of Education		
	All Respondents	Older Partners	Younger Partners
High School graduation or less	12.0 (11)	4.3 (2)	19.6 (9)
Some higher education (including AA degrees)	26.1 (24)	15.2 (7)	37.0 (17)
Baccalaureate degree	30.0 (28)	32.6 (15)	28.3 (13)
Master's degree	19.6 (18)	26.1 (12)	13.0 (6)
Doctoral degree	12.1 (11)	21.7 (10)	2.2 (1)
T O T A L S	99.9 (92)	99.9 (46)	100.1 (46)

TABLE V. Employment in Adulthood (Percentaged Vertically)

Respondents' Employment in Adulthood

	All Respondents	Older Partners	Younger Partners
Student	3.3 (3)	0.0 -	6.5 (3)
Laborer Operative Craftsman	9.8 (9)	0.0 -	19.6 (9)
White collar work	14.1 (13)	8.7 (4)	19.6 (9)
Sales	9.8 (9)	15.2 (7)	4.3 (2)
Technician or semi-professional	15.2 (14)	6.5 (3)	23.9 (11)
Artist	5.4 (5)	6.5 (3)	4.3 (2)
Manager	13.0 (12)	19.6 (9)	6.5 (3)
Professional	29.3 (27)	43.5 (20)	15.2 (7)
TOTALS	99.9 (92)	100.0 (46)	99.9 (46)

TABLE VI. Income at the Time the Relationship Began, by Older-Younger Partners (Percentaged Vertically)

Income Brackets	Combined Income of Couples		Older Partners' Income		Younger Partners' Income		Total of Older and Younger Partners' $	
Less than $7,000	6.5	(3)	10.9	(5)	41.3	(19)	26.1	(24)
$7,000 - 14,999	4.3	(2)	23.9	(11)	32.6	(15)	28.3	(26)
$15,000 - 24,999	17.4	(8)	26.1	(12)	21.7	(10)	23.9	(22)
$25,000 - 49,999	45.7	(21)	23.9	(11)	4.3	(2)	14.1	(13)
$50,000 - 99,999	15.2	(7)	4.3	(2)	0.0	-	2.2	(2)
$100,000 or more	10.9	(5)	10.9	(5)	0.0	-	5.4	(5)
T O T A L S	100.0	(46)	100.0	(46)	99.9	(46)	100.0	(92)

191

and $25,000, and more than a fifth (21.7 percent, N = 20) earned $25,000 or more. Five in the latter group earned $100,000 or more.

Income, Older vs. Younger Partners. Almost three-quarters of younger partners (N = 34) had incomes in the two lowest brackets. Conversely, almost two-thirds of older partners' incomes (N = 30) were in the four highest categories in Table VI. These data indicate that older partners tended to be in a position to exchange extrinsic resources with younger partners, and that the latter tended to be in a position to need such resources.

The reader is reminded that these were the incomes at the time of the couples' courtships, some of which were a long time ago. It is a limitation of this study that the incomes reported were not adjusted for rates of inflation.

Income, Couples (left-hand column in Table VI). The combined income of the partners ranged similarly from less than $7,000 to $100,000 or more; the median income for all couples, however, lay in the range between $25,000 and $49,999, while a quarter (N = 12) had combined incomes of $50,000 or more. (Unemployment was implicated for the three couples with incomes under $7,000.)

Religion. The data revealed strong contrasts between subjects' religious orientation in childhood vs. adulthood. Catholic observance was reduced by 40 percent, Jewish observance by almost 70 percent, and Protestant or spiritual observance by 39 percent. In marked contrast, the proportion of subjects claiming "no" religion in adulthood increased from a childhood percentage of 3.3 percent to 44.6 percent. The cross-tabulations for older-younger partners indicate that changes from organized religion to no religion were even more pronounced among younger than older partners (see Table VII).

Summary and Questions about the Description of the Sample. The sample is predominantly well-educated, white, middle socio-economic class (as measured by occupation and income). As adults, 45 percent do not now identify with any religion, in contrast to 97 percent who were raised is an organized religion.

Seven-tenths of the older partners (N = 32) are artists, professionals, and managers, in contrast to only a quarter (N = 12) of younger partners. All three occupational groups have a greater degree of autonomy than most other occupations. Does that autonomy render these older partners somewhat more immune to possible public disapproval of their age-divergent relationships? Conversely, given the fact that more than two-fifths of the younger partners are in occupations at the opposite end of the status and wage continuum, does the higher status, greater autonomy occupa-

TABLE VII. Religion in Childhood and Adulthood (Percentaged Vertically)

	All Respondents' Religion		Older Partners' Religion		Younger Partners' Religion	
	Childhood	Adulthood	Childhood	Adulthood	Childhood	Adulthood
Catholic	27.2 (25)	16.3 (15)	15.2 (7)	10.9 (5)	39.1 (18)	21.7 (10)
Jewish	10.9 (10)	3.3 (3)	15.2 (7)	4.3 (2)	6.5 (3)	2.2 (1)
Protestant (or Spiritual)	58.7 (54)	35.9 (33)	67.4 (31)	47.8 (22)	50.0 (23)	23.9 (11)
None	3.3 (3)	44.6 (41)	2.2 (1)	37.0 (17)	4.3 (2)	52.2 (24)
T O T A L S	100.1 (92)	100.1 (92)	100.0 (46)	100.0 (46)	99.9 (46)	100.0 (46)

tions of the aggregate of older partners make them especially attractive to the younger men? Do the two groups exchange the greater intrinsic resources of the younger for the greater influence, prestige, income and autonomy of the older?

The Interviews

The interviews sought qualitative data to test the hypothesis of social exchange of extrinsic and intrinsic resources. Responses of a number of couples were highly congruent with the postulated exchange, but there are some counter-indications, discussed below. In a majority of cases, the younger partner was far more likely than the older to use the power to grant or refuse sexual gratification as a means of securing, or maintaining, equity in the exchange, even though sexual attraction was rarely one-sided. In more than three-quarters of the couples who had capital assets, the latter had been provided by the older partner. In approximately half the couples the partners contributed roughly equally to daily living costs. This suggests that sexual resources are not necessarily exchanged for non-sexual resources.

Further, not infrequently the *intrinsic* resources offered by the older partner (intelligence, sophistication, social accomplishments and the like) were as strongly attractive according to the younger partner as material possessions.

To illustrate these findings, we present a number of vignettes which illuminate the nature of the exchanges revealed in this sample. We begin with the "purest" example of interview data which supported the hypothesis:

> Gene is a bright, attractive man of 27 (who looks years younger). As a member of a progressive political organization, he first encountered his future lover, 40-year-old Frank, speaking from the platform at political gatherings. Gene speaks of these encounters: "I don't know that I was that sexually attracted to him. He wasn't like anybody I ever fantasied about. I *was* interested in him, but more so because of his prominence, at first. Sexual attraction is kind of a funny thing. It has various forms. I guess I wanted to [get in on] some of his prominence. That was part of it. Usually it is the intellectual qualities that I find attractive in older men. Initially that was especially one of my reasons for getting into this relationship—just to be around him, and learn. Especially when you're young, the thing I was able to barter was youthfulness, and the people I was involved with *like* youthfulness, and it was like a kind of *exchange*. I

was [receiving their wisdom and prominence] and giving whatever they found attractive: The status some feel they acquire by having a youthful lover; the sexual excitement some get from younger people; whatever kind of joy they get out of a younger person's personality. I 'traded' that for more worldliness and exposure to intellectual development.

Also there's a real sexual attraction I have for older men. They seem calmer and more solid and I find that sexy. (The older men I'm talking about are around 35. In the gay male culture, particularly, that's a very sexy age. A lot of porno stars are that age and not thought to be unattractive at all.) This is really sexist but, when we talk about manliness we talk about strength. Not just physical strength, but strength of character is very important and very attractive."

Without any knowledge of the hypothesis of the study, this young man documents its validity insofar as it applies to himself and his partner. As is evident, he feels very comfortable about exchanging or "bartering" his youthful sex appeal for the intellect and associated prestige of an older partner. And then, almost as an afterthought, he discovers that he enjoys the sex as well. But many respondents are not nearly so sanguine about such exchanges.

"Sugar Daddy": Stereotype or Reality?

A prevalent stereotype in the gay male world characterizes the older man in an age-stratified partnership as a "sugar-daddy," who "keeps" a younger man in an exchange of money for sex appeal and sexual favors. (This is not unlike the familiar assumption in the heterosexual world of a "kept" woman in an older man-younger woman relationship.) Since the "sugar-daddy" stereotype comes so close to embodying the study hypothesis, we found it useful to organize the presentation and discussion of the vignettes around it.

As revealed above, roughly half the couples in the sample repudiate this stereotype because—setting capital assets aside—neither partner is economically dependent upon the other. As for the balance, the data suggest that older partners cherish the sexual excitement afforded by their younger partners, and younger partners find the economic resources of their older partners very comfortable, but in all the relationships the story goes beyond this simple exchange. Most younger partners report being, at least to some extent, sexually aroused by their older partners. And some, like Gene, also report being attracted by *additional, intrinsic* qualities of the older partner. In a significant number of couples (see Table VI) there is no large gap in the older and younger partners' incomes. The "sugar daddy" stereotype is further confounded by the insistence of some partners — sometimes younger, more often older — that the younger partners *not* be financially dependent upon the older, even when they earn less. As in Gene's case, many couples in the sample split their financial costs down the middle, or close to it. A significant problem for some younger partners is keeping up with the older partners' spending patterns. Conversely, some older partners are troubled by what in their view is the profligacy of younger partners who define luxuries (e.g., a VCR) as necessities.

In addition, sensitive issues of self-image frequently impinge upon the question of "sugar daddies." Some older partners do not seem discomfitted by the image that they are "keeping" their younger partners, but others deplore the stereotype and, as a result, are at pains to point out the non-cash contributions which younger partners make to the household and the relationship.

For many older partners self-image is at risk when people outside the relationship hint that the only way the older man can attract a younger partner is with economic bait. Some couples collaborate to reduce this risk by creating either the illusion or fact of economic equity; others live indefinitely with the pain. Several relevant examples follow:

> Karl, a very affluent 49-year-old engineer, is consumed with delight and passion for Ted, a warm, good-natured 22-year-old Chicano student with great charm, warmth and good looks. When it was agreed, two years ago, that Ted move into Karl's upper middle-class home in the suburbs of a southwestern city, Karl prevailed upon Ted to give up his campus job. Good-naturedly bemused, Ted acquiesced and was thus free to meet Karl's wish that they take frequent short holidays together in tropical climes. Independently, each reports that their love-making is immensely gratifying to Karl, and satisfactory to Ted. There is an agreement between them that Ted is in charge of keeping up the garden, his primary contribution to the household. This enables them both to repress any notion that Ted is being "kept" in return for sex.

The following vignette provides some interesting contrasts. Now well beyond college age, Glen was effective at making a living even before he and Peter met almost seven years ago.

Peter, 53 years old, is also impassioned with his lover, Glen, a 29-year-old with the appearance of an Adonis. At the time they met, Peter was already a successful realtor. He brought Glen into the business and they have prospered together. Their house is glamorous. Two expensive, late model cars sit in the driveway. Peter comments that "I was drawn to his youthfulness, which has been a factor in all my relationships—his body, his mode of living, and a very definite sweetness. Through the years Glen's maturing has brought some of the hardening that comes to us all with life experience. But Glen's sweetness is still there."

There is one major exception to their happiness, and it looms large for Peter. The amount of love-making afforded by Glen falls seriously short of meeting Peter's needs. In consequence, Peter finds it necessary to seek sex extramurally but states he would much prefer to make love solely with Glen. For his part, Glen is cognizant of the problem but feels utterly unable to do anything to rectify it.

Both older men, Karl and Peter, are forthright in regard to their passion for men half their age. However, they deal differently with the economic transfer from older to younger partner. Karl and Ted act as if there is equity between the gardening performed by Ted, and Karl's substantial economic investment, both in Ted's necessities and in luxuries. Under Peter's leadership, however, Glen has concrete economic gains to show for his efforts. True, he got his start in real estate as a result of being taken in under Peter's wing, but, *economically*, he is carrying his own weight quite well. It seems reasonable to conclude that *their* unpredicted exchange, i.e., mutual exchange of extrinsic resources, and far more intrinsic being sought by the older than the younger is able to provide, is inconsistent with the hypothesis.

These two vignettes reveal contrasting methods for "eliminating" economic inequities. In the instance of Karl and Ted, it is done by avoiding the evidence. In the case of Peter and Glen, the older partner's patronage is real, but so also is Glen's genuine economic contribution. Karl and Ted may trade some sexual gratification for economic benefits but they maintain the fiction that Ted makes an equitable exchange of labor for economic assets. As for Peter and Glen, it would be facile to conclude that their expectation of a substantial economic contribution from the younger partner results from the older partner's sexual frustration. The economic arrangement was worked out at the outset of their relationship, before the emergence of Glen's inability to satisfy Peter sexually.

Sexual "Refusal": Inequitable
Exchange by Some Youths

The condition of older partners wanting more sex than their alluring younger partners afforded them, as in the case of Peter and Glen, was quite widespread in the study. This was even evident between some partners as young as 33 and 21 years old, respectively. Many younger partners were unable to maintain the unwritten and usually unspoken contract. While their older partners were living up to the letter of the contract — providing ample extrinsic resources — these younger men fell short of satisfactorily delivering the sexual component of the intrinsic, thereby rendering the social exchange quite inequitable. In gay male culture, from time to time, one hears older gay men say about a hypothetical younger partner, "If he didn't *'put* out,' I'd *throw* him out." The older men in this study showed far more forbearance. In most instances, as the quote from Peter illustrates, they emit a sense of melancholy rather than anger.

The following excerpts illustrate with striking variations the responses of older partners to the inequity they experience.

Jack, 41 years old, is a professor at an Ivy League university. Brad, 27, has had a remarkable history. He was reared in an upper-middle class home. In the fever of the counterculture, his left-wing passions led him to run away from both a New England prep school and a mental hospital. He had a relatively brief period of surviving by selling his beautiful body on city streets (and consoling himself with sex with fellow hustlers when trade was slow). He has a keen mind and, in his early 20s, committed himself to a leftist political analysis of the gay rights movement. He defines himself as a writer, and his letters — and periodic articles for which he is not paid — are published several times a year in the gay press.

Jack and Brad met via an impersonal sexual encounter when the latter was 20. Jack was impassioned by the youth and, shortly after, invited him to share his highly advantaged home, a lovely old house, filled with artwork, oriental rugs, and dark woodwork, in a city on the Eastern Seaboard. The interview with Brad took place in his second floor study in the back of the house, overlooking a garden. Brad places great value on this as the private setting for his scholarship and writing. He picks up the story:

"We haven't had sex together since our first year, [seven years ago. The cessation of sex] was at my initiative. I didn't want to hurt him and I think I may have, some.

We're very different people but we are very close, and I think it was a great piece of good luck that I met him. [For me] it wasn't 'romance' with a big 'R.' It really was common interests: political and intellectual commitments; loving art; having certain common views about the best way to live a life. That's as important — *more* important — than sex, in the long run. It's really what makes a relationship, I think. If the sexual relationship had lasted, that would've been fine. But I feel deprived by monogamy, and we've never attempted it. We both 'see' [have sex with] other people, but every night, no matter how late I get home from the bars, we always sleep together, with sensual, not sexual, contact.
[As to why I stopped having sex with him,] he is good-looking. He's got a big cock. He's a sexy man, but he's not my type. Not *sexually*. [There were times when] we enjoyed sex thoroughly, but I wasn't fully comfortable with it. I liked lots of other things in sex [besides the predictable, "traditional" acts Jack wanted to perform]. Also, for Jack sex meant something romantic, but it didn't mean that for me. For me sex is *pleasure*. These are some of the differences in our attitudes."

Currently Jack is sadly resigned to Brad's decision. But 63-year-old Monroe's reaction to some withholding of sex by Adam, his youthful partner, is very different from Jack's. He is loathe to settle for sensuality:

Monroe's appearance and personality remind one of a Wall Street broker. He recently inherited a small fortune from his late lover (who had been roughly the same age). Adam is a tall, handsome blond with great charm, warmth and infectious humor. Their age gap is 40 years, the largest in the study. Adam recently graduated from art college. When they met two years ago, Adam was living independently in his own apartment, and Monroe in a hotel. Five months later Monroe moved into Adam's apartment but, considering it déclassé, rented a penthouse, in due course, for $2,000 per month. Adam complained vigorously because Monroe hadn't consulted him on the final choice. Although each was paying half the expenses at the former apartment (which pained Adam to give up), Monroe pays the full cost of the penthouse because what Adam could contribute would only amount to a drop in the bucket.
Monroe, in the initiator role, requests sex frequently. Adam genuinely enjoys sex with him, but much less often. On the nights when Adam refuses because he isn't in the mood, Monroe, in an aroused

state, moans with sexual frustration. Adam encourages him to mas-
turbate but Monroe rejects the idea, viewing it as unseemly since his
sexual partner is lying in the same bed with him. There are nights
when Adam is awakened by Monroe trying to have sex with his
sleeping form. This makes Adam feel used and angry. He puts his
foot down and Monroe desists—for a while.

The sexual relationship of quite a few couples in this sample follows the
pattern described by Blumstein and Schwartz (1983) in *American Couples*, as characteristic of many husbands and wives. They note that, typically, wives are disadvantaged when it comes to money and theorize that,
historically, the control which may be called *"refusal,"* which wives exercised over husbands' sexual access to them, has evolved as a counterbal-
ance to husbands' control over wives' access to money (Blumstein and
Schwartz, 1983, pp. 206-214).

There appears to be an arresting similarity in gay male age-stratified
couples. There is a strong tendency for younger partners to be financially
dependent (though for different reasons than wives), and a corollary tendency for younger partners to exercise "refusal" over the older partner's
access to sex.

If wives are disadvantaged financially because of limitations placed by
husbands and society on their access to money, younger gay male partners
tend to be disadvantaged primarily by their age—and no doubt also by
possessing less talent: They simply haven't had as many years, or gifts, as
their older partners to build lucrative careers. The causes are different but
the *results* are often parallel.

There is no evidence that Adam, Brad, Glen, or other younger partners
are deliberately trying to frustrate their older partners. Monroe provides
Adam with a penthouse lifestyle. Peter has been instrumental in Glen's
"getting in on" the posh, suburban way of life. Jack is literally Brad's,
the writer's, patron—these facts do not automatically produce the hypothesized exchange.

Importunate Youth, Reluctant Older Partner

For opposite reasons, the hypothesis does not hold up in instances such
as the following (far less characteristic than the above):

Charles, an attorney, and John, a student computer operator, are 37
and 25 years old, respectively. John is totally deaf and totally without speech. The two men have been together for five years. To a
considerable extent John's deficits have veiled his keen, alert mind

from the world-at-large—though not his sparkling personality and captivating smile. In the bloom of his mid-20s, John is extremely handsome. Charles, who is trim and nice-looking, appears somewhat younger than his 37 years.

According to Charles, "John is more sexually active, and has a higher sex drive, than I. True, after five years together, his sex drive isn't as constant—or demanding of satisfaction as frequently—as it used to be. It's taken a lot of pressure off me to perform.

Within the last two years our sexual interaction has soothed off to where we both feel more comfortable [with our pattern of frequency]—though there's still a difference in our sexual needs. When I don't feel horny I feel very frustrated that I have to put up with John wanting sex. I'd rather just hug him and go to sleep. Other times it's fine because we both want sex at the same time. [But otherwise] I feel I don't perform up to John's desired standards—both in frequency and quality. In fact, there's an inverse relationship between the two. When the frequency is down to a level where I feel a stronger urge to have sex, the quality is higher; probably a little more satisfying to John. Recently I've been taking more initiative, which I feel very happy about. I don't know how to explain the change, except that his demands [are no longer] nightly—something I don't feel comfortable with.

After five years, the same thrills aren't there as in the excitement and ecstacy of the courtship. [Most couples] settle down together and have sex once or twice a week, enjoying *sensuality* in between." The problem is that when Charles initiates sensuality it gets John all fired up for full-blown sex.

It is of interest to note, but based only on anecdotal observations, that a number of age-gap relationships exist in the deaf gay world between older, hearing partners and younger, deaf partners. As a basis for systematic inquiry, one may postulate the following application of exchange and equity theories, to wit: That deaf gay men in the bloom of youth exchange their sexual allure for the *substantial* emotional and economic security afforded by older, hearing men as well as the many other concrete social supports unavailable to so many deaf people as they attempt to negotiate the hearing world.

Furthermore, it may be argued that the learning of sign language by an older, hearing partner during courtship is a telling example of "earning" the sexual favors of the younger—in this case, deaf—partner.

Youths Detest "Sugar Daddy" Stereotype

The reactions of younger partners to the "sugar daddy" stereotype are far more uniform than those of older partners. In short, the younger men *detest* it because it wounds their self-image to be seen as someone who would either "sell" himself, or financially exploit the person he loves. And some just don't want their self-sufficiency to be called into question. Some are offended by the assumption that they can only make it on their looks, not their brains. This is particularly true of those absorbed in creative expression. The stereotype serves to demean their achievement. They develop various defenses against the stereotype (though some say they have never consciously dealt with the question until faced with the research interview).

Younger partners have other defenses. Some argue they are productive vocationally but are not remunerated for writing, political activism, or the performing arts. They just don't happen to earn money at it. A few *do* feel more legitimate, however, when an occasional story or article is published, or they get to perform before an audience. They work hard in, and place great value upon, their den, studio or shop located in the older partner's home.

In the case of some younger partners who contribute significantly less than half to household expenses, an entirely different defense is offered— by older and younger partners, alike. The rationale is that the older partner uses much *more* than half the household space. Therefore it is not inequitable for him to pay more than half the mortgage payments and other expenses.

Calms and Storms Over Financial Inequity

About half the couples were very conscious of issues of financial inequity. Two examples follow, illustrating equanimity (between Fergus and Dwyer) and conflict (between Miguel and Ken).

Fergus, a stock broker, and Dwyer, a writer 20 years his junior, do nothing to rationalize their disparate financial states. For almost two years they have been living together in Fergus' very comfortable home, high on a hill of an elegant western city.

Dwyer states that, "When we started talking about moving in together, I just wanted to know what sort of financial arrangement Fergus would like. He seemed very [laid back about it] but I made sure that it was very clear beforehand. It was for him to say whether he wanted me to pay rent. With my [modest] income I had to know, so we made it very concrete. Even if I did have a lot of money it makes things easier if everyone understands." After moving in, Dwyer reduced his full-time employment at a social agency to 10 hours per week so that he could devote more time to writing. "Fergus always says, 'Don't worry about money. Don't worry about it. I'm making *lots* of money.' But I still like to pay my own way.

There was one day a couple of months ago when Fergus made in commissions almost what I made last year, and that was like, I thought, 'Oh my God! He made $3,000 in commissions today, and I made $3,500 last year.' I mean, it's my *own* choice. I could make more money *not* writing. Hopefully, eventually I'll make more money *writing*. [At the interviewer's request, Dwyer showed him a story of his, published in a collection.] But in the meantime it's frustrating to be so poor, and to have to be aware of money all the time." As for the impact upon him of Fergus' wealth, and its effect upon their relationship, Dwyer said, "I think that, between us, it's not more noteworthy than when I see *anyone* who makes a lot of money. And he, also, seems to be very comfortable [about the disparity]. Actually, what's hard is that sometimes people *assume* that I'm being 'kept'; that Fergus is a 'sugar daddy.' Their attitude seems to be, 'Oh well, you don't have to worry,' and I find that very unappealing. I protest that I pay my own way but it's embarrassing [to have to be defensive]."

Although Dwyer is obviously bothered by such reactions, it is not an issue within the relationship. But such is not the case for Ken and Miguel.

Ken, now in his mid-30s, is a native of the midwestern state where he and Miguel met, and have lived together (except for stormy separations) for six years. He is very attractive, in both personality and appearance. Miguel, a highly-paid professional, is a native of Spain but has lived in the United States for decades. He has just turned 50.

No couple in this study is more relationship-centered. They do everything they can together, from grocery shopping to foreign travel. For Miguel it is an almost unbearable emotional burden to be separated from Ken—even when driving to the airport to meet a relative's plane. When Miguel goes to work each morning, the phone rings at home within the hour. The same will usually recur in midday and mid-afternoon. As for Ken, he would be more willing to take off on his own but almost never does. For example, despite a close relationship with a sister in New England, either the two men go together or Ken doesn't go at all. The same is true of visits to New York City to Miguel's sister and nephew, whom he has legally adopted.

Miguel is a gourmet cook and prepares sumptuous meals, not only when they entertain guests, but also, from time to time, when they are dining alone. Ken serves willingly as his scullery.

Yet a central problem looms over their relationship. Despite Miguel's high income (well into six figures), the disparity in their resources is a periodic source of tension. Rationally, Miguel knows that he earns more than enough for both to be able to live on very comfortably. He further acknowledges that if Ken were a female he wouldn't have the least bit of conflict about supporting him. But Ken's being a male changes all that for Miguel. The notion of supporting another man—even the man he shares his life, home and bed with—periodically drives him to distraction. He readily acknowledges that his Hispanic cultural background probably has a lot to do with his reaction.

The heat of this issue waxes and wanes. When it is "hot" it serves as a lightning rod for conflict between them. Ken argues that he invests a high proportion of his modest income in household expenses, in contrast to a very small proportion of Miguel's income. More importantly, he is Miguel's lover, friend, traveling companion, driver, co-shopper, and provides a sounding board in regard to the latter's many problems at work. In addition, he furnishes other resources which are highly valued by Miguel, among them emotional support, keeping all Miguel's accounts, and safely investing Miguel's money at highest yield.

There are periods when Miguel's distress about financial inequity drives Ken to seek paid employment (which Miguel is then likely to disparage because of a wage which falls so far short of his own). This employment usually lasts from a few months to upwards of a year. Ken's primary contributions to family life just don't happen to be monetary.

There are long periods when Miguel is not exercised about the financial inequity. But he says that he worries about Ken's future "when I am gone." Ken argues that this problem is easily taken care of if Miguel will simply provide for him in his will. But there is the adopted nephew to think about. And so it goes.

CONCLUSION

The evidence included above — supported by multiples more than space allows — furnishes clear signs that the study hypothesis cannot be rejected categorically. It is apparent that younger partners are aware of how attractive their intrinsic resources are to many older men. However there is no constant which serves to standardize the nature of their responses. Conversely, many older men know the value of their extrinsic resources to many younger men. But the plentitude of these resources does not translate into a fully-identified, *consistent* model of the relevant social exchange.

Human affairs and social dynamics are so complex and multifaceted that it comes as no surprise to discover intervening, explanatory or confounding variables which are likely to "intrude" upon the equation.

Further exploratory research in this area, with a larger sample size and, if possible, a comparison group of same-age couples, is needed to refine the major hypothesis, and more precisely specify the nature of the exchanges.

REFERENCES

Berger, R. M. (1982). *Gay and gray: The older homosexual man.* Urbana, IL: University of Illinois.

Berger, R. M. (1980). Psychological adaptation of the older homosexual male. *Journal of Homosexuality, 5* (3), 161-175.

Berman, P. W., O'Nan, B. A. & Floyd, W. (1981). The double standard of aging and the social situation: Judgments of attractiveness of the middle-aged woman. *Sex Roles, 7* (2), 87-96.

Berscheid, E., Walster, E. & Bohrnstedt, G. (1973). The body image report. *Psychology Today, 7*, 119-131.

Blau, P. M. (1967). *Exchange and power in social life.* New York: Wiley.

Blood, E. (1972). *The family.* New York: Macmillan.

Blumstein, P. & Schwartz, P. (1983). *American couples: Money, work and sex.* New York: Morrow.

Cain, B. S. (1982, December 19). Plight of the gray divorcee. *The New York Times Magazine,* pp. 89-93.

Coombs, O. (1979, December 3). Portrait of an aging hustler. *New York,* pp. 46-54.

Francher, J. S. & Henkin, J. (1973). The menopausal queen: Adjustment to aging and the male homosexual. *American Journal of Orthopsychiatry,* pp. 670-674.

Gagnon, J., & Simon, W. (1973). *Sexual Conduct.* Chicago: Aldine.

Grinnell, R. M. Jr., (Ed.). (1981). *Social work research and evaluation*. Itasca, IL: Peacock.

Harry, J. (1982). Decision-making and age differences among gay male couples. *Journal of Homosexuality, 8* (2), 9-21.

Harry, J. (1983). Gay male and lesbian relationships. Chapter 10 of Macklin, E. & Rubin, R. (Eds.), *Contemporary families and alternative lifestyles*. Beverly Hills: Sage, pp. 216-234.

Harry, J. & DeVall, W. (1978). Age and sexual culture among homosexually oriented males. *Archives of Sexual Behavior, 7* (3), 199-209.

Homans, G. (1950). *The human group*. San Diego: Harcourt, Brace, Jovanovich.

Hoult, T. F. (Ed.). (1969). *Dictionary of modern sociology*. Totowa, NJ: Little-field Adams.

Kelly, J. (1977). The aging male homosexual: Myth and reality. *The Gerontologist, 17* (4), 328-332.

Kimmel, D. C. (1979). Life-history interviews of aging gay men. *International Journal of Aging & Human Development, 10* (3), 239-248.

Laner, M. R. (1978). Growing older male: Heterosexual and homosexual. *The Gerontologist, 18* (5), 496-501.

Marx, K. (1978). Economic and philosophic manuscripts of 1844. In E.C. Tucker (Ed.), *The Marx Engels reader*. (2nd ed.). New York: Norton.

Momeni, D. A. (1976). Husband-wife age differentials in Shiraz, Iran. *Social Biology, 23* (4), 341-348.

Patel-Gira, V. (1974). A study of marital happiness in Hindu Gujrati women. *Indian Journal of Psychiatric Social Work, 3*, 37-40.

Presser, H. B. (1975). Age differences between spouses: Trends, patterns and social implications. *American Behavioral Scientist, 19* (2), 190-205.

Sigall, H. & Landy, D. (1973). Effects of having a physically attractive partner on person perception. *Journal of Personality and Social Psychology, 28* (2), 218-224.

Symons, D. (1979). *The evolution of human sexuality*. New York: Oxford University Press.

Walster, E., Walster, G. W. & Berscheid, E. (1978). *Equity: Theory and research*. Boston: Allyn & Bacon.

Weinberg, M. S. (1970). The male homosexual: Age-related variations in social and psychological characteristics. *Social Problems, 17* (4), 527-537.

The Impact of Age
on Paid Sexual Encounters

Livy Anthony Visano, PhD

York University, Toronto

Age, I do abhor thee
Youth, I do adore thee

—William Shakespeare, *The Passionate Pilgrim xii*

As in many other contexts of modern society, aging appears to be a liability in the illicit business of hustling sex. Even though hustling emphasizes fleeting, emotionally-detached and mercenary exchanges, these sexual encounters are far from indiscriminate. The value placed on youthfulness conditions the selection of partners, fees, and performances.

The literature on male prostitution, from empirical inquiries (Butts, 1947; Jersild, 1956; Ross, 1959; Reiss, 1961; Ginsburg, 1967; Drew & Drake, 1969; Harris, 1973; Coombs, 1974; Lloyd, 1977; Hoffman, 1979; Linedecker, 1981; Jackson, 1983; Benjamin, 1985; Luckenbill, 1986) to more popular novels (Andros, 1969, 1982; Rechy, 1977; Aldyne, 1980; Hamilton, 1981; Levy, 1982; Phillips, 1982; Mackay, 1985), pays considerable attention to the views of hustlers. Interestingly, the other side of this cash-for-sex relationship, the clientele, is simply depicted as a mass of undifferentiated "old trolls" or overlooked altogether. In an effort to partially fill this gap and thus provide a more balanced account, this paper explores hustler-client relations. Specifically, this research answers the question: How much role distance and/or commitment do these participants maintain? In advancing this issue, this paper demonstrates that the maintenance of neutrality is highly problematic. Age, it will be argued,

Livy Anthony Visano, is Assistant Professor, York University, Toronto, Ontario, Canada. The author is indebted to Joseph Harry and Stephen Murray for their generous and insightful comments. A special note of gratitude is extended to Wally Hopkins for collecting data on American hustlers and clients.

influences the negotiation of these roles. Lastly, the difficulties encountered by older participants are analyzed in terms of wider issues—the reproduction of cultural values in the glorification of youthful bodies.

This study deals with a limited form of prostitution—street hustling, which is different from escort/call, photography, bar, "kept," or party services (Ross, 1959; Pittman, 1971; Simpson et al., 1976; Mandate, 1977; Luckenbill, 1986). According to early accounts, notably by Butts (1947), Jersild (1956), and Reiss (1961), hustling is presented as an occasional activity of lower-class, delinquent peer groupings of heterosexual boys. This finding, however, has been contradicted by more recent evidence which documents the participation of both heterosexual and homosexual boys, the absence of gang formations and the diverse socio-economic backgrounds of hustlers (Harris, 1973; Lloyd, 1977; Hoffman, 1979; Linedecker, 1981; Johnson, 1983; Visano, 1987). The disavowal of homosexuality, so rampant in early approaches, is understandable given the general antipathy towards homosexuality among officials and apprehended youths within the juvenile justice system during the 1950s and early 1960s. These early studies were solely conducted on captive hustlers—those who were officially processed by the police, psychiatrists, and social workers.

The clients in this study are far from representative of gays or even older gays. They are gay and straight men who prefer boys and who, for a variety of reasons, find them unavailable. Clearly, not all homosexual men want younger partners, especially teenage hustlers (Harry, 1982a).

METHOD

This article is part of a larger ongoing longitudinal project designed to investigate the variety of relations that hustlers develop with socializing agencies. In the course of transforming their identities, hustlers are involved with street peers, clients, police officers, social workers, families, and other social networks located in the wider community. This current study on hustler-client relations incorporates a multi-method design of informal interviews, observations of street corner transactions and structured diaries. We adopted a flexible "theoretical sampling" scheme (Glaser & Strauss, 1967) that was well-suited and convenient. The sample was collected primarily by a "snowball" technique that generated leads to well-informed contacts. Independent introductions were also made by going directly to the natural setting. My research assistant conducted systematic observations and interviews in the following cities: Honolulu (August-September, 1986), Tampa, Miami, and Atlanta (April-August,

1986), and Portland (June-November, 1984). I collected data in Vancouver (June, 1984), Montreal (September, 1985), and Toronto (February-August, 1986).

The sample consisted of 120 hustlers—93 gay and 27 straight young men. Forty-eight hustlers were over 22 years of age (older hustlers) and 72 boys were 22 years old or younger (younger hustlers). The gay-identified cohort included 49 younger and 44 older hustlers. The straight group, however, was comprised of 23 younger and only four older hustlers. Sixty clients were interviewed, 40 men were over 40 years of age while 20 men were 40 years old or younger. Thirty-five percent of all clients identified themselves as gay. Parenthetically, both hustlers and clients routinely employ the above age-specific distinctions. Irrespective of the validity of their claims regarding youthfulness, these younger/older characterizations were consistently invoked as an objective reference. What hustlers and clients say, imagine or believe regarding age, however distorted, is very integral to the way they relate to each other. Lastly, interviews were also conducted with 30 key informants drawn from gay support groups.

THE STREET CULTURE: IMAGES OF YOUTHFULNESS

Hustling exists within a youth-oriented street culture. And yet, the influence of this culture has been overlooked in studies of hustlers. As a result of repeated interactions, newcomers learn from their more seasoned street colleagues how to "take the edge," that is, to maximize gain with a minimum of effort. In fact, 66 percent of hustlers indicated that they enjoyed the congenial company of fellow hustlers with whom they shared accommodation and leisure activities. The remainder socialized with others who were not "in the trade"—family, friends, or lovers. The former group of hustlers developed a loyalty to those boys from whom they learned values and techniques.

The street culture, replete with myths, provides a general frame of reference which is used to justify hustling. This framework is a source of direction with prescribed roles and expectations which guide client relations and activities. Moreover, the subterranean values of the street culture act as a defense mechanism which protects hustlers from the negative attitudes of outsiders toward them.

A central element of the street culture concerns the youthfulness of participants. According to 75 percent of hustlers, the street culture devalues older hustlers and older clients. Discrimination is evident in two dominant street images—the physical body and the game orientation to hustling.

First, age for these boys is synonymous with the conditions of the physical body. Commercial sexuality reformulates the physical body into an item of exchange. Consequently, the body is dressed, stylized, flaunted and objectified. An obsession with bodies is apparent in the manner in which boys display themselves—tight-fitting jeans, open shirts, rolled-up sleeves, tattoos adorning their muscles, to name only a few. By flashing a fresh and vivacious body, hustlers render older bodies sexually and physically less attractive. Within the economy of hustling and the culture of the street, the body is transformed into a source of income and a provider of valued goods, such as drugs.

Besides bodily images, youthfulness is also projected in general attitudes toward play. A game perspective is articulated by younger members on the street. According to 80 percent of the hustlers, the "wild parties," the psychic lure of the "fast lanes" and the use of cocaine, acid, or marijuana reflect youthful pursuits. Images of play predominate in various street adventures. Peter, a 17-year-old hustler typified the sentiments of a majority of younger boys:

> Hey, I'm young—I ain't dead. I wanna live—enjoy life. A piece of the fast action. I'm only young for now. Fun city, man. Let the older jerks get jealous! My body can take this scene. I don't, like, wanna be old.

These streetwise thrill seekers perceive themselves as living expressions of an exciting street culture.

An excessive preoccupation with youthfulness sets limits on the expectations of older clients and older hustlers. As boys lose their youthfulness, it becomes increasingly difficult for them to compete with scores of younger and more attractive newcomers. Likewise, older clients experience rejection despite their willingness to pay for sexual favors.

On the street, aging signifies a reduced level of participation in the pleasures of the body. Youthfulness validates sexual prowess. For example, hustlers view older boys as "losers," that is, as less successful because they restrict themselves to older and less desirable clients. Ninety percent of hustlers believed that older clients and older prostitutes relate to each other by default, due to their failure to attract more favorable sex partners. Serving an older clientele symbolizes failure, desperation and an overall attenuation of street bonds. But, aging is a master status only insofar as it becomes part of one's self-image. Nevertheless, even a youthful self-image does not protect older hustlers from rejection by clients.

Younger Gay Hustlers

Younger gay hustlers are tough-minded opportunists who extol street culture virtues. Moreover, hustling represents a vocation laden with occupational perspectives and skills. This enterprise requires them to develop innovative techniques in selecting work sites, securing a steady flow of clients, managing private encounters, and delivering a wide array of sexual services. These boys package themselves as attractive commodities with inviting body language — a grin, prolonged eye contact, and clothing which emphasizes youthful physical appearance. Also, they protect their marketable assets — their bodies, by safeguarding against sexually transmitted diseases. Eighty-two percent of gay hustlers reported using condoms while 86 percent of them refused to perform certain sex acts, ranging from "fisting" to more rough S/M games.

Younger gay hustlers are more selective in the choice of sexual partners. Richard, a 20-year-old hustler, justified his refusal of older clients:

> I'm a real looker — the best. Young and a beauty. I need to protect my trade. If I go with the older guys, I'll get a bad reputation. If you're a good looking stud, you want to go with the best. You don't go for losers.

A preference for younger clients signifies an emotional overinvolvement with the trade. This disclosure, however, runs contrary to the norm of neutrality. Emotional attachment jeopardizes a boy's chances of maximizing financial gain. As Larry, a 19-year-old hustler elaborated:

> These witches are lucky we even talk to them. They give us a hard time — yeah, they really do. So the money ain't as good! It's still better to get it on with a cuter dish. But I'm not gonna say this to my pals. I'm here, like I said, to make some fast bucks with the nicer shit out here.

Jody, a 17-year-old boy who was described by two more seasoned hustlers as the "best kid on the track," explained the difficulties of professional detachment:

> Like, if you're a good hustler you shouldn't stick it only to some stiffs. Fuck, you'll starve, if you give it to the younger folks only. The bread is shit. But you know, it feels good!

Gay-identified younger hustlers actively participate in the gay community. They avail themselves of numerous facilities and activities. Moreover, 79 percent of these hustlers lived with their lovers, many of whom were other hustlers. Unlike other studies (Pittman, 1971; Winslow & Winslow, 1974), our data suggest that these boys are not stigmatized by the gay community. Rather, a highly responsive community exists which is prepared to assist hustlers disengage from this illicit pursuit. According to 12 gay counselors, these hustlers experience considerable problems in approaching agencies that operate within a more heterosexual mandate. Similarly, hustlers reported that traditional youth-serving agencies fail to provide the support necessary for a successful withdrawal from hustling.

Younger gay hustlers occupy distinct territories—congenial work sites in close proximity to bars and baths. As a result of their geographic location and limited involvements in other illicit street activities, they rarely associate with straight hustlers. During our field observations, several straight hustlers wandered into "turfs" occupied by gay hustlers. Although the exchanges were trivial, such as requests for cigarettes, relations between these hustlers were overshadowed by feelings of distrust.

Several striking differences exist between younger American and Canadian hustlers. The presentational style and client preferences of these hustlers vary considerably. Canadian hustlers adopt a street argot that is widely used by their female counterparts on the street. They are inclined to use pejorative terms like "scores," "tricks," or "johns" more often than American boys who depict clients as "dates," "engagements," or "appointments." Also, there appears to be a larger number of effeminate hustlers in Canadian cities. These boys, attired in tights, slippers, and bright colors often employed terms of endearment such as "honey," "sweetie," or "dearie," in their exchanges with clients. And yet, these same Canadian hustlers projected a more dour demeanor. American hustlers, on the other hand, were inclined to be more friendly and civil toward clients. They engaged in considerable banter while negotiating prices and activities. Clients and hustlers were asked to comment on these differences. According to Eugene, a well-traveled 52-year-old client:

> These kids [in Toronto] would starve in the States. They're too mean-looking. Sure, they cover it up. Even the queens are tough. Too hungry out here. A lot of punks.

Louis, a 61-year-old client, further asserted:

> The laws are a bitch here. The kid in Vancouver compared to Seattle works harder. No nonsense. Cops are on their tail a hell of a lot. It's more relaxed in Seattle.

Similarly, Alexander, a 21-year-old hustler who has worked in Los Angeles and Toronto, added:

> The hookers in L.A. don't look like poor slobs. In Toronto you can spot a hustler. They look like a bunch of bums. No class!

Joseph, a 20-year-old hustler in Tampa, remarked:

> A lot depends on the gay scene. The bigger the scene the more you see a lot of different fucking screwballs. From queens to leather. Like, if it's more big you get all kinds. That's it.

Although younger hustlers discriminate in favor of younger clients, the pool of younger clients is relatively small. Choices are limited in many cases. In general, the data suggest that Canadian hustlers discriminate less than their American counterparts.

Repeat patronage is the foundation of successful commercial enterprises. Relations with regular clients are more predictable, manageable, and rewarding financially. In fleeting encounters with anonymous clients, younger gay hustlers frequently "pass as straights" in order to keep their rates high. Lester, a 49-year-old client, declared:

> Sex with a hunk costs more. A really masculine — a butch, a real looker is expensive. They charge more. Greater demand for them.

Hank, a 19-year-old hustler, concurred:

> The queen is a cheap fart. But I can pull more bread if I hide it. I can double the score like when I go tough. I go straight with the closet and get a lot of bread.

Older Gay Hustlers

Older hustlers are less committed to prevailing street values. Despite their skills, seasoned boys lose the youthful energy, spontaneity, and naive sensuality that once characterized their appeal. Typically, a hustler has three years on the street before nature begins to affect his earning capacity. The longer one weathers the street life as a hustler, the greater the likelihood that one's youthfulness will quickly disappear. Years on the street, drug use, long hours on street corners, poor nutritional habits, inadequate sleep, heavy cigarette smoking, anxieties concerning subsistence, and the affliction of sexually transmitted diseases exact a price on the physical well-being and attractiveness of a hustler.

As age and steady work take their toll, boys gradually end up offering services to the most difficult and undesirable clients, or with no clients at all. Their productivity and wages are reduced drastically as clients discard them for younger boys.

Older hustlers, that is men 22 years or over, respond to the pressures of competition by adopting a number of tactics. First, older boys learn to adjust their appearances. They manipulate their demeanor—clothing, hair, and language in a manner that invites more favorable assessments by clients. They "hang out" with newcomers to whom they fabricate stories about their vigor and continued accomplishments. Fifty-nine percent of older gay hustlers became supportive "father figures" or "big brothers" to the younger and more impressionable hustlers. In turn, the latter shared the proceeds of their business with older boys.

Older hustlers fail to be noticed by clients, let alone secure their business. Consequently, they feel compelled to adopt a more persistent and strident form of solicitation. Eighty-four percent of older hustlers claimed that once a deal was struck, they were extremely accommodating. They offered a "serve-yourself approach" wherein a wide variety of intimate sexual services was offered. Unlike younger hustlers, they would grant "extras," charge less money and permit their clients to pay on credit. Older hustlers were also more tolerant of their clients' misconduct. All of these concessions were designed to encourage repeat encounters.

Along with the above age-specific distinctions which hustlers construct, there are striking differences among hustlers which are attributable to their sexual orientation. Boys who are defiantly straight resort to violence whereas gay-identified hustlers strive to maintain a more professional level of involvement with clients.

Rough Trade

For "rough trade," hustling sex is simply an instance of street survival. This temporary means of making quick cash is a substitute for other delinquent activities—dealing in drugs, stolen merchandise, or stealing. These boys internalize the values of the street to a dangerous extreme.

The "peers" of Reiss's (1961) study have not disappeared. They continue to hustle in smaller numbers. Interestingly, 23 percent of hustlers not only identified themselves as straight but also belonged to close-knit homophobic reference groups. These boys frequently work together and offer a group service. This group service heightens the vulnerability of clients (Harry, 1982b). According to 66 percent of these boys, "queer bashing" is a celebrated form of entertainment. These boys attempt to secure their client's money without engaging in sex. When they work as a team, one boy usually flirts with a client while his colleagues steal the client's possessions. By skillfully appraising their client's weaknesses, these boys lure an unsuspecting client into a quiet alley, park, or abandoned building and proceed to beat and rob him either after or instead of sex. Eighty-five percent of these boys proudly admitted that they assaulted or threatened older clients in order to rob them of their possessions — jewelry and wallets. Images of violence prevail in their recollections of past accomplishments. As Jerry, a 16-year-old, disclosed:

> You see, like shit, these old stiffs are good. 'Cause they're old, you can throw the boots at 'em. Make 'em scared. Stupid bitches trying to pick kids up.

Violence against older clients, however, may simply be a focused expression of their homophobic sentiments.

Straight hustlers perform very limited sex acts. By assuming an insertor role — using clients as female substitutes — they claim that their masculinity remains intact. According to this logic, they also bully their clients to prove their straight identity. Their reputation as violent hustlers is of little consequence to them for several reasons.

First, they refuse to deliver sexual services on a regular basis to a steady clientele. Repeated encounters with the same client undermine their heterosexuality. Second, violence reaffirms their authority over clients as well as ownership of their bodies. Violence against clients demonstrates their membership in tough peer groupings. But, 74 percent of these boys argued that they were only interested in the immediate material rewards of hustling. Why then should this group of hustlers be concerned with the client's age? Older clients are less likely to be violent and less likely to be undercover police officers. Moreover, they can be easily persuaded to pay higher prices due to their vulnerability. Clearly, rough trade exists "in" the world of street prostitution but is not "of" it. For these boys, the benefits derived from violence exceed the rewards attendant with hustling sex. As prostitutes they are irrational, but as opportunistic street survivors they seize upon any situation that offers them a "fast buck." Hustling sex is simply one of many short-term "con" games they routinely pursue. Other "scams" include panhandling, welfare fraud, shoplifting, drug dealing, and mugging. More importantly, these boys are grossly homophobic. They adamantly refuse to identify themselves as prostitutes — a designation they pejoratively attach to homosexual boys on the street. Last, they perform for the benefit of their street peers who expect this disparaging treatment of clients.

Furthermore, passing as straight is not surprising given the heterosexual emphasis of these youthful peer groups. In contrast to Reiss's (1961) findings, it is argued that heterosexuality, not homosexuality, is a situational contingency. Admission of homosexuality is delayed until more supportive structures have been discovered. In interactions with their peers, these boys project straight self-conceptions. Similarly, in encounters with the police they pass as straight in order to be treated more leniently as exploited or victimized youths. Tom, a 22-year-old hustler, admitted that he posed as a straight hustler for two years. He did so not necessarily because he was insecure about his sexual orientation but because a failure to embrace heterosexuality would have led to violent confrontations with some of his more seasoned straight street buddies.

Clients

Clients and hustlers are not committed to similar role expectations. According to all hustlers and 71 percent of clients, older clients are extremely vulnerable. They are subjected to considerable psychological, emotional, or physical abuse. Hustlers acknowledged that this discriminatory treatment is not only legitimate in the street culture but it also remains societally endorsed. That is, they believed that these potential "targets" are not well protected in the wider community. They are perceived as double failures. On the one hand, older clients are at a disadvantage in the gay community. Admittedly, there are a number of support networks which assist older gays to participate more meaningfully in the community. But, older men seeking more fleeting sexual relations with younger men or boys routinely face rejection in bars. Donald, a 66-year-old client, commented:

> Sure, a lot of older men aren't cruising. They found peace with guys their own age. Well, I don't. Should I be thrown out? The bar scene is noise – too many games. I'm not appreciated, I know that. What else is there? Listen, I wouldn't be paying for it if I could find it for free.

On the other hand, older clients are considered marginal to the street scene. With the exception of more regular clients, older men are generally viewed by hustlers as docile bodies that can be easily manipulated. Witness, for example, the derogatory remarks made by Michael, a 20-year-old hustler:

The old bitch was really ugly. At least 50, or 60 years old. A real bastard. Weak and disgusting. I really can do what I want with these older guys 'cause nobody cares. If he complains, I'll ruin him, that's all!

A general contempt for older clients was expressed by 69 percent of hustlers. Although the physical activities requested by older clients are less demanding, these relations are also threatening emotionally. Stephen, a 19-year-old hustler, argued:

Man, it's scary. All the bread in the world ain't worth it. Old faggots will give you anything. That's scary. They're too nice.

Likewise, Carmen, a 57-year-old client, elucidated:

They hate us. I know—I had a lot of boys. They're dangerous if we get too close. Too intimate. We talk, shower them with gifts—you name it. Not always for sex. That frightens them.

Interestingly, older clients also debase themselves by assuming a degree of blame. Feelings of shame contribute to their own pacification (Ryan, 1971). Rather than risk further rejections at bars (Lee, 1978; p. 264), older clients seek sexual refuge among hustlers. George, a 49-year-old client, provided an insightful assessment of this problem:

Our colossal mistake is to fall into a trap we created. We look for younger studs—but we know they don't care for us. It's the bar scene all over. But, get this—we think that money can buy any sex. We do to others what others are doing to us—looking for boy wonder.

Clients delude themselves into thinking that their money will reduce, if not eliminate negative stereotypes. Although they feel rejected, older clients claim that they can "work it out" with younger hustlers. Money for them becomes emancipatory; liberating them from discredit. Graham, a 60-year-old client, affirmed this perspective:

These guys are hookers and hypocrites. They're supposed to do it for money. I'm a shopper—so for my money—a lot of money, I buy the best. My money should buy the best. I'm not like the others—I pay.

But, clients quickly discover that when they fail to provide greater financial rewards, they will once again be rejected. Rather than resist stigma, older clients tend to be more accommodating. Instead of challenging these negative evaluations 87 percent of older clients simply resorted to "paying more for less." Although they felt uneasy with the taunts and insults hurled at them, they remained passive, and at times deferential to these young hustlers. Jordan, a 52 year-old client, trivialized these criticisms:

> Why should I get upset? Let these kids — some delicious-looking ones, make fun of me. So what? As long as the boy delivers the goods, it doesn't hurt. They're not all that important to me. Besides, we get what we deserve.

Resistance is difficult for clients who fear public disclosure, police reporting and physical threats. Maurice, a 42-year-old client, added:

> As long as we're afraid to go to the cops or even come out, we'll always give in. Can't blame the kids for taking advantage. So taking this shit from these kids is nothing compared to losing your wife or job.

Paradoxically, accommodation simply invites more offensive treatment or rejection. Whenever younger prostitutes suspect that their clients feel vulnerable, they inflate fees, perform fewer services, or worst of all, bait them. Despite their disregard for older clients, younger hustlers enjoy the ease with which they can secure a successful "pick-up" of these prospective clients.

Younger clients that is, men under 40, are less tolerant of trivial exchanges. They direct their initial remarks to the immediate concerns of fees and services. On the other hand, older clients are inclined to engage in more idle talk. Also, given the premium placed on youthfulness, younger hustlers can easily pick up older clients without staging a number of rituals designed to promote their bodies. Less manipulation of appearance, speech or gestures is required. Nonetheless, 47 percent of younger gay hustlers deliberately flaunted their bodies to older clients on street corners. These demonstrations were not intended to secure a pick-up but rather to clearly indicate to their clients that they were fortunate in connecting with such a highly valued youthful body.

Once encounters move away from the more public street corner locations into more private settings, the content of these interactions changes. In these latter sites, hustler-client relations are replete with insecurity and concerns for personal safety. In these private settings hustlers attempt to establish control over their clients. They maintain a position of power by arrogating an exaggerated sense of sexual prowess. Armed with this expertise, they take charge by imposing their preferences and by directing the tempo of sex acts. This control minimizes the danger of being exploited by clients who refuse to pay and threaten to use violence. Also, control serves to reduce any ambiguity about the roles established by hustlers. In addition to direct commands, hustlers rely on more persuasive techniques. Hustlers routinely play on their charms and "stroke" clients into submission. By flattering their masculinity and performance, these boys hope to be rewarded. Younger boys will also concoct ingenious stories of hardships on the street in order to elicit favorable responses from their clients. Fifty percent of the boys indicated that they fabricated information about themselves to encourage client disclosures. In turn, older clients talked about their responsible jobs, heterosexual marriages and other more private topics, which if publicly revealed would court tragic consequences. Clients fail to realize that hustlers are not reluctant to use this disclosure to victimize them should encounters become more problematic. As Foucault (1977, 1980) argues, a 'confessional" examination is more effective than physical punishment in achieving power and discipline. Once hustlers strip clients of their anonymity, they are able to ensure a greater degree of compliance. In addition to creating dependency relations, client self-disclosures are more dangerous because of the principle of least interest — the hustler has less to lose from the indiscretion by a client than the client. A departure from the obligations of the hustler role may even give the client, who can deny having had to pay trade, leverage. Conversations take time away from the sex act. Young hustlers use street jargon to manipulate relations with older clients. This foreign argot compels clients to seek clarification from these boys. In responding to their clients' curiosities, boys impose their definitions. Conversation also gives hustlers more time to assess the relative strengths and wealth of their prospective client.

The regulation of any behavior is difficult without some threats of sanctions. Should persuasive techniques prove to be ineffective, threats become a primary means of restoring order. The most common tactic used by hustlers to control recalcitrant older clients includes verbal intimidation designed to embarrass and create fear. As Frank, an 18-year-old prostitute, admitted:

> I told this old fool who was fresh that I bashed a lot of heads. Just to let the idiot know that I'd do it again. If that doesn't work — time to rip him off.

The low visibility of these encounters enables hustlers to use threats of physical violence. Although all hustlers candidly expressed a willingness to use force, only 20 percent of them admitted that they applied force to secure compliance. Interestingly, all of these boys belonged to the "rough trade" designation. Gay hustlers, on the other hand reported that admonitions suffice. However, 40 percent of the gay hustlers believed that reprimands affirm adversarial roles which, in turn, enhance emotional detachment. Carl, a 46-year-old client, eloquently discussed these double standards:

> There is no safe sex for older johns. Street hustlers expect them to be more polite while putting them down. I regret going to a hustler. It's downright humiliating. It's difficult to explain. We think because we pay for it, we should be treated with respect. Not quite! Instead, these kids are out to screw us. Why should I be made to feel helpless or even stupid?

Interviews with clients and hustlers further illustrate differences in age-specific profiles of clients. According to rough estimates elicited from hustlers in Tampa, Montreal, and Portland, 80 percent of their clients were over 40; 10 percent of clients were under 40 and another 10 percent were simply categorized as "ugly" regardless of their age. In Honolulu, Vancouver, and Atlanta, boys estimated that only 40 percent of clients were over 40; 40 percent fell in the under 40 years old group, and the remaining 20 percent constituted the undifferentiated age category of undesirable ugly clients. In Toronto and Miami, hustlers noted that 70 percent of their clients were over 40 years of age, 10 percent were under 40 and another 20 percent belonged to the more devalued classification of "ugly" clients. An overwhelmingly large number of clients (86%) felt that the above projections understated the size of the "over-40 years old" category of clients. Rather, they suggested that 95 to 100 percent of all clients fall within this age category.

Furthermore, general client comparisons reveal that, unlike their American counterparts, Canadian clients are more cautious, timid and deferential toward hustlers. Jacques, a 38-year-old client, explained:

> Sure I'm active in the gay life in Quebec—I live it. But on the street I have to be careful. I don't know who I'm dealing with. Watch the police and of course the crazy kids. In Montreal you got all types. It's not safe when you got religious nuts running the city. The police, for sure, always watch too. It's not safe—no way!

Commenting on the discrepant operating styles of clients, John remarked:

I ain't no closet. Why give a shit. In this city [Portland] hustlers know what you want. You go to their hangouts. I'm blunt with them. When I think of Canada — it's the British thing. More uptight people. More right-wing. Probably more bashers and more cops. It'll change.

Last, hustlers develop categories of older clients. These typologies facilitate the maintenance of order since hustlers use them as predictable clues from which quick inferences about older clients can be drawn. In general, hustlers classify older clients in terms of gay/straight distinctions. Clients are further subdivided according to age and levels of cooperation.

Straight Clients

In general, hustlers classify straight clients according to the following categories: the indecisive, or "circle jerk"; the unfriendly, or "gas queen"; the careless, or "lonely old man;" and the inexperienced, or "tourists."

The indecisive or "circle jerk" group consists of older clients who regularly patrol the tenderloin districts. They derive sexual pleasures from watching young hustlers at a distance. Once they muster sufficient courage to pick up a hustler, they become extremely indecisive about services and fees. They require considerable persuasion in negotiating a deal. According to hustlers, these clients chat excessively, demand too much attention, and frequently refuse to strike a bargain. Whenever deals are struck, they question the benefits received, criticize the hustler's performance and often request a refund or discount. They challenge a basic feature of hustling — the exchange of money. Moreover, the haggling which characterizes these situations invites other passersby to take notice. These clients, therefore, jeopardize the initial pick-ups by rendering them more public and presumably more visible to the police.

The unfriendly or "gas queens" include impudent single, unattractive, middle-aged, and lonely clients. According to hustlers, these men demand "fast action." They disregard rules concerning the superior roles assumed by hustlers. Given their numerous experience with hustlers, their positions of wealth or prestige in the wider community, and their levels of education, they insist on imposing their definitions of appropriate sexual activities. Hustlers view them as incorrigible, unreliable and arrogant, thereby worthy of verbal abuse.

The careless or "lonely old men" designation refers to the married, cooperative, and considerably older clients who are equally insensitive to the "trade." They disrupt the business by allowing themselves to become emotionally attached to the sex act. Essentially, these clients are looking for lovers. They require repeated reprimands regarding the inappropriateness of their passionate outbursts. Despite such demonstrative gestures as intimate fondling, caressing, or embracing and endearing flirtation, these clients are not depicted as odiously as the "circle jerks" or "gas queens." Hustlers simply dismiss their advances as careless and stupid. Intimate physical contact is often managed and manipulated for further financial gain.

Clients defined as too friendly, or "sugar daddies," also seek more loving relationships and equally challenge the norms of emotional detachment. Although hustlers publicly discredit these clients, they welcome their companionship. Hustlers view them as fertile sources of emotional and material support. They associate with these men off the street and outside of their working hours. But, on the street and in the company of their street peers, hustlers ridicule and embarrass them.

"Tourist" is a designation used primarily by hustlers in Honolulu. These groups include a broad cross-section of wealthy teenagers, first-time pleasure seekers, and young military personnel. Although they are financially secure, they end up paying less for services delivered primarily because hustlers prefer them to all other straight clients.

Gay Clients

Detachment is highly problematic for hustlers serving younger gay clients. Role conflict emerges whenever hustlers become embedded in more affectively-oriented ties. Within these contexts hustlers demonstrate a sensitivity to the evaluation of their clients. By affirming a more mature gay consciousness, younger gay clients assist hustlers in restructuring their self-conceptions. These relations, however, pose problems for hustlers especially since these roles are less predatory and mercenary.

Hustlers prefer younger gay clients for a number of reasons. First, hustlers consider them more interesting, attractive, and well-experienced on and off the street. Second, these clients act both as mentors in tutoring boys in innovative sexual practices, and as sponsors in introducing them to contacts beyond the limited confines of the workplace. In turn, hustlers not only spend more time with them but also grant them more "extras" at reduced rates. Lorne, a 19-year-old hustler, minimized the importance of financial rewards in these exchanges:

> The younger date is all right. You know—kinkier sex. Money's no big deal. We do dope, booze, fool around a lot. When I get in on— it's not work for me. It's fun with them.

Likewise, Dan—a 32-year-old client, explained:

> I'll pick a kid up. Rap for awhile. Talk him out of charging. Show him a new life outside of the stinkin' street. He doesn't hustle me. We turn each other on. No money. Just great sex.

According to estimates provided by hustlers and clients alike, younger gay clients represent a small fraction of the total client population; that is, from one to five percent of all clients. In this study contact was made with only two younger clients, or 3.3 percent of our client sample.

Older gay clients, however, constituted 32 percent of our client sample. More than any other client group, older gays conformed to the norms of hustling in a disciplined and cooperative manner. Like their younger counterparts, but unlike older closeted and/or straight clients, they introduced hustlers to a variety of people from whom boys received emotional and material assistance in securing employment, skills development and education. In fact, 18 percent of hustlers reported a close rapport with these men, especially with the more wealthy and well-connected benefactors. But, 82 percent of hustlers resented older clients who encouraged the pursuit of alternative lifestyles; they rejected the stabilizing influences of these well-intentioned clients. Twenty-six percent of these clients believed that hustlers were lower-class losers who need some form of positive direction.

Unlike other client category groupings, older gay clients paid hustlers to accompany them to bars or parties. Thirty-seven percent of older gay clients used hustlers as "show-pieces" to demonstrate their ability to attract younger companions. Moreover, two hustlers indicated that they were "kept" by older men who tried to "tame" them. An overwhelming 74 percent of older gay clients were "regulars," that is, clients in good standing who were offered greater concessions. In general, hustlers view gay clients as more competent interactionally than their closeted counterparts.

No Safe Refuge: Aging as a Cultural Constraint

The idealized world of hustling clashes sharply with the realities of discrimination. The behavior of hustlers contradict the objective values inherent in hustling—universal and emotionally-detached sexual relations. In a painstaking process, older clients and older hustlers realize that the value placed on youthfulness contributes to their segregation and alienation.

Older participants are unable to influence market conditions, the flow of younger clients and hustlers, and cultural stereotypes. Despite their numerous adjustments, older interactants were unable to secure satisfactory sexual engagements. Ageism mars the contours of hustling.

The value placed on youthfulness contributes to an impoverishment of self-concepts. Thirty clients admitted that they selected hustling as a solution to the difficulties they encountered in bars. Consequently, they enlisted the support of hustlers who would ratify a renewed sexual identity. Instead of finding a liberating, safe, and accepting refuge, they experienced further rejection. They could not buy sex, at any price! But, rather than restructure their self-identities, they conceded to the negative attitudes held by hustlers. Instead of discovering companions off the street, older clients desperately sought to transform their relations with hustlers by developing sentimental ties. But as long as they paid for companionship, they felt that their choices remained relatively open. Unlike older clients, older hustlers turned to the outside community. As they participated more fully in the general life of the gay community, informal relations opened up which were supportive of disengagement from prostitution. Drop-in centers, counselors, and the "gay scene" in general provided them with meaningful bonds wherein sexual, material, and emotional needs were met. Older clients intermittently drifted back into bars and baths only to experience further rejection. As they withdrew from these settings they continued to explore what money can buy on the street.

The dominant culture celebrates youthful bodies. Larger societal values legitimate the promotion of youthful sex icons (Fontana, 1984). A youth-oriented culture pervades all social relations. Myths flourish about despondent older gays (Berger, 1981; Harry & Devall, 1981; Alhonte, 1981). Age is a cultural marker which degrades older persons as pathetic sexual actors (Clifford, 1961; Cory & Le Roy, 1963; Teal, 1971; Kelly, 1979; McPhersen, 1983). These stereotypes penetrate the world of prostitution. In fact, prostitution reproduces as well as reinforces ageism. The imposing character of culture is apparent in the discriminatory attitudes of both hustlers and clients which prize youthfulness. Specifically, 80 percent of all hustlers wanted younger clients while 85 percent of clients preferred younger hustlers. Interestingly, older clients, the most discriminated group was also extremely discriminating. Money alone does not necessarily attract a body as a sexual object. For older clients, money does not qualify them to rent any sexual object. For older hustlers, their bodies cannot be rented even at lower rates.

CONCLUSION

Hustling is a cultural reproduction. Hustling subordinates rather than liberates sexual expressions. Positive sexual self-identities for older men are difficult to attain within a culture that sanctions appropriate age-specific behavior. As Murray (1984, p. 12) advises, the cultural sexual script warrants re-examination. Culture enhances ageism, a form of elder abuse.

This paper sheds light on the attempts of hustlers and clients to structure relations on the basis of age. As with the taboo of childhood sexuality, the myths that older persons are unattractive, asexual, lonely, and incompetent require further analysis. Older client-younger hustler encounters are also at odds with deeply rooted societal values which condemn man-boy relations. Discrimination is not only situated in the context of hustling. Rather, this ageism is derivative of wider cultural influences which loom large in these invisible encounters. In addition to youthfulness, the valuation of heterosexuality is reproduced by closeted and/or straight clients and hustlers who claim to be operating within a physically and emotionally "untouchable" framework—a lingering homophobia.

REFERENCES

Aldyne, N. (1980). *Vermilion*. New York: Avon.

Alhonte, M. (1981). Confronting ageism. In D. Tsang (Ed.), *The Age Taboo*. Boston: Alyson.

Andros, P. (1969). *Stud*. Boston: Alyson.

Andros, P. (1982). *Below the belt and other stories*. San Francisco: Perineum.

Benjamin, M. (1985). *Juvenile prostitution: A portrait of the life*. Toronto: Ministry of Community and Social Services.

Berger, R. (1981). *Gay and gray*. Urbana: University of Illinois.

Butts, W. (1947 April). Boy prostitutes of the metropolis. *Journal of Clinical Psychopathology* 8 (6): 673-681.

Clifford, A. (1961). The aging homosexual. In I. Rubin (Ed.), *Third Sex*. New York: New Book.

Coombs, N. (1974). Psychosocial view of behavior. *American Journal of Orthopsychiatry* 44(5): 782-789.

Cory, D. & J. Le Roy. (1963). *The homosexual and his society: A view from within*. New York: Citadel.

Drew, D. & Drake, J. (1969). *Boys for sale*. New York: Brown.

Fontana, A. (1984). The stigma of growing old: Or Ponce de Leon is alive and well and lives in leisure haven, USA. In J. Douglas (Ed.), *Sociology of Deviance*. Boston: Allyn and Bacon.

Foucault, M. (1977). *Discipline and punish*. New York: Vintage.

Foucault, M. (1980). *History of sexuality*. New York: Vintage.

Ginsburg, K. (1967). The meat rack: A study of male homosexual prostitutes. *American Journal of Psychotherapy* 21(2): 170-185.

Glaser, B. & A. Strauss. (1967). *The discovery of grounded theory*. Chicago: Aldine.

Hamilton, W. (1981). *Kevin*. New York: Signet.

Harris, M. (1973). *The dilly boys*. London: Groom Helm.

Harry, J. (1982a). *Gay children grown up*. New York: Praeger.

Harry, J. (1982b). Derivative deviance: The cases of fag-bashing, blackmail, and shakedown of gay men. *Criminology* 19: 546-64.

Harry, J. & W. Devall. (1978). Age and sexual culture among gay males. *Archives of Sexual Behaviour* 7: 199-208.

Hoffman, M. (1979). The male prostitute. In M. Levine (Ed.), *Gay men: The sociology of male homosexuality*. New York: Harper and Row.

Jackson, E. (1981 December). Street kids: Nobody's priority. *Body Politic* : 7.

Jersild, J. (1956). *Boy prostitution*. Copenhagen: G.E.C. Gad.

Johnson, E. (1983). *In search of God in the sexual underworld*. New York: Quill.

Kelly, J. (1979). The aging male homosexual: Myth and reality. In M. Levine (Ed.), *Gay Men: The Sociology of Male Homosexuality*, New York: Harper and Row.

Lee, J.A. (1978). *Getting sex*. Ontario: Musson.

Levy, O. (1982). *A brother's touch*. New York: Pinnacle Books.

Linedecker, C. (1981). *Children in chains*. Boston: Little, Brown.

Lloyd, R. (1977). *Playland*. London: Blond and Briggs.

Luckenhill, D. (1986). Deviant career mobility: The case of male prostitutes. *Social Problems* 33(4).

Mackay, J. (1985). *The hustler*. Boston: Alyson.

Mandate. (1977 December). Gay hustle for love and/or money (3), 32.

McPhersen, B. (1983). *Aging as a social force*. Toronto: Butterworths.

Murray, S. (1984). *Social theory, homosexual realities*. New York: Gai Saber.

Phillips, E. (1982). *Sunday's child*. Toronto: Bantam Books.

Pittman, D. (1971 March). The male house of prostitution. *Trans-Action* 8: 21-27.

Rechy, J. (1977). *The sexual outlaw*. New York: Grove Press.

Reiss, A. (1961). The social organization of queers and peers. *Social Problems* 9: 102-120.

Ross, H.L. (1959). The hustler in Chicago. *Journal of Student Research*: 113-19.

Ryan, W. (1971). *Blaming the victim*. New York: Pantheon.

Simpson, C., Chester, L., & Leitch, D. (1976). *The Cleveland street affair*. Boston: Little, Brown.

Teal, D. (1971). *The gay militant*. New York: Stein and Day.

Visano, L. (1987). *This idle trade*. Concord: Vita Sana Books.

Winslow, R. & Winslow, V. (1974). *Deviant reality*. Boston: Allyn and Bacon.

Sappho and the Crack of Dawn (fragment 58 L-P)

John J. Winkler, PhD

Stanford University

One of the scraps of ancient papyrus found in the wastedumps of the Egyptian city of Oxyrhynchus[1] contains 26 broken lines from a poem by Sappho concerning old age.[2] The page is torn down the middle of a column of writing and there remain only the closing words of the lines. Lines 25-26 can be completed from a quotation in Klearchos' essay on erotic desire,[3] but the remainder of this fragmentary poem can only be restored by an intelligent use of parallels and conjectures. This has not often been attempted; the fragment, beautiful as it is, has largely escaped critical notice. The reading proposed here, tentative and hypothetical as all such reconstructions must be, is that in fragment 58 Sappho used traditional Greek mythology in a striking way to picture herself in old age cradled and enfolded in the loving arms of the great goddess.

First, to demonstrate to Greekless readers how scrappy are the legible remains and how cautious we must be in restoring their connected sense, I will give the text itself in transliteration. Square brackets mark missing papyrus: what was there can sometimes be restored or plausibly conjectured when the surrounding letters limit the possibilities. Dots mark the approximate number of missing or illegible letters. After that I give the fragment in English translation.[4] Parenthetical question marks in the translation indicate uncertainties of restoration.

John J. Winkler was Professor of Classics, Stanford University. Professor Winkler died of complications resulting from AIDS in April 1990. Correspondence may be addressed to Professor A. A. Stephens, Department of Classics, Stanford University, Stanford, CA 94305-2080.

TRANSLITERATION

5   ]ugoisa [   ]
6   ].[..]..[   ]idachthên
              ]chu th[.]oi[.]all[. . . . . .]utan
              ].chtho.[.]ati.[. . . . .]eisa
              ]mena tan[. . . . ô]numon se
10   ]ni thêtai st[u]ma[ti] prokopsin
              ]pôn kala dôra paides
              ]philaoidon liguran chelunnan
              pa]nta chroa gêras êdê
     [leukai d' egeno]nto triches ek melainan
15   ]ai, gona d' [o]u pheroisi
                 ]êsth' isa nebrioisin
                 a]lla ti ken poeiên?
                 ] ou dunaton genesthai
                 ]brodopachun Auôn
20   [es]chata gas pheroisa[
                 ]on umôs emarpse[
              [athan]atan akoitin
                 ]imenan nomisdei
                 ]ais opasdoi
25   egô de philêmm' abrosunan, [   ]touto kai moi
     to la[mpron eros tôeliô kai to ka]lon le[l]onche.

TRANSLATION

5   . . . .fleeing (?)
     . . . .was bitten/taught (?)
     . . . .
     . . . .
     . . . .you of (many?) names
10   . . . .give success to (my) mouth
     . . . .beautiful gifts. . .children
     . . . .song-loving (player?) of keen-voiced tortoise-lyres
     . . . .old age already (has withered?) all (my) flesh
     (my) hairs from black (have become white?)
15   . . . .my knees do not carry (me?)
     . . . .(to dance?) like fawns
     . . . .but what could I do?
     . . . .not possible to become (ageless?)

. . . .rosy-armed Dawn
20 . . . .carrying to the ends of the earth
. . . .yet (old age?) seized (him?)
. . . .(immortal?) spouse
. . . .supposes
. . . .would offer
25 But I cherish soft delicacy, ...For me as well,
passionate love
has made this sun's splendor
and its beauty
mine.

The mythological reference lying behind the words "Dawn," "carrying to the ends of the earth," and "spouse" can only be Tithonos.[5] His story is well known from lines 218-238 of the *Homeric Hymn to Aphrodite*.[6] êôs (in Aeolic Greek, Auôs), the goddess of the dawn, carried off a divinely handsome ephebe named Tithonos to be her consort and to live with her in her palace at the eastern horizon, "the ends of the earth." She asked father Zeus to grant him eternal life. But she forgot to ask also for eternal youth. As he grew older and older, his hair becoming white and his limbs too weak to carry him, she continued to feed him on ambrosia but no longer shared his bed. Eventually he so withered away that she could put him in a cupboard and close the door forever. His voice could still be heard, however, chirping away like a cricket in the woodwork. The myth of Tithonos was a familiar folktale, told to explain the origin of the cicada, which was believed to survive with no other food than a few sips of dew and yet to be endowed with an amazingly vibrant power of song.

We should, of course, always leave open the question of just how closely the "I" of any poem is to be identified with the actual poet-singer who composed it, but it is fairly clear that Sappho, the "I" of this fragment, speaks of herself (or imagines herself) as having reached old age (*gêras*, 13). It is visible on her flesh, in the whiteness of her once-black hair, and is felt in the weakness of her knees, for she can no longer gambol and leap in dancing choruses like the agile fawn she once was (14-16). The reference of this description of old age to the Sapphic "I" is pretty well guaranteed by the first-person verb of the next line (17): "But what can I do?"[7] That strong and determined Sapphic "I" opens the last couplet as well. In contrast to something before she declares, "but I . . . ," just as in the famous fragment 16 L-P she lists various masculine opinions about what is most beautiful on earth—a formation of cavalry or soldiers or ships—"but I assert that it is whatever a person desires."

That last couplet had long been known from its independent quotation by the fourth-century Peripatetic scholar Klearchos, excerpted by Athenaios *Deipnosophists* 15.687A-B.[8] With the discovery of P. Oxy. 1787, various conjectures became possible about its sense in context. These readings raise interesting questions about method. Bowra hypothesized that it was spoken by Dawn herself, though he quietly omitted that suggestion from the second edition of his book.[9] J. A. Davison confidently asserts, on the flimsiest of grounds, that the lines were spoken by Tithonos. The only basis for his conjecture is that Tithonos occurs earlier in the poem and that he was, in mythological genealogy, related to Ganymede and Paris, which gives him "a congenital tendency to *abrosuna* [delicacy], not to mention *malakia* [softness, implying feminine sexual receptiveness]."[10] One of the fascinating aspects of studying fragments is to watch the Rorschach effect whereby scholars reveal their underlying attitudes about what is possible or acceptable in life and poetry. Davison makes no secret of his contempt for a man who is carried away by a powerful woman, and his allusion to Ganymede and to Tithonos' supposed 'congenital tendency' colors that old patriarchal attitude with the language of modern homophobia.

The opposite extreme to such interpretative reading is the mindless positivism that would equate the meager surviving record with what actually existed. For an extreme instance, D. Meyerhoff notes that Tyrtaios fragment 12 W. (middle seventh century) refers to Tithonos' handsome youth, while Mimnermos fragment 4 (contemporary with Sappho, about 500 b.c.e.) mentions his old age; from this he concludes that the story of Tithonos' endless aging was not known in the generation before Sappho![11] A positivistic critic of this stripe might similarly propose that since Tithonos' identity as the original cicada is not explicitly mentioned until a later period it is unjustifiable to import that connection here.[12] It would be possible to mount a reasoned, extensive (and inevitably tedious) set of arguments against such ponderous carapaces of self-immobilizing dogma. For present purposes, let it suffice to say that if any reader truly believes that the exiguous written scraps of archaic poetry are an adequate basis for delineating the extent of what was known or unknown at that time, he or she should stop here. Particularly when the matter is folkloric there is every likelihood that elite poetry will allude to or record only stray bits of the extensive body of tales and figures known to its audience. That is the assumption upon which I shall proceed.

Returning to the poem, it seems clear that Sappho writes as a famous and successful poet. The Muses have given "success to (my) mouth"

(10). Reference to her own fame as a poet fits with her self-portrayal as white-haired and old. A woman so widely celebrated after her lifetime and well-known in her own must have achieved her fame long before she retired from active dancing. The musical theme of lines 10-12 may be carried through in the mythological example of lines 17-22, for there Sappho refers to Tithonos, and here my reading slips into the realm of conjecture and tentative restoration.

The standard reading of Tithonos' role in fragment 58 is that he is a negative example.[13] Sappho supposedly reminds herself that her aging is a universal and inevitable experience. In effect, she is saying "But why should I complain, since even the handsome Tithonos, Dawn's consort, was compelled to grow old?" It is entirely possible that this is what the poem originally contained, but if it did we must admit that the thought is wholly conventional and uninspired. Rather than abandon fragment 58 to the worst fate of all, namely, that it was built around a lame and unexciting cliche, I would like to offer the suggestion that Sappho saw more in Tithonos than a negative example of aging.

The great erotic goddesses who acted on their passions—Dawn, Aphrodite and Selene (the Moon)—apparently received considerable attention in Sappho's collected works. In addition to her treatment of Dawn's love for Tithonos, she related the old tales of Selene's love for Endymion (frag. 199) and Aphrodite's passions for Adonis (frag. 211 b iii) and for Phaon (frag. 211c). This last is particularly interesting since Phaon, like Tithonos, represented both extreme old age and the bloom of ephebic youth. (Aphrodite restored him to youth with a powerful plant, the sea-holly.) In earlier Greek poetry, the same goddesses have other mortal lovers as well. Dawn snatched up not only Tithonos but Orion (*Odyssey* 5.121), Kleitos (*Od.* 5.250) and Kephalos (Hesiod *Theogony* 986); Aphrodite picked up, in addition to Phaon and Adonis, Phaethon as her paramour (*Theogony* 988-91). Rather than see the exemplum in fragment 58 as simply about the aging of Tithonos, we should allow the possibility that the great goddess herself, Dawn in this instance, might well have occupied a share of Sappho's attention and that it was not just Tithonos but the analogy Tithonos:Dawn: Sappho:goddess that structured her allusion to the myth.

Such a framing would allow us to maintain that the relevance of Tithonos' story to Sappho is that she envisions herself growing physically weaker but poetically stronger. Like Tithonos she sees herself on a trajectory of increasing old age, with stiff joints and slower movement, but it is at the same time a path towards ever-greater fame as a poet. She is on her way to becoming, like Tithonos, the embodiment of song and she imagines herself as she will be one day—and actually is for us—a famous name, a collection of songs, and no longer a physical presence. This makes the exemplum more than a negative lament. Instead, Sappho transcends that utterly conventional cliche to see in Tithonos two positive features—his identification with pure song and his everlasting union with the goddess.

To take one more step in this direction, I would dwell on the picture of Tithonos/Sappho being carried away by the powerful goddess. It is, like much in Sappho, a discrete but unmistakable lesbian image. Sappho allows us briefly to see herself in the role of Tithonos, wrapped in the rosy arms of Dawn and rapt away to the goddess' home in the Far East to be her "spouse" (22) forever. It is a rather extraordinary picture of woman-to-woman passion and rapture.

Finally, the phrase "this sun's splendor and beauty" (25-26) in the closing couplet suggests that the imagined scene of the poem's performance is in the sunlight. Since Dawn is the subject, we might, with no stretch of the imagination, see Sappho singing this song as the sun first rises, meditating on her physical old age as she watches the rosy crack of light widen on the eastern sky-line. Not only for Tithonos but "for me too" (25), passionate love (*erôs*)—by the goddess and for the goddess—has given Sappho a permanent share of fame's bright sunlight.

NOTES

1. *Oxyrhynchus Papyri*, vol. 15, number 1787 (London 1922). I quote the text from Edgar Lobel and Denys Page *Poetarum Lesbiorum Fragmenta* (Oxford 1955), fragment 58, pp. 41-42, omitting the illegible traces of the first four lines. The same fragment is number 79 in Bergk's collection, 65a in that of Diehls.

2. For a general discussion of life-stages and old age in early Greek poetry, see W. Schadewaldt, "Lebeszeit und Griesenalter im frühen Griechentum" *Die Antike* 9 (1933) 282-302 = *Hellas und Hesperien* vol. I, ed. 2 (Zürich/Stuttgart 1970) 109-27.

3. *Klearchos*, volume 3 of *Die Schule des Aristoteles*, ed. Fritz Wehrli (Basel 1948), fragment 41 (= Athenaeus *Deipnosophists* 687b). Klearchos was a member of Aristotle's Peripatetic school, active in the late fourth and early third centuries b.c.e.

4. The most useful edition is now that of David A. Campbell in the Loeb Classical Library series (Cambridge, MA and London, 1982), with all the known fragments of Sappho, extensive testimonia concerning her life and work (though gossip and fiction play a large part in these), and a reliable prose translation.

5. First detected by F. Stiebitz, "Zu Sappho 65 Diehl" *Berliner Philologische Wochenschrift* 46 (1926) 1259-62.

6. English translations: Thelma Sargent *The Homeric Hymns* (New York and London, 1973) pp. 51-52; H. G. Evelyn-White *Hesiod, The Homeric Hymns and Homerica* (Loeb Classical Library: New York and London 1904) pp. 421-423.

7. The word translated "do" is also the Greek word for "compose poetry." The half-line might therefore mean "What should I compose poetry about?", implying that it is perfectly right that a poet in her old age should sing about aging and not about the conventional themes of Greek lyric—youth, dancing, and the first blooming of beauty and desire.

8. S. Nicosia *Tradizione testuale diretta e indiretta dei poeti di Lesbo* (Filologia e critica 19: Rome 1976) 111-19.

9. C. M. Bowra *Greek Lyric Poetry* (London 1936) 236; second edition (1961) p. 226.

10. J. A. Davison *From Archilochus to Pindar* (1968) 239 n.1.

11. Dirk Meyerhoff *Traditioneller Stoff und individuelle Gestaltung: Untersuchungen zu Alkaios und Sappho* (Beiträge zur Altertumswissenschaft 3; Hildesheim 1984) 191-92.

12. For a general survey of Tithonos, see J. T. Kakridis "Tithonos" *Wiener Studien* 48 (1930) 25-38.

13. H. Eisenberger *Der Mythos in der äolischen Lyrik* (diss. Frankfurt am Main 1956) 93-95.